The Story
of the
"Mary Celeste"

The Story of the "Mary Celeste"

By Charles Edey Fay

DOVER PUBLICATIONS, INC.
NEW YORK

Published in Canada by General Publishing Company, Ltd., 30 Lesmill Road, Don Mills, Toronto, Ontario.

Published in the United Kingdom by Constable and Company, Ltd.

This Dover edition, first published in 1988, is an unabridged, slightly altered republication of the work originally published by Peabody Museum, Salem, Massachusetts in 1942 (unabridged first edition, limited to 1000 copies). For this Dover edition, some of the pictorial plates have been placed back to back. The engraving of the *Mary Celeste* originally appeared in color, with caption on a previous page. Two foldouts (the chart following page 114, and Appendix H) are now presented as double-page spreads.

Manufactured in the United States of America

Dover Publications, Inc., 31 East 2nd Street, Mineola, N.Y. 11501

Library of Congress Cataloging-in-Publication Data

Fay, Charles Edey.
  [Mary Celeste]
  The story of the "Mary Celeste" / by Charles Edey Fay.
      p.   cm.
  Reprint. Originally published: Mary Celeste. Salem, Mass. : Peabody Museum, 1942.
  Bibliography: p.
  Includes index.
  ISBN 0-486-25730-4 (pbk.)
  1. Mary Celeste (Brig)   2. Shipwrecks—North Atlantic Ocean.   I. Title.
G530.M37F38   1988
001.9′4—dc19   88-6513
                                                        CIP

INTRODUCTION

From time immemorial, Man has inhabited two worlds: one, the objective world about him which he could see and touch; the other, the realm of dreams and fancies, in the exploration of which his eager mind found fascinating employment. Although the frontiers of the Unknown have continued to recede before the advance of scientific knowledge, there still remains a wide domain, where Mystery allures and beckons, and Man, ever delighting in that which eludes and baffles, still pursues.

In a world largely subjugated to his will, it is the Sea which, with infinite variety of mood, either mocks, beguiles or resists him. Now submissively bearing his far-flung commerce, and now, with insatiable ferocity, devouring his proudest creations, it is the Sea, which, holding within her vast treasure-house the secrets of her multitudinous dead—"unknelled, uncoffined and unknown"—defies his challenge and intrigues his imagination.

For almost threescore years and ten, the story of the Mary Celeste—a small, seaworthy, American half-brig found wandering, ghostlike, without master or crew, over the waters between the Azores and the coast of Portugal—has continued to allure the interest of people all over the world, and to excite seemingly endless speculation on the part of "those who go down to the sea in ships."

A surprisingly large amount of literature has grown up around this vessel and her total company of ten persons. Much of it is notable for its inexactitude. Not a little of it is remarkable for the ingenuity displayed in the invention of names and places non-existent, but useful in investing the narrative with a garment of verisimilitude. Some of it displays an apparent readiness to defame the dead as well as to hoax the living. The eagerness to tell a thrilling story has, at times, overpowered the sense of obligation to tell the truth.

One of the purposes of this volume, which represents several years of careful study and investigation, is to state in orderly fashion the facts derived from authoritative sources, and to cite as far as possible the authorities from which the facts have been drawn. Not a little of the material is now published for the first time. Considerable information has been gathered from the archives of the Atlantic Mutual Insurance Company of New York and of the United States and Canadian Governments as well as other trustworthy sources. There is also the further purpose of suggesting the most probable solution of the most widely known of all marine mysteries, which has become the "cause célèbre" in the annals of the sea.

Even as a ship is never the work of one man only, but is the product of the combined efforts of many, in like manner this volume represents the efforts and the good-will of a number of persons animated by a common desire and purpose. Into the framework of it, the supervising shipwright has endeavored to put only such timber as would stand the test of wind and wave—the analysis and the criticism—which inevitably attend such launchings upon the literary seas. There has been no need to trim the sails for any special breeze. With the sole desire to state the facts, this adventure has been entered upon in a spirit akin to that of the ancient Tyrrhenian mariner in his invocation:

> O Neptune!
> You may save me if you will;
> You may sink me if you will;
> But, whatever happens,
> I will keep my rudder true.

Sunny Crest Farm,
Woodbury, Connecticut,
June 1941.

October 14, 1940

Dear Mr. Fay:

I think it would be a public service
to ascertain and publish the facts in the
alluringly famous "Mary Celeste" case, and
you may be assured of my best wishes and
cooperation in such grand work.

If I have a picture of this ship in
my collection I will be very much pleased to
have you photograph it. For the moment, I
cannot recall such a picture which possibly
may be at Hyde Park. I am having a complete
catalogue prepared in connection with the
museum being built there, and I suggest that
some months hence you communicate with the
museum on the subject.

I will of course be quite delighted
to have a copy of your forthcoming book to
add to the museum library.

Very sincerely yours,

Franklin D. Roosevelt

Charles Edey Fay, Esq.,
Sunny Crest Farm,
Grassy Hill Road,
Woodbury,
Connecticut.

CONTENTS

PART I

CONTENTS

PART II

CONTENTS

PART III

Appendix

CONTENTS XV

ILLUSTRATIONS

TEXT ILLUSTRATIONS

ACKNOWLEDGMENTS

THE author is indebted to a considerable number of persons and organizations for the material which went into the making of this volume. Responses to inquiries have been generous, with manifestations of interest in the subject, and of a readiness to collaborate in the effort to make a full, factual presentation of the case.

Although care has been exercised to make acknowledgment herein of every one of these friendly auxiliaries, the author, conscious of his limitations, bespeaks the indulgence of any who may inadvertently have been omitted.

For information relating to Captain and Mrs. Briggs and their home life at Wareham and Marion, Massachusetts, the author is under an incalculable debt of gratitude to Dr. Oliver W. Cobb of Easthampton, Massachusetts, their first cousin, and to Mr. J. Franklin Briggs of New Bedford, Massachusetts, nephew of Captain Briggs. Without the time and effort generously given by them in numerous letters and in personal consultations it would have been impossible to present a clear and trustworthy picture of the most important figure in this tragedy of the sea. Dr. Cobb's interesting and informing article in *Yachting* (February 1940) and his book entitled *Rose Cottage* have provided the author with a great deal of factual material. To Mr. Briggs the author is also deeply indebted for the pictures of Captain and Mrs. Briggs, their two children, and of the melodeon and the sword, as well as for permission to publish some of the family letters. From both Dr. Cobb and Mr. Briggs, the author has received much helpful information relating to the masts, sails and rigging of sailing vessels.

For important documentary material relating to the case, special acknowledgment is made of the obligation to Mr. J. C. Anakin of Liverpool, England, whose investigations, conducted over a number of years, have materially helped to extricate the facts from the mass of legendary matter, particularly with reference to the proceedings at Gibraltar.

To Mr. R. Lester Dewis and Captain William M. Collins, both of West Advocate, Nova Scotia, the author is under deep obligation for detailed information relating to the building of the *Amazon* and her early history before she became the *Mary Celeste*. Mr. Dewis is a grandson of Joshua Dewis, boss-builder of the *Amazon,* named in the vessel's first register as "shipwright" and owner of sixteen sixty-fourths interest in the vessel, which made him the largest shareholder. Through the courtesy of Mr. Dewis, it has been possible to obtain a photograph[1] of a painting of the *Amazon,* made at Marseille in November 1861. This painting is owned by Mr. Dewis and is on exhibition at the Fort Beauséjour Historic Site, Aulac, New Brunswick, Canada. Captain Collins, a veteran of the sea, has devoted a good part of a long lifetime to a study of the *Amazon–Mary Celeste* case, and has frequently been consulted by writers and other persons interested in the subject.

From the Deputy Minister of the Public Archives of Canada were received, without charge, photostats of the two registers issued by the Canadian government to the vessel while she was the *Amazon* and under the British flag.

For the picture of Albert G. Richardson, first mate, we owe acknowledgment to Mrs. George Loblein of Brooklyn, New York, whose father was a brother of Mrs. Albert G. ("Fannie") Richardson. For other information regarding Mate Richardson and his family, we are indebted to the following persons and organizations: Miss Betty Arp and Mrs. Anna Fisher of Brooklyn, New York; Mr. Clar-

1. In the author's possession.

ence P. Greene, Portland, Maine; Samuel T. Reed, Hamden, Connecticut; Mrs. Grace I. Trundy and W. F. Trundy, town clerk, both of Stockton Springs, Maine; Adjutant-General of the State of Maine; Navy Department, War Department, Treasury Department, and Veterans Administration, Washington, D. C.

The archives of the Atlantic Mutual Insurance Company have proved a rich source of authentic information relating to the construction of the vessel: the repairs made from time to time; the insurance effected by the company at the time of the vessel's fateful passage, and the final adjustment of the loss on hull and freight interests, involving four other American companies. Its file of contemporary newspaper comment on the mystery surrounding the vessel's abandonment and the disappearance of the entire ship's company contains a wealth of interesting material. Without the encouragement of the author's friend and former associate, Mr. William D. Winter, now president of the Atlantic Mutual Insurance Company, this work would not have been attempted, and it is due in no inconsiderable measure to his continuing interest and co-operation that it has been brought to completion.

No acknowledgment of the author's varied obligations would be complete without reference to that rich repository of factual information, the National Archives, and also to the many courtesies received from the Maritime Association of the Port of New York and the New York Maritime Register.

Mr. Lincoln Colcord of Searsport, Maine, has very kindly read the galley proofs of this book, and has made a number of useful suggestions.

Record should also appropriately be made of helpful information received from and services rendered by the following: Lieutenant-Colonel J. Agostinho, Director of the Servico Meteorologico dos Açores, Angra do Heroismo, Azores Islands; Mr. George Alexander Armstrong, United States Consul, Malaga, Spain; Commander John B. Barrett, Branch Hydrographic Office, New York City; Mr. Fred L. Blatchford,[2] Wrentham, Massachusetts; Captain G. S. Bryan, United States Navy, Hydrographic Office, Washington, D. C.; Mr. J. W. Cantillion, Secretary, American Bureau of Shipping, New York City; William E. Chapman (former United States Consul at Gibraltar), Norman, Oklahoma; Collector of Customs, New York; Miss Elizabeth Cullen, New York City; Mr. T. J. Dalnodar, of the Maritime Association of the Port of New York; Mr. Ernest G. Driver, Secretary, New York Board of Underwriters; Reverend C. A. M. Earle, Rexton, New Brunswick, Canada; Mr. J. Edward Geddie, Editor of *Chambers's Journal*, Edinburgh, Scotland; Mr. P. M. Hamer, Chief Division of Reference, The National Archives, Washington, D. C.; Reverend C. R. Harris, Rector, St. George's Church, Parrsboro, Nova Scotia; Harvard College Library, Harvard University; Mr. Harry E. Hawley, United States Consul, Gibraltar (temporarily at Marseille); Hydrographic Office, Navy Department, Washington, D. C.; Insurance Department of the State of Maine; Insurance Department of the Commonwealth of Massachusetts; Insurance Department of the State of New York; Mr. A. G. Law, New York; Maritime Register, New York; The National Archives, Washington, D. C.; Captain M. L. Pittman, Atlantic Mutual Insurance Company; Mrs. Thomas J. (Florence Appleby) Port, Stapleton, Staten Island, New York; Public Library of the City of Boston; Public Library of Buffalo, New York; Mr. Paul North Rice, Chief, Reference Department, Public Library of the City of New York; Plymouth Cordage Company, North

2. Since deceased.

Plymouth, Massachusetts; Marjorie Dent Candee and Anne W. Conrow of the Seamen's Church Institute of New York; Captain Howard A. Flynn, Governor, The Sailors' Snug Harbor, Staten Island, New York; Mr. Robert Harrison, United States Shipping Commissioner's Office, New York City; Miss Kathleen M. Smith, Brooklyn, New York; Mr. John B. C. Sprague, Centre Moriches, Long Island; Mr. and Mrs. Benjamin W. Strachan, New York; Mr. E. Pizzarello, Registrar, Supreme Court, Gibraltar; Mr. S. N. Taylor, Town Clerk, Marion, Massachusetts; and my wife, Hélène E. C. Fay, wise counsellor and keen but kindly critic, without whose sympathetic collaboration this work could hardly have been accomplished. To each and all of these, the hearty thanks of the author are hereby extended.

NOTE

For the greater convenience of the reader, this work
has been divided, like ancient Gaul, "into three parts."

In PART I will be found the record of the main course
of events from the launching of the vessel in 1861, up to
her tragic experience in November 1872.

PART II contains factual matters directly relevant to the
subject, but which, if introduced into Part I, would retard
the smooth flowing of the narrative in its progress toward
the dramatic climax. This second part consists largely of
events occurring in the after years, but considered important in view of the light they shed on some of the principal characters and on the motivation of their conduct.

In PART III will be found copies of records, important
documents and matters more or less statistical in character.

Mary Celeste

PART I

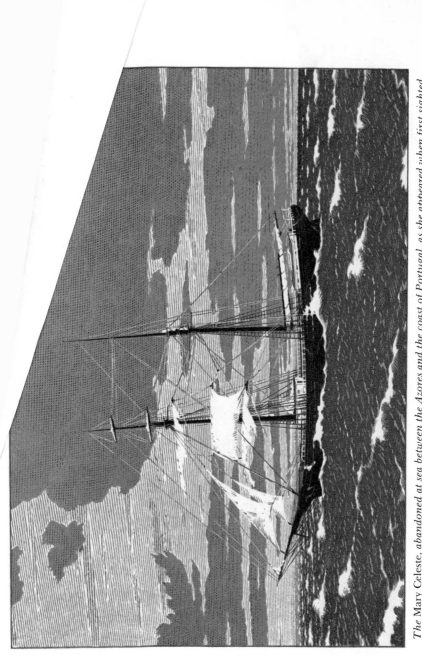

The Mary Celeste, abandoned at sea between the Azores and the coast of Portugal, as she appeared when first sighted by the Dei Gratia, on 4 December 1872. A wood engraving by Rudolph Ruzicka.

CHAPTER I

Mary Celeste begins Her Voyage

IN the fall of 1872, Captain Benjamin Spooner Briggs purchased an eight twenty-fourths interest in a small half-brig named *Mary Celeste*. At about the same time, extensive repairs,[1] including an extra deck and the rearrangement of the cabin, were made at a cost of $11,500 causing an increase in the vessel's tonnage from 206.29 to 282.28.

It was on or about 19 October[2] that Captain Briggs left his home in Marion, Massachusetts, for New York to supervise the loading of the vessel and make final arrangements for the voyage.

On Saturday, 26 October,[3] Sarah Elizabeth Briggs, the captain's wife, accompanied by their two-year-old daughter, Sophia Matilda, left Marion via Fall River for New York. Arriving on Sunday morning at the Fall River Line's North River Pier, they were met by Captain Briggs who conveyed them and their baggage across town to the *Mary Celeste* which was lying at Pier 50 East River.[4]

From the captain's letter of Sunday, 3 November 1872,[5] to his mother, Mrs. Nathan Briggs, it is known that on Saturday night, 2 November, the vessel finished loading.

1. Excerpt from Atlantic Mutual Inspection record: "¾ poop extended over all. Severl [*sic*] New timbers new transoms part new Knightheads stern & stem New Bends—top Sids [*sic*] & Stern & patch Y. M. Oct. 1872."

2. See letter of 3 November, from Captain Briggs to his mother, page 4.

3. Letter of 27 October 1872 from Sarah Elizabeth Briggs to her son Arthur. This letter is in the possession of Mr. J. Franklin Briggs, New Bedford, Massachusetts.

4. *Maritime Register*, 30 October 1872.

5. Letter of 3 November 1872. See page 4.

Letter of Captain Briggs to His Mother*

New York, Nov. 3d, 1872

MY DEAR MOTHER,

It is a long time since I have written you a letter and I should like to give you a real interesting one but I hardly know what to say except that I am well and the rest of us dito. It is such a long time since I composed other than business epistles. It seems to me to have been a great while since I left home but it is only little over two weeks but in that time my mind has been filled with business cares and I am again launched away into the busy whirl of business life from which I have so long been laid aside. For a few days it was tedious, perplexing, and very tiresome but now I have got fairly settled down to it and it sits lightly and seems to run more smoothly and my appetite keeps good and I hope I shan't lose any flesh. It seems real home-like since Sarah and Sophia have got here and we enjoy our little quarters. On Thursday we had a call from Willie[6] and his wife—took Sophia and went with them on a ride up to Central Park. Sophia behaved splendid and seemed to enjoy the ride as much as any of us. it is the only time that they have been away from the vessel. On account of the Horse disease the horsecars have not been running on this side of the city so we have not been able to go and make calls as we were so far away from anyone to go on foot, and to hire a private carriage would have cost us at least $10.00 a trip which we didn't feel able to pay and we couldn't walk and carry Sophia a mile or two which we should have had to do to get to ferry for Iva [word unintelligible] or E-port.[7] It has been very confining for S. but I hope when we return we can make up for it. We seem to have a very good Mate and Steward and I hope shall have a pleasant voyage We both have missed Arthur and I believe I should have sent for him if I could have thought of a good place to stow him away. Sophia calls for him occasionally and wants to see him in the Album which by the way is a favorite book of hers She knows your picture in both Albums and points and says Gamma Bis. She seems

---

* By permission of Mr. J. Franklin Briggs, from photostat (in author's possession) of original letter.

6. Rev. William H. Cobb, brother of Mrs. Briggs, and for many years librarian of Congregational House, Boston, Massachusetts.

7. Presumably Elizabethport.

New York. Nov. 3ᵈ 1872

My dear Mother

It is a long time since
I have written you a letter and
I should like to give you a
real interesting one but I hardly
know what to say except that
I am well and the rest of us
dito it is such a long time
since I composed other than
buisness Epistles. It seems to
me to have been a great while
since I left home, but it is only
little over two weeks but in that
time my mind has been filled
with buisness cares and I am
again launched away into the
buisy whirl of buisness life from
which I have so long been laid
aside, for a few days it was

tedious/perplexing. and very tiresome
but now I have got fairly settled
down to it and it sits lightly and
sums to run more smoothly and
my appetite keeps good and I
hope I shan't lose any flesh. It
sims real home like since. Seele
and Sophia have got here. and we
enjoy our little quarters on Thursday
we had a call from. Weller and
his wife took. Sophia and went with
them on a ride up to Central
Park Sophia behaved splendid and
seemed to enjoy the ride. as much
as any of us it is the only time
that they have been away from the
vessel., on account of the Horse
disease the horse cars have
not been running on this side
of the city so we have not been
able to go and make any calls
as we were so far away from

anyone to go bad feet and to hire a private Carriage would have cost us at least $10. a trip which we didn't feel able to pay and we couldn't walk and carry Sophie a mile or two which we should have had to to get to ferry for Ipswich or Ezport it has been very confining for S. but I hope when we return we can make up for it. We seem to have a very good mate and Steward and I hope shall have a pleasant voyage we both like Mitford Arthur and I believe I should have sent for him if I could have thought of a good place to stow him away. Sophia calls for him occasionally and wants to see him in the Album which by the way is a favorite book of hers She knows your picture in both Albums and points and says Grandma Pa's Sis

Shall leave Tuesday morning

seems real smart has got over that bad
Cold she had when she came and has
a first rate appetite for hash and bread and
butter I think the voyage will do her
lots of good. we enjoy our melodeon and
have some good sings I was in hopes Oli
might get in before I left but am afraid
not now. we finished loading last night
and shall leave on Tuesday morning if we
don't get off tomorrow night the Lord
willing. our vessel is in beautiful
trim and I hope we shall have a
fine passage but as I have never
been in her before can't say how she'll
sail we shall want you to write us in
about 20 days. to Genoa. care of Am. Consul
and about 20. days after to Messina care of.
Am. Consul who will forward to us if we don't
go there. I wrote James to pay you for A's
board and rent if he forgets call on him
also. for any money that may be necessary
for Clothes. please get Eben to see his skates
are all right and the holes in his new

real smart—has got over the bad cold she had when she came and has a first rate appetite for hash and bread and butter. I think the voyage will do her lots of good. We enjoy our melodeon and have some good sings. I was in hopes Oli[8] might get in before I left but I'm afraid not now. We finished loading last night and shall leave on Tuesday morning if we don't get off tomorrow night, the Lord willing. Our vessel is in beautiful trim and I hope we shall have a fine passage, but as I have never been in her before can't say how she'll sail. Shall want you to write us in about 20 days to Genoa, care of Am. Consul and about 20 days after to Messina care of Am. Consul who will forward to us if we don't go there. I wrote James to pay you for A's board and rent: if he forgets, call on him—also for any monney that may be necessary for clothes. please get Eben to see his skates are all right and the holes in his new thick boot heels.

I hope he'll keep well as I think if he does he'll be some help as well as company for you. love to Hannah. Sophia calls Aunt Hanna often: I wish we had a picture so she could remember the countenance as well as name—hoping to be with you again early in the spring, with much love I am

Yrs affly.   BENJ

[At the top of the fourth page appear the following words.]

Shall leave Tuesday morning

On Monday, 4 November, he went to the New York office of the United States Shipping Commissioner and signed the "Articles of Agreement"[9] and the "List of Persons Composing the Crew"[10] of the *Mary Celeste.*

It was on the same day that an Atlantic Mutual underwriter initialled the insurance for J. H. Winchester & Co. for $3,400 on the vessel's freight on charter from New York to Genoa, Italy, at the rate of two and a half per cent. He little dreamed of the tragic events destined to follow

---

8. Captain Oliver E. Briggs, brother of the master of the *Mary Celeste.*

9. See Appendix I.

10. See Appendix J.

in the wake of the *Mary Celeste*, nor could he have had reason to suppose that, after the passing of fifty years, the Atlantic Mutual would be the only survivor of the five American companies interested in her insurance on her fateful passage.

From the letter dated Thursday, 7 November,[11] "Off Staten Island," written by Captain Briggs's wife to his mother, it is established that on Tuesday morning, 5 November,[12] the vessel left her dock at Pier 50 East River, but, owing to unfavorable weather, "anchored about a mile or so from the city," off Staten Island, where they remained until the morning of the seventh,[13] when, "with wind light but favorable," they made a fresh departure.

It was customary in those days for the Sandy Hook pilot boat to take letters for mailing in New York, and it is apparent that Sarah's letter, the valedictory character of which could not then have been realized, was transmitted in that manner.

About ten years before, in the schooner *Forest King*, the captain and his wife had gone to the Mediterranean on their honeymoon. Later, in the bark *Arthur* and the brig *Sea Foam*, they had made other voyages together. On each occasion, Captain Briggs was in command. In between voyages, two children had been born: Arthur Stanley on 20 September 1865, and Sophia Matilda on 31 October 1870.[14] [Plates II and III.]

Practical New England housewife that she was, and profiting, no doubt, by previous sea experience, Sarah Briggs had her sewing machine shipped to New York

11. Letter from Mrs. B. S. Briggs to Mrs. Nathan Briggs, page 11.

12. Ibid.

13. Ibid.

14. See copies of birth certificates from town records, Marion, Massachusetts, Appendices V and W.

Captain Benjamin Spooner Briggs
Master of the Mary Celeste

PLATE I

Mrs. Benjamin Spooner Briggs
wife of the Master of the Mary Celeste
and their son Arthur Stanley Briggs

PLATE II

along with her melodeon and music books to accompany them on the long voyage. [Plate XII.]

The captain and his wife looked forward with bright anticipation to the trip which promised to be financially profitable, especially as the vessel had already been chartered to carry a return cargo, presumably of fruit, from Messina[15] to New York.

Letter from Wife of Captain Briggs to His Mother*

BRIG MARY CELESTE

Off Staten Island Nov. 7th 1872

DEAR MOTHER BRIGGS,—

Probably you will be a little surprised to receive a letter with this date, but instead of proceeding to sea when we came out Tuesday morning, we anchored about a mile or so from the city, as it was strong head wind, and B.[16] said it looked so thick & nasty ahead we shouldn't gain much if we were beating & banging about. Accordingly we took a fresh departure this morning with wind light but favorable, so we hope to get outside without being obliged to anchor. Have kept a sharp look-out for Oliver,[17] but so far have seen nothing of him. It was rather trying to lay in sight of the city so long & think that most likely we had letters waiting for us there, and be unable to get them. However, we hope no great change has occurred since we did hear and shall look for a goodly supply when we reach G.[18]

Sophy thinks the figure 3 & the letter G. on her blocks is the same thing so I saw her whispering to herself yesterday with the 3 block in her hand—Gam-gam-gamma. Benj. thinks we have got a pretty peaceable set this time all around if they continue as they have begun. Can't tell yet how smart they are. B. reports a good breeze now, says we are going along nicely.

* By permission of Mr. J. Franklin Briggs, from photostat (in author's possession) of original letter.

15. See letter from Captain Briggs, 3 November 1872 to his mother, page 4.

16. Benjamin.

17. Oliver Everson Briggs, brother of Benjamin.

18. Genoa.

I should like to be present at Mr. Kingsbury's ordination next week. Hope the people will be united in him, and wish we might hear of Mrs. K's improved health on arrival. Tell Arthur I make great dependence on the letter I shall get from him, and will try to remember anything that happens on the voyage which he would be pleased to hear.

We had some baked apples (sour) the other night about the size of a new-born infant's head. They tasted extremely well.

Please give our love to Mother & the girls, Aunt Hannah, Arthur and other friends, reserving a share for yourself.

As I have nothing more to say I will follow A. Ward's advice, and say it at once.

Farewell　　Yours aff'ly　SARAH

Before her marriage to her cousin Benjamin Briggs, Sarah Elizabeth Cobb had sung in the choir of the Congregational Church of Marion, of which her father, the Reverend Leander Cobb, was pastor. She was fond of music and had a good voice. Dr. Oliver W. Cobb of East-hampton, Massachusetts,[19] recalls hearing his father praise her after a Sunday morning service, for the excellent quality of her singing. Both Sarah Cobb and her husband were first cousins of Dr. Cobb.

Around the family piano—one of the few then in town—there had been many a family "sing," and in his letter to his mother, written on the Sunday prior to their departure from New York, we find Captain Briggs saying: "We enjoy our melodeon, and have some good sings." In a letter written from the vessel[20] 27 October to her son Arthur in Marion, Mrs. Briggs says: "After a while, Mother was playing on the melodeon, and she (Sophy) wanted Sarah Jane, her doll, to play too." Perhaps the only shadow over the happiness of the captain and his wife was the seemingly

19. Dr. Cobb to the author.

20. Letter in the possession of Mr. J. Franklin Briggs, New Bedford, Massachusetts.

(1872)

Brig Mary Celeste
Off Staten Island Nov 7th

Dear Mother Briggs,-

Probably you will be
a little surprised to receive a letter with
this date, but instead of proceeding to sea
when we came out Tuesday morning, we
anchored about a mile or so from the
city, as it was strong head wind, and
B. said it looked so thick & nasty a
head we shouldn't gain much if we
were beating & banging about. Accordingly we took a fresh departure this morning with wind light but favorable, so
we hope to get outside without being

obliged to anchor. Have kept a sharp
look out for 6 lines, but so far have
seen nothing of him. It was rather
trying to lay in sight of the city so
long & think that most likely we
had letters waiting for us there, and
be unable to get them. However
we hope no great change has occurred since we did hear, and
I shall look for a goodly supply
when we reach G.

Sophy thinks the figure 3 & the letter
G. on her blocks is the same thing,
so I saw her whispering to herself
yesterday with the 3 block in her
hand — Gam Gamy Gamma.
Benjo thinks we have got a pretty
peaceable set this time all round.
if they continue as they have begun
can't tell yet how smart they are
B reports a good breeze now, says
we are going along nicely.

I should like to be present at Mrs Kingsbury's ordination next week. Hope the people will be united in him, and wish we might hear of Mrs R's improved health on arrival Tell Arthur I make great dependence on the letter I shall get from him, and will try to remember anything that happens on the voyage Which he would be pleased to hear.

We had some baked apples (done) the other night about the size of a new-born infant's head. They tasted extremely well.

Please give our love to mother & the girls, aunt Hancock, Arthur, and other friends reserving a share for yourself.

As I have nothing more to say I will follow A. Ward's advice, and say it at once.

Farewell & Yours Affy Fred

necessary separation from their son Arthur, aged seven, and therefore of school age. To the Briggs family, education was a matter of major importance, and in committing the boy to the capable hands of his Grandmother Briggs, they took comfort in the realization that everything needful for his welfare would be done.

When, on Thursday morning, 7 November, the *Mary Celeste* left her Staten Island anchorage, she began a voyage destined to lift her from comparative obscurity to a place of enduring fame in the chronicles of the sea.

CHAPTER II

The Master of the *Mary Celeste*

Almost four weeks were to pass before the next reported appearance of the *Mary Celeste*.

Before proceeding with that phase of her adventure, it will be necessary to deviate from the direct course of the narrative, in order to study the background of the events that follow.

Even under ordinary circumstances, it would be important to know something of the antecedent history and experience of the principal persons involved. Under the circumstances attending the present case, having in mind the unjust aspersions upon the character and reputation of Captain Briggs in some of the legendary literature of recent years, it seems particularly desirable, in the interest of justice as well as for purposes of information, to make known the facts as to the sources whence he came and the environmental influences of his earlier years.

Benjamin Spooner Briggs was born at Wareham, Massachusetts, on 24 April 1835. He was the second of the five sons born to Captain Nathan Briggs and his wife, Sophia Cobb. All of the sons but James were brought up by their father to follow the sea, and two of the four became master mariners at an early age.

Maria, the eldest child and only daughter, in conformity with the family tradition of being "wedded to the sea," married Joseph D. Gibbs, also a sea-captain.

Benjamin's father, Captain Nathan Briggs, appears from his letters and voluminous sea journals to have been poet and philosopher as well as practical and successful master-mariner. Although kind and affectionate in all his

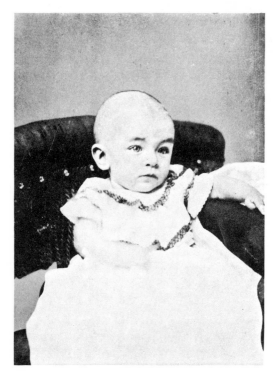

Sophia Matilda Briggs
daughter of Captain and Mrs. Benjamin Spooner Briggs
and lost with them at sea

PLATE III

family relationships, he was a strict disciplinarian aboard ship. From time to time, his own sons and other relatives shipped under him, "but on ship-board [as a still living member of the family writes of him],[1] the etiquette of the sea ruled, and one would not have known but that they were strangers." The same writer says of him: "He was as careful of his personal appearance on ship-board as at home. He navigated his ship with great care. There was no slacking with him. He did not order his sailors about or talk to them. All his orders were given to his mates and they were held responsible for the execution of the same. When the Captain walked the quarter-deck, no sailor ever thought of passing on the weather-side. If going to or from the wheel, they always went on the lee side, or if a sailor had work to do on the weather side, he would, in passing, touch his cap in salute and pass to leeward, never going between the Captain and the wind." . . . "He was a Spartan father when it came to having his sons on shipboard. They had to do the regular work of sailors, take their trick at the wheel, stand watch, help reef and furl sails.

"The Captain expected his boy to be the first man aloft in an emergency. In addition to this, the boy had regular lessons to study and to recite to the Captain; navigation, geography, history, literature. There was no idleness on these voyages."

"In 1824, Captain Nathan Briggs made his first voyage across the ocean, as master of the schooner *Betsy & Jane* When he shipped his crew, he wrote into the articles of agreement; 'No grog will be allowed on board.' Others copied this, and in 1840, it became part of the standard form of agreement." This attitude toward liquor, both on land and sea, also became one of the fixed principles of his son Benjamin.

1. Dr. Oliver W. Cobb, *Rose Cottage.*

When he was about four years old, Ben and his mother, with three others of her children, were compelled to make their home with the children's maternal grandfather, the Reverend Oliver Cobb, at the Manse of Marion's Congregational Church of which he was the Pastor. This change was due to severe financial reverses suffered by Captain Nathan, who had invested his sea-earnings in a commercial enterprise in Wareham which had failed. The minister had other children of his own. Both the walls of the Manse and the pastor's income must have had unusual flexibility to accommodate and provide for such a large assembly, but the measure and warmth of his hospitality knew no limitations, and Benjamin, along with the other children and their mother, spent five happy years there.

The influence of such surroundings on the life of a small boy during his most impressionable years cannot be measured.

In the meantime, his father, Captain Nathan, had regained employment as shipmaster, and by 1844, when Ben was nine years old, Captain Nathan had so far retrieved his fortunes as to be able to make a new home for his wife and children, now numbering six. In the fall of that year, they moved into their newly-built home "Rose Cottage" at Sippican Village, about a mile distant from the Manse. [Plate VI.]

Both during the years spent in the Manse and afterwards, Benjamin's life was redolent of the sea, in the tradition of which most of the local families were born and bred. It was chiefly to the sea that the enterprising youth of the time looked for their careers. It was in that quarter that opportunity beckoned. Along the town wharf, doubtless, loitered many a village Jason, dreaming of the years when he, too, would venture across the furrowed seas, and bring home deep-burdened ships, laden with the produce of distant Ind and far Cathay.

Relatives and friends were arriving after long voyages to distant lands, with stories of foreign ways and customs, and, not infrequently, with tales of shipwreck experienced or hardship endured. Letters to and from the loved ones away at sea kept up a ceaseless flow of correspondence. Melbourne, Montevideo and Messina; Smyrna, Santos and Singapore; manifests, bills of lading and charter-parties; rivers, capes and harbors; geography was not only studied but inhaled—it was in the very air they breathed. Stimulating food and drink it was for a young lad, and the stuff of which dreams are made.

It is not definitely known whether Benjamin, like his brothers, shipped under his father, but he was brought up in a home where a kindly discipline was maintained, and careful training in manners and deportment were considered essential. In the formation of his character, his mother, who it will be remembered was a minister's daughter, was always a powerful influence. The bond between them was unusually strong, and the last letter written by him, of which there is any record, was addressed to her in tender and affectionate terms, evincing solicitude for her comfort during his absence. This letter was sent just a few days prior to his sailing from New York.

She lived to a ripe old age, and is remembered by those still living as a woman of strong character whose Christian faith enabled her to withstand, with grace and fortitude, the successive shocks caused by the loss at sea of two sons and a daughter by shipwreck; two sons by yellow fever while at sea, and by the death of her husband, Captain Nathan, struck by lightning as he stood in the doorway of their home.

On 9 September 1862, Benjamin Spooner Briggs, aged

twenty-seven, and Sarah Elizabeth Cobb, aged twenty, were united in marriage at Marion, Massachusetts, the ceremony being performed by the bride's father, the Reverend Leander Cobb, pastor of the Congregational Church of Marion.

It was the first and only marriage for both of the contracting parties, as attested by the Town Records of Marion.[2] "Benjamin and Sarah had been boy and girl sweethearts. It was a love match, and they always remained deeply devoted to each other."[3]

Ben is described by a member of the family as "a man who spoke in a quiet tone of voice, and with an inclination to reticence."[4] He was very familiar with the Bible, which he read regularly. On occasion, he "gave testimony" at prayer-meetings according to the custom of those times. On one of his trips to Gibraltar, he joined a Masonic Lodge there.

When he took command of the *Mary Celeste* in the fall of 1872, he was in his thirty-eighth year. He had previously commanded the schooner *Forest King* (the vessel which took him and Sarah on their honeymoon to the Mediterranean), and also the bark *Arthur* and the brig *Sea Foam*. His reputation as a master mariner by this time was well established. United States Consul Horatio Jones Sprague, writing[5] from Gibraltar to the Department of State at Washington, states that Captain Briggs "was well known" and that "he bore the highest character for seamanship and correctness." Consul Sprague, in his letter of 3 April 1873, to N. W. Bingham, Treasury Department Agent at Boston, wrote: "The missing master, Briggs, I had known

2. See Appendix U for certified copy of record of marriage.
3. Letter of 13 June 1941 from J. Franklin Briggs to the author.
4. J. Franklin Briggs to the author.
5. Letter No. 130, 20 January 1873.

for many years, and he always bore a good character as a Christian, and as an intelligent and active shipmaster." The same writer, in his letter of 12 August 1873 to Mr. James C. Briggs, expressed sympathy in his affliction, concluding with the statement: "Your Brother was well-known to me and therefore I was able to appreciate his merits." Gentle and affectionate in his family relations, it seems reasonable to suppose that he would be just and considerate toward the men serving under him. He could be stern when occasion required it, and was not a man to be intimidated or imposed upon.

Born of sturdy, God-fearing New England stock; reared in an atmosphere of wholesome refinement, and trained as well in the salty curriculum of the sea as in ways of right living, Benjamin Briggs was well prepared to undertake the responsibilities of the command of the *Mary Celeste*.

CHAPTER III

The Crew

THE master of the *Mary Celeste* is not the only member of the ship's company who has suffered at the hands of some of the previous chroniclers of the vessel's tragic experience. The crew has been described as "about as bad a looking lot as ever swabbed a deck" and as "a company of cutthroats for whom every civilized nation has a gallows in waiting." These are a few of the contemporary newspaper comments. Some of the writers have peopled the decks of the vessel with ghostly crews that never existed except in the imaginations of the writers themselves. A crew of "thirteen" has been a popular theme with some, in the hope, no doubt, of investing the story with a greater air of mystery. Even comparatively recently, they have been variously described as drunken, dissolute, and murderous. To those who desire the facts, it will be of interest to know that all the available evidence points directly the other way. It is a matter of official record that a crew of seven, including first and second mates, steward and four seamen, was shipped at New York.

The first mate was Albert G. Richardson, of Stockton Springs, Maine. [Plate VII.] According to the crew list signed at New York 4 November 1872 by H. E. Jenks, Deputy United States Shipping Commissioner, Richardson was "28[1] years of age, 5 feet 8 inches tall, with light complexion and brown hair; wages $50."

He was the son of Theodore and Elizabeth Richardson, and had a brother Lyman who was a sea captain. A Certif-

1. The age differs slightly from that given at the time of enlistment in 1864. See Appendix J.

icate of Service issued by the Office of the Adjutant-General of the State of Maine,[2] dated Augusta 16 December 1940 gives his Civil War record. "It is hereby certified that it appears from the records of this office that Albert Richardson of Quota of Stockton, Maine, enlisted February 27, 1864, mustered March 18, 1864, in Company A, Coast Guard Infantry, Maine Volunteers, at Belfast, Maine for three years. Honorably discharged May 25, 1865 at Portland, Me., a Private. Said Albert Richardson was born in Charlestown, Mass; age at enlistment 18 years, 2 months; light complexion, blue eyes; dark hair; by occupation a seaman."

According to a communication received from the War Department[3] he was a private in "Captain Baker's Independent Company for Coast Defences, subsequently known as Company A, Coast Guard Maine Infantry."

A letter from the Veterans Administration[4] at Washington states that a claim for death pension benefits, based on the Civil War Service of Albert Richardson, was filed on 6 August 1890 by Fannie N. Richardson as the veteran's widow,[5] and she was awarded death pension benefits until 29 April 1937, the date of her death.[6]

From the same authority,[7] it is learned that "There is also on file the joint affidavit of James H. Winchester and Joseph C. Noyes, dated Oct. 29, 1890, in which they state that 'Albert G. Richardson sailed in our employ for about

2. Letter to the author, 16 December 1940.

3. Letter to the author, 21 April 1941.

4. Letter of 6 January 1941 to the author.

5. Mrs. A. G. Richardson died at 1962 Brown Street, Brooklyn, New York, at the age of ninety-one.

6. Letter of 6 January 1941 from Veterans Administration to the author.

7. Letter of 31 January 1941 from Veterans Administration to the author.

two years, and the said Albert G. Richardson was lost, drowned, from our Brig *Mary Celeste* on or about Nov. 24, 1872.' The affiants were doing business in New York under the firm name of J. H. Winchester & Co."

The *New York Sunday World*[8] quotes Captain J. H. Winchester as saying: "The Mate of the vessel, Mr. Richardson, was the husband of my wife's niece, a man of excellent character."

Richardson had previously sailed under Captain Briggs. Dr. Oliver W. Cobb, a physician now residing at Easthampton, Massachusetts, whose boyhood days were spent in Marion, Massachusetts, and who lived part of the time with the Briggs family, recalls[9] hearing Captain Briggs congratulate Mrs. Briggs upon their good fortune in having Richardson go with them as first mate on the *Mary Celeste*.

The particulars of Richardson's association with this voyage of the *Mary Celeste* are given in detail in view of the fact that, in one of the most widely circulated narratives purporting to be the true account of the vessel's experience, a fictitious character, apparently known only to the author of that narrative, appears actively throughout as the vessel's first mate, whereas Richardson is not acknowledged as mate, or even as a member of the ship's company, his name being only casually mentioned, in the last chapter, as one of "a string of names" previously put forward by others as belonging to "people who might have been on board."

Of the second mate, Andrew Gilling, little is known except the information furnished by the official record: "Birthplace, New York; age 25; Height, 5 feet, 8 inches:

8. 24 January 1886.
9. To the author 10 July 1940.

Captain Benjamin Spooner Briggs as a young man

PLATE IV

Captain Benjamin Spooner Briggs as a young man

PLATE V

Complexion, light; Hair, light: Wages per month, $35."
In the engagement book, the address of 19 Thames Street,
New York, is given.

On 8 July 1873, the pastor of the parish of Kathy, Samso,
Denmark, addressed the Royal Danish Consul at Gibraltar, inquiring in behalf of "the bereaved and sorrowful
mother" of Andrew Gilling for news regarding his fate,
and requesting instruction as to the proper procedure in
order to have the effects of the missing seaman sent to his
mother.

The "Steward and Cook," Edward Wm. Head, according to the record, was born in New York. He is therein described as: "Age, 23: Height, 5 Feet, 8 inches: Complexion, light: Hair, light: Wages per month $40." Captain
Winchester in the same interview as that quoted above
said of him: "The steward was a white man who belonged
to Williamsburg, where he was respected by all who knew
him, and he had just been married when the brig sailed."
In the "Engagement Book" of the United States Shipping
Commissioner, under date of 5 November 1872, his address is given as "145 Newell Street, Greenpoint" (a section of Brooklyn).

In view of the fact that a book published in 1929 by
Laurence J. Keating is largely, if not entirely, based upon
the alleged representations of a person named "John Pemberton," who at the age of eighty-two (or ninety-two as reported by the *London Evening Standard*) claimed to have
been cook or steward on the *Mary Celeste* at the time of her
abandonment, the following letter addressed to United
States Consul Sprague at Gibraltar, should be of interest.

New York, July 31, 1873.

DEAR SIR:—
Will you have the kindness to forward to the address of Messrs.
J. H. Winchester & Co., the effects belonging to my husband, Ed-

ward W. Head, late Steward of the Brig *Mary Celeste* — please advise them of the shipment and oblige,

Yours very resp'y,

[signed] MRS. EMMA J. HEAD.

Hon. Horatio J. Sprague
  U. S. Consul, Gibraltar, Spain

The letter is written on the official letterhead of J. H. Winchester & Co., 52 South Street, the principal owners of the vessel. Apparently, Mrs. Head called there in order to arrange for the shipment, from Gibraltar, of her late husband's effects. The letter appears to have been prepared by some one in the Winchester office as the writing in the body of the letter differs from that of the signature of Mrs. Head.

Under date of 19 August, Consul Sprague acknowledged Mrs. Head's communication, and referred therein to her husband as "late Steward of the Brig *Mary Celeste*," and instructed her as to the necessary procedure to obtain his effects.

In the United States Shipping Commissioner's official crew list, dated 4 November 1872, the name of "Ed. Wm. Head" is given as "Std. & Cook. . . ." This list contains no such name as "John Pemberton" or anything similar to it. Even if it should be supposed that "Pemberton" shipped under an assumed name, it is significant that "Pemberton" was unable to give the right names of any of his alleged companions on the passage except those of Captain and Mrs. Briggs. In the circumstances, it would seem that the whole structure of the narrative in question, which depends upon the alleged statements of the nebulous "Pemberton," stands revealed in its true light.

The remaining members of the ship's company are described in the crew list and other official records as follows:

Name	Birthplace	Age	Hgt.	Comp.	Hair.	Wages per month
Volkert Lorenzen[10]	Germany	29	5′ 9″	Lght.	Lght.	$30
Arian Harbens[11]	Germany	35	5′ 8″	Lght.	Lght.	30
Boz Lorenzen[12]	Germany	25	5′ 9″	Lght.	Lght.	30
Gottliecbs Goodschaad[13]	Germany	23	5′ 8″	Lght.	Lght.	30

In another part of the same record, all in the same handwriting, the name of the second seaman is entered in one place as Adrian Martens and in another as Andrew Marten; the fourth, as Gottleb Goudschaad and Gottlieb Goodschall. In still another official record, executed at the same time, these two names appear as "Arian Mardens" and "Gottlieb Goudschaal." The addresses of all four appear in the "Engagement Book" as 19 Thames Street (New York).

In the Inventory (Appendix R) sent on 10 March 1873 by Consul Horatio J. Sprague, to the Assistant Secretary of State, Washington, D. C., reference is made to a seaman's chest marked "Adrian Martens" which differs again from the other versions. In still another communication to the State Department, Consul Sprague gives the name as "Arian Hardens."

Reference to the character of three members of the crew is made in a communication No. 142, dated 4 April 1873 from United States Consul Sprague at Gibraltar to the Department of State at Washington.

"I beg to enclose copy of a communication which I have this day received from Prussia, asking for information regarding some of the missing crew of the derelict *Mary Celeste*. It is somewhat gratifying to learn three out of the five men composing the crew of the *Mary Celeste*

10. Correct name Volkert Lorenzen.
11. Correct name Arian Martens.
12. Correct name Boz Lorenzen.
13. Correct name believed to be Gottlieb Goodschaad or Goodschaal.

were known to the writer of that communication as being peaceable and first-class sailors, as it further diminishes the probability that any violence was committed on board of this vessel by her crew."

Following is a copy of the letter mentioned by Consul Sprague:

ON [*sic*] THE AMERICAN CONSUL
    Gibraltar   UTERSUM, ISLE OF FÖHR, PRUSSIA,

DEAR SIR: *March 24, 1873.*

Please excuse me of writing these few lines of information regarding two sailors (brothers) belonging to the American Brig *Mary Celeste,* their mother and their wives wish to know in which condition the ship has been found, whether the boats were gone or not, whether the log-book has been found on board or not, so as to find out on what day they have left the ship, and further do they like to know whether any signs of disturbance have been found on board. I know three of the sailors personally and know them to be peaceable and first-class sailors. Please favor us with an answer and let us know your opinion why they left said Brig.

           I remain, Yours, truly,   T. A. NICKELSEN,[14]

direct Utersum, auf Föhr, Prussia, Via Hamburg.

It is noticeable that this letter does not refer to any of the sailors by name. The reference to "two sailors, brothers" would seem to apply to the Lorenzens, Volkert and Boz. In the course of testimony given at Gibraltar, mention is made of the fact that "There were four berths in the fore-castle with bedding, but only three sea-chests" with the explanation by Mate Deveau that, "often, two sailors chum for one chest." It would not be unnatural for the two Lorenzen brothers to do this.

14. A letter of 7 February 1885 from R. I. Lorenzen, Chief of the Parish, Utersum, Isle of Föhr, Prussia, to the German Consul Ferdinand Schott at Gibraltar, refers to "the letter of the late Chief of the parish, Nickelsen," who, apparently, was a German island official in 1873.

Further evidence as to the character of the crew comes from the letter written[15] by Captain Briggs, just two days before his vessel left her East River pier, wherein he states: "We seem to have a very good Mate and Steward," and, four days later (7 November) Mrs. Briggs writes to her husband's mother: "Benjamin thinks we have got a pretty peaceable set this time all around, if they continue as they have begun," adding, with characteristic Yankee caution, "Can't tell yet how smart they are."

There can be no question about the *Mary Celeste* being adequately manned. She carried a crew of eight, including the captain, which was in conformity with the recommendations of a Seamen's Congress held some years later in England, when a total of seven was recommended for sailing vessels of 200 tons register, and a crew of nine, all told, for vessels of 300 tons.[16] It is reasonable to assume that Captain Briggs, experienced mariner that he was, would exercise more than ordinary care in the selection of a crew for a voyage on which his wife and two-year-old daughter were to accompany him.

15. 3 November 1872 to Mrs. Nathan Briggs.
16. *Marine Journal* (New York), 7 November 1891.

CHAPTER IV

A Startling Cable from Gibraltar

IT is Saturday, 14 December 1872, and the Disaster Clerk of the Atlantic Mutual Insurance Company, whose duty it is to make daily record of all maritime casualties reported in the newspapers, has been handed a copy of a cablegram from Gibraltar, addressed "Parker, New York" and signed "Morehouse." The entry made in the Disaster Book[1] reads as follows:

FOUND FOURTH AND BROUGHT HERE "MARY CELESTE" ABANDONED SEAWORTHY ADMIRALTY IMPOST NOTIFY ALL PARTIES TELEGRAPH OFFER OF SALVAGE.

Morehouse who sent the cable was Captain David Reed Morehouse, master of the brigantine *Dei Gratia* which had sailed on 15 November,[2] eight days after the *Mary Celeste*. Parker, presumably, was John W. Parker of the firm of Heney & Parker, brokers, 25 Coenties Slip, New York, part-owners of the *Dei Gratia*.

This message, announcing the finding on 4 December of the half-brig *Mary Celeste,* abandoned but seaworthy, was no doubt the first report received in America of a marine tragedy destined to become the most widely known of all the mysteries of the sea.

In all likelihood, the contents of the cable were immediately communicated by "Parker" to J. H. Winchester & Co., 52 South Street, agents of the vessel and owners of a twelve twenty-fourths interest, and by them transmitted

1. Disaster Book No. 93, page 192.
2. *Maritime Register,* 20 November and 27 November 1872.

to the various companies who had insured the hull and freight interests.

The entry in the Atlantic Mutual's Disaster Book continued as follows:

Atlantic's interest, Freight or Charter $3,400.00, Gold, November, 1872, New York to Genoa, for J. H. Winchester, cargo 1700 barrels Alcohol shipped by Meissner, Ackerman & Co. of 48 Beaver St. insured in Europe.[3]

This, being interpreted, meant that J. H. Winchester & Co. as principal owners and agents of the vessel had engaged to take a cargo of alcohol to Genoa in the *Mary Celeste,* and that, for the performance of such service, they expected to earn freight money amounting to $3,400 contingent upon the delivery of the cargo at Genoa.

Confronting the vessel owners was the possibility that, through perils of the sea, the vessel might be prevented from earning her freight money, with resultant pecuniary loss to them. It was this risk which J. H. Winchester & Co. as managing owners, had insured at the rate of two and a half per cent with the Atlantic Mutual Insurance Company.

On the same day that Captain Morehouse had telegraphed to the agents or owners of his vessel, as already noted, Consul Sprague sent the following telegram:

GIBRALTAR, 13TH DECEMBER 1872
BOARD OF UNDERWRITERS, NEW YORK
BRIG "MARY CELESTE" HERE DERELICT IMPORTANT SEND POWER ATTORNEY TO CLAIM HER FROM ADMIRALTY COURT.
[SIGNED] HORATIO J. SPRAGUE

Consul Sprague also despatched the following message to O. M. Spencer, Consul at Genoa:

3. Atlantic Mutual Insurance Company, Disaster Book No. 93, page 192.

GIBRALTAR, 13TH DECEMBER 1872

AMERICAN CONSUL, GENOA

AMERICAN BRIG "MARY CELESTE" HERE DERELICT IM-
PORTANT SEND BILL LADING CARGO TO CLAIM FROM AD-
MIRALTY COURT.   [SIGNED] SPRAGUE, CONSUL

On making inquiry of J. H. Winchester & Co. at 52 South Street, it was learned that the insurance on the vessel's hull was carried by four American companies in amounts as follows:

Maine Lloyds	$6,000.00
Orient Mutual Insurance Company	4,000.00
Mercantile Mutual Insurance Company	2,500.00
New England Mutual Insurance Company	1,500.00
Total amount insured on hull	$14,000.00

This, added to the Atlantic's insurance of $3,400 on freight on charter, made a total of $17,400 on the hull and freight interests, all insured in this country. The value of the cargo, said to have been insured abroad, was reported as £6,522–3–0.

After consultation among the local underwriters, the following cablegram was despatched on the same day by the Board of Underwriters to Horatio J. Sprague, United States Consul at Gibraltar:

PROTECT BRIG "MARY CELESTE" WANT VOYAGE PER-
FORMED   OGDEN[4]

"Ogden" undoubtedly was Mr. Alfred Ogden, who, in 1872, was the Chairman of the Standing Committee on Salvages, Losses and Averages of the Board of Under-writers of New York. Mr. Ogden was also vice-president of the Orient Mutual Insurance Company, one of the five American companies previously mentioned.

4. Atlantic Mutual Insurance Company Disaster Book No. 93, page 192.

"Rose Cottage," boyhood home of Captain Benjamin Spooner Briggs at Marion, Massachusetts

PLATE VI

Albert G. Richardson, First Mate of the Mary Celeste

PLATE VII

Thus far, reference has been made only to the reception of the news by the insurance companies and their consequent action to protect their interests. It is not difficult to imagine the effect of the startling intelligence when it was communicated to the families and friends of Captain Briggs and of other members of the ship's company.

The fact that the cable message reported the vessel as seaworthy only served to deepen the mystery. The vessel had left New York, well found and well provisioned, with an experienced master and an adequate crew. As Captain Briggs expressed it,[5] "our vessel is in beautiful trim." About the only hopeful prospect was that, having abandoned the vessel in some sudden emergency, the company of ten persons had later been picked up by a passing vessel, and, according to the destination and the speed of the rescuing vessel, would ultimately be reported as having safely arrived in port. In case of rescue by a sailing vessel, it was realized that the time of waiting for such news might be considerably prolonged.

It was not unnatural that speculation should be rife as to the cause for abandonment of a seaworthy vessel by a competent mariner such as Captain Briggs was known to be, and various were the theories which, in the public press, along the wharves and wherever seafaring folk foregathered, continued to be advanced during the succeeding weeks and months, while the families and friends of the ten missing persons waited with anxious interest for some message that would announce their whereabouts or disclose their fate.

For the record of events leading to the finding of the *Mary Celeste* by the *Dei Gratia,* and the circumstances attending the successful salvage operation of bringing the derelict to Gibraltar, we shall turn to the following chapter.

5. Letter, dated 3 November 1872 from Captain Briggs to his mother.

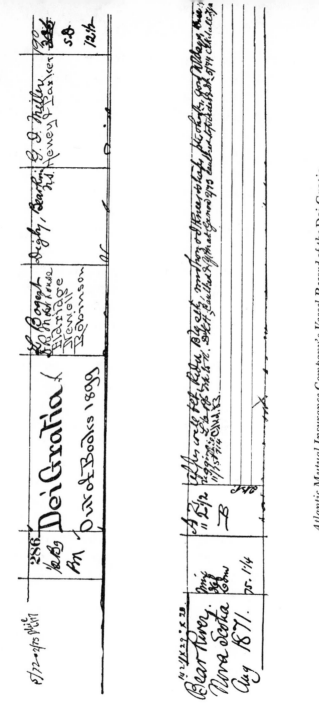

Atlantic Mutual Insurance Company's Vessel Record of the Dei Gratia

CHAPTER V

The *Dei Gratia* has an Unexpected Adventure

One ship drives East, and one drives West,
By the selfsame wind that blows;
It's the set of the sails, and not the gales,
Which determines the way it goes.

ELLA WHEELER WILCOX

IT was on 15 November 1872,[1] just eight days after the departure of the *Mary Celeste,* that the British brigantine *Dei Gratia,* 295 tons [Plate VIII], of Bear River, Nova Scotia, under command of Captain David Reed Morehouse [Plate IX], left New York with a cargo of petroleum.[2] She was bound for Gibraltar, where she was to stop "for orders," which meant that, on arrival at Gibraltar, Captain Morehouse would find a telegram from the vessel owners, telling him where to proceed to deliver his cargo. The *Dei Gratia* carried eight men all told. Oliver Deveau [Plate X] and John Wright were first and second mates respectively. Four days later (19 November), she was spoken[3] in latitude 40° 55′ N, and longitude 66° W, which would have brought her about 360 miles on her journey. She proceeded on her course until Wednesday, 4 December.

On that day, soon after the beginning of the afternoon watch, Captain Morehouse was on deck. With him were Second Mate Wright and Seamen Augustus Anderson and John Johnson. Johnson was at the wheel. It was either

1. *Maritime Register,* 20 November, 27 November and 4 December 1872. "Br., Morehouse, N. Y. Nov. 15 for Gibraltar."

2. Ibid., 30 October 1872. Freight Report, "Funch, Edye & Co. Ship Brokers. Br. Brig *Dei Gratia* 250, hence to Gibraltar, f. o., with petroleum at 6s. 9d.—7s. 9d."

3. *Maritime Register,* 27 November 1872.

Captain Morehouse or Johnson who first sighted[4] a sailing vessel about four to six miles distant, on their port or windward bow. The state of her sails, and the fact that she yawed some, attracted their attention. She was under very short canvas. Captain Morehouse summoned Mate Deveau, then below and off duty, and pointed the vessel out to him. Scanning her through the glass, they were unable to descry anybody on board. She was making about one and a half to two knots, headed *westward* and therefore proceeding in a direction *opposite* to their own. According to Wright, second mate, "our head was then S.E. by East—the head of the other vessel was N.W. by North—as far as I could judge." According to the *Dei Gratia's* log, they were then in latitude 38° 20' N, longitude 17° 15' W.[5] The conclusion was that the stranger was in distress and required assistance, although no signal of distress was displayed. Captain Morehouse proposed to "speak" the vessel in order to render assistance if necessary, and gave orders to haul his wind. They accordingly hauled up and on nearer approach hailed her, but received no response. The captain then ordered a boat lowered, and Mate Deveau, accompanied by Wright and Johnson, rowed over to the stranger. The sea was running high, the weather having been stormy, although the wind was then moderating.

On reaching the vessel, Deveau and Wright clambered aboard, leaving Johnson in the small boat alongside. By this time, no doubt, they had observed the vessel's name

4. According to court testimony, both Deveau and Wright stated the hour as one o'clock sea-time, but the entry on the *Dei Gratia's* log, made apparently by Captain Morehouse himself, states: "Saw a sail to the E. 2 P.M." See Appendix L. Deveau later corrected his testimony, stating that it was 1:30 when the Captain called him.

5. The *Dei Gratia's* log on 4 December at noon — about two hours before Captain Morehouse's entry, quoted above—gives the vessel's location as "Lat. 38° 20': Long. 17° 37' D. R. 17° 15'." See Appendix L.

Mary Celeste on her port bow, or possibly on the vessel's quarter. Shortly thereafter, the vessel's log, found in the cabin, would disclose both her name and her hailing port, New York. It was then about three o'clock. Making a thor-

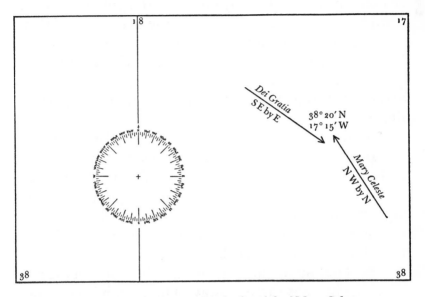

Diagram showing where Dei Gratia *first sighted* Mary Celeste
4 December 1:30–2:00 P.M. (Civil Time), 5 December (Sea-time)
Latitude 38° 20′ North, Longitude 17° 15′ West

"Our head was then S.E. by E.—the head of the other vessel was N.W. by N.—as far as I could judge." *Testimony of* JOHN WRIGHT, *Second Mate of the* Dei Gratia, *on 20 December 1872.*

"The wind was to the northward—her head to the westward—She was then going in opposite direction to ourselves—We met her." *Testimony of* OLIVER DEVEAU, *First Mate of the* Dei Gratia, *on 18 December 1872.*

Entry on Log of Dei Gratia, *5 December (Sea-time) gives course as SE½E at time of meeting.*

ough search of the vessel, they failed to find a single soul on board. There were no boats.[6] The one ship's boat, which, there was evidence to show, had lain across the

6. *Maritime Register*, Disasters, 15 January 1873. Also court testimony and letter No. 123 of 13 December 1872 from Consul Horatio J. Sprague at Gibraltar to Department of State.

main hatch, was missing. They found about three and a half feet of water in the hold, a quantity which was considerable in such a small vessel, but, with seventeen hundred barrels of alcohol[7] in the hold, would not have been particularly noticed except by sounding the pumps. The forward-house was full of water up to the coaming, and there was a great deal of water between decks. Both the fore hatch and the lazarette hatch were off. The binnacle (which was a stand of wood for the compass to rest in) was knocked out of its place and injured; the compass was destroyed.

The wheel was not lashed but was undamaged. Her jib and fore-topmast staysail were set on the starboard tack. Two of her sails—the fore-sail and upper fore-topsail —had been blown away; the lower fore-topsail was "hanging by the four corners"; the main-staysail had been hauled down and was lying loose on the forward-house.[8] All the rest of the sails were furled.

The standing rigging was all right, but some of the running rigging was carried away. The captain's chronometer, sextant, navigation book, ship's register and other papers were missing. The log book was found on the desk in the mate's cabin, and the log slate was found on the cabin table. There was nothing to eat or drink in the cabin on the table, and there was no cooked food in the galley. There were six months' provisions in the storeroom and plenty of drinking water. These, and other con-

7. Lecture at Yale University, 22 February 1904 by Mr. Anton A. Raven, President of Atlantic Mutual Insurance Company, published by *Yale Alumni Weekly*, 2 March 1904; also *Maritime Register*, Disasters, 18 December 1872; *Gibraltar Chronicle*, 31 January 1873; letter No. 134 of 25 February 1873 from Consul Sprague to Department of State; letter of 7 March 1873 from N. W. Bingham, Special Agent, United States Treasury, to Consul H. J. Sprague.

8. Deveau stated that it had fallen down on the stovepipe of the galley.

ditions noted by Deveau and Wright during the half-hour they spent on board the vessel, will be mentioned at greater length, in a subsequent chapter.

Their brief inspection finished, they climbed down into their small boat and, with Johnson, returned to the *Dei Gratia* where they reported to Captain Morehouse the result of their investigation.

According to the record, Deveau then proposed that the captain permit him to take two men and sail the derelict into Gibraltar. It there appears that Captain Morehouse, who was a prudent master, at first demurred. As master of the *Dei Gratia*, he was responsible to the owners for the safety of the vessel and her cargo of petroleum, as well as for the safety of the men under his command. To spare a sufficient number of his seven men to sail the *Mary Celeste* to Gibraltar might endanger both vessels and their crews. Between themselves and Gibraltar lay some six hundred[9] miles of ocean, with all the unpredictable perils that might overtake two comparatively small sailing craft on the broad Atlantic in the December season.

However, the opportunity of earning a salvage award for bringing into port a derelict with a cargo of considerable value was not to be lightly passed by, and after consultation between captain and crew, it was decided to make the attempt. Captain Morehouse directed Deveau to take with him Seamen Charles Lund and Augustus Anderson, making three men, all told, to sail the *Mary Celeste* to Gibraltar and leaving Captain Morehouse with four men to run the *Dei Gratia*. (It will be noted that Lund and Anderson were not the men who accompanied Deveau on the first trip to the derelict.) The captain let them have the ship's small boat, a barometer, compass and watch,

9. Letter of 7 December 1940 from Hydrographic Office, Navy Department, Washington, D. C., to the author.

along with some food the steward had prepared. Deveau, who, according to his own statement had previously been master of a brig, took his own nautical instruments. According to the record, it was about four o'clock in the afternoon of this memorable Wednesday, 4 December (or 5 December, according to sea-time as, at sea in those days, the date changed at noon) when Deveau, Lund and Anderson boarded the *Mary Celeste* and proceeded to put her in readiness for the remainder of the journey. Between eight and nine o'clock in the evening of the same day, the vessel was pumped out, sail was set on her, and they got under way. They found a spare trysail which they set in place of the fore-sail which was gone. It took them two or three days "to set her to rights," so as to proceed on the voyage and "make any headway." They had fine weather until they got into the Strait of Gibraltar, when "it came on a storm." Up to that time, they had seen the *Dei Gratia* almost every day, and had spoken her three or four times. On the night of the storm, however, the two vessels lost sight of each other. When the *Mary Celeste* arrived at the port of Gibraltar early in the morning of Friday, 13 December,[10] they found that the *Dei Gratia* had arrived there in the evening of the day before.[11]

On the same day that the *Mary Celeste* arrived, she was taken into custody by T. J. Vecchio, Marshal of the Vice-Admiralty Court. On 18 December the Court began its hearings on the claims of "David Reed Morehouse, Master of the British brigantine *Dei Gratia* and for the Owners,

10. Letter of 22 January 1873 from Frederick Solly Flood to Board of Trade, London. *Maritime Register*, 8 January 1873 and court testimony.

11. Court testimony and Letter No. 123, 13 December 1872 from Consul Sprague to Department of State. Erroneously reported in *Maritime Register* as having arrived on 11 December. Letter of 22 January 1873 from Frederick Solly Flood to Board of Trade, London.

Officers and Crew of the said brigantine, claiming as Salvors."

In view of the radical change in the status of the *Mary Celeste* within the period of about five weeks, dating from the time of her sailing on 7 November, when she left New York, to the time of her arrest as a derelict at Gibraltar 13 December, it seems desirable, before proceeding further with the narrative of events, to make inquiry into her previous history with a view to discovering, if possible, some explanation of her sudden abandonment. Here was a vessel, fully provisioned with food and water; with hull, masts, spars, and standing rigging in good order: with only a normal leakage, and, with the exception of two sails blown away, "fit" as Seaman Anderson expressed it, "to go round the world." Some commentators have tried to make it appear that she was an ill-starred ship, and many theories as to the cause of abandonment have been advanced. Of these, some will be considered in a succeeding chapter. In the circumstances, a careful survey of the principal facts of her career from the time her keel was laid at Spencer's Island in 1860, up to her departure from New York, may prove rewarding.

CHAPTER VI

Early History of the *Mary Celeste*

Build me straight, O worthy Master,
Staunch and strong, a goodly vessel.

LONGFELLOW

1. *Building and Original Ownership*

FROM the record of events, it is manifest that, had there been no Joshua Dewis, there would have been no *Mary Celeste*. Son of a farmer, he was born in the little village of Economy, Nova Scotia, on the Bay of Fundy about twenty miles east of Parrsboro. There, in his early manhood, with the help of a few neighbors, he built a small vessel. Shortly thereafter, he came down the shore to West Advocate and bought a tract of about one thousand acres, including a farm and a lot of fine timber land. At Spencer's Island,[1] about seven miles west of West Advocate, lived the Spicer brothers—Isaac and Jacob—who also owned large tracts of timber land. Included therein was a clean, open space, which, to the appraising eye of Joshua Dewis, seemed an ideal spot on which to start a shipbuilding yard. Gathering about him his relatives in Advocate Harbor, his former neighbors in Economy, and also the merchants Cox & Bigelow (who carried on a small business at the Island) he unfolded his plan to launch a shipbuilding enterprise.

At that time, all along the Nova Scotian shores, shipbuilding gave promise of becoming an increasingly important and remunerative industry. In the circumstances, Joshua Dewis had little trouble in convincing his rela-

1. Spencer's Island is a small, rocky island about one-half mile distant from the shore. The village, with its shipyard, is located on the mainland.

tives and neighbors of the practicability of the plan, and soon the project was under way. It is a matter of record that the work began and continued under favorable auspices. Joshua Dewis, described by those who knew him as the "soul of honesty," selected for his helpers capable and reliable men who worked well together. Among them was William Thompson, a mariner from Economy, who superintended the rigging and was owner of an eight sixty-fourths interest. After building the foundations, they laid the keel of their first ship during the fall of 1860. She was ready for launching in the spring of 1861 and sometime in May glided safely down the ways, receiving the name *Amazon*, a name she bore until 1868 when she was renamed *Mary Celeste*. On 10 June 1861, she was registered at Parrsboro, twenty-five miles further up the Bay of Fundy, in which district Spencer's Island was included. She was the first vessel built at Spencer's Island, and the only one built there by Joshua Dewis, although, during the years that followed, twenty-seven other vessels were built there on the same foundation blocks by other parties.

In this, her first register,[2] she is described as "brigantine rigged," having two masts, the foremast being square-rigged, and the mainmast, fore-and-aft or schooner-rigged. In the Atlantic Mutual Vessel Record[3] she is described as a "half-brig." She had a billet-head and a square stern and, at that time, only one deck. She was of "carvel-build"[4] with a wood framework. Her measurements were: length, 99.3 feet; breadth, 25.5 feet; depth, 11.7 feet. Gross tonnage,

2. Appendix D.

3. See page 52.

4. Carvel-build means: "a manner of building boats so that the planking is flush or smooth-sided, the opposite to clinker or clinched-built, where the planks overlap." *Patterson's Illustrated Nautical Encyclopedia*, page 76.

198.42 tons. She was built mostly of native wood such as birch, beech and maple up to light load-line: then spruce to the rails, with pine to finish the cabins. Timber of this sort was big and handy. She received the official number 37,671. Her first owners were as follows:

George Reid of Parrsboro, Province of Nova Scotia		
Farmer		8/64 shares
Joshua Dewis of Parrsboro Shipwright		16/64 shares
Isaac Spicer of Parrsboro Farmer		8/64 shares
Jacob Spicer of Parrsboro Farmer		8/64 shares
Robert McLellan of Economy Mariner		4/64 shares
William Thompson of Economy Mariner		8/64 shares
and		
William Henry Bigelow of Parrsboro		
Daniel Cox of Cornwallis		
William Henry Payzant of Cornwallis		
merchants and joint owners of		12/64 shares
Total		64 shares

Cox & Bigelow, the Spencer's Island merchants, superintended the construction of the vessel. The building of the *Amazon* was of the nature of an inter-family affair, inasmuch as Joshua Dewis, boss-builder and owner of sixteen sixty-fourths of the vessel, married Naomia Reid, daughter of George Reid, owner of eight sixty-fourths interest. Another daughter, Mary Reid, married Jacob Spicer, owner of eight sixty-fourths interest. Robert, son of Joshua Dewis, married Emily, daughter of Isaac Spicer, owner of eight sixty-fourths interest.

There are living, today, in West Advocate and neighboring towns, descendants and other relatives of the original company which embarked with Joshua Dewis upon his ambitious enterprise.[5]

5. Mr. R. Lester Dewis, grandson of Joshua Dewis, and Mrs. William M. Collins, granddaughter of George Reid, both live at West Advocate,

These sturdy, forthright Nova Scotia folk do not hesitate to voice their salty and vigorous disapproval of a certain writer who has published false statements concerning the *Amazon (Mary Celeste)*. To quote Captain William M. Collins, a retired sea-captain of West Advocate,[6] "We have been talking and breathing *Amazon* and *Mary Celeste* for two generations."

The Spencer's Island people were proud of their little vessel into the building of which went not only the skill and honest workmanship of capable Nova Scotian shipwrights, but also the faith and hope and good-will of an entire community.

Their descendants feel that a vessel, like a person, has a name and a reputation to be kept clean and bright. They deeply resent the attempt to besmirch the *Mary Celeste*. In view of the controversial aspect of this particular phase of the case, we quote from a letter[7] received from the Reverend C. R. Harris, Rector of St. George's Church, Parrsboro, Nova Scotia: "One thing seems perfectly clear, and that is, that the *Amazon* (later the *Mary Celeste*) was built at Spencer's Island. The place was pointed out to me several years ago by most reliable people who have lived all their lives at Spencer's Island, and whose father as a boy could have remembered the actual building. Miss Dennis,

Nova Scotia. Dr. Edmund Stanley Spicer, grandson of Jacob Spicer is a dentist at Kentville, Nova Scotia. Dr. John Dewis, an examining physician for the John Hancock Mutual Life Insurance Company, Boston, is a son of the master-builder, Joshua Dewis. Professor H. E. Bigelow of Mount Allison University, Sackville, New Brunswick, is the son of William Henry Bigelow, one of the original builders and owners of the vessel. Inasmuch as the most widely circulated book on the subject wrongly attributes the building of the vessel to other parties, apparently fictitious, at another part of Nova Scotia, the author has deemed it desirable to give the names of actual, living persons related to the original owners and builders.

6. Letter of 26 October 1940 to the author.

7. Letter of 13 May 1941 from Reverend C. R. Harris.

in *More About Nova Scotia,* bases her remarks on the *Mary Celeste* on a conversation with Captain George Spicer (whom I have met). He lived to be a very old man. I think her account can be regarded as correct. She gives Joshua Dewis as the builder in 1861. She certainly wasn't built at Parrsboro."

As the question of the name of the builder of the *Amazon* and the place of construction has become a subject of controversy, the following account by Miss Clara Dennis[8] of her interview with Captain George Spicer of Spencer's Island, and eldest son of the Jacob Spicer who was one of the original owners of the vessel will be of interest. Said Captain Spicer: "The *Mary Celeste.* I was second mate on her for two years. . . . The *Mary Celeste* was the first vessel built here at Spencer's Island. Joshua Dewis built her in 1861. She was a brigantine, and was launched down here on the beach just beside the mill, on a day in May. She was 184 tons burden, and was named the *Amazon.* Those men are making hay now on the spot where the builder got timber for the *Amazon* seventy-five years ago. . . . I sailed with the *Amazon* to Five Islands where she was to be loaded with deals for London. . . . There was nothing unusual about the ship; she went along very well. I did not get any farther than Five Islands, that time, however, for I took sick and had to return home. The *Amazon* herself got no further than Quaco, near St. John, N. B. Captain McLellan took ill and they sailed back here.

"The Captain was brought up to our house where he passed away. He was sick only a few days. He was just a young man. We took his remains over to his home in Economy. I remember his young wife came down to the shore to see what was in the boat.

"Captain Jack Parker was given charge of the *Amazon*

8. *More About Nova Scotia* (Toronto: Ryerson Press, 1937).

and he took the deals over to London. Later, I sailed as mate in the *Amazon*. We went to the West Indies, England and the Mediterranean—what we call the foreign trade. Not a thing unusual happened. We finally brought a load of corn from Baltimore to Halifax—Halifax imported corn then—and I came home to see the folks after a voyage of two years and three months in the *Amazon*. A week later, the *Amazon* had gone to Cow Bay, Cape Breton, to load coal for New York. There came a gale o' wind and she went ashore. . . . She was finally purchased by the Americans. They repaired her and changed her name to *Mary Celeste*."

2. *Experiences Under the Name of* Amazon

The *Amazon's* first trip, begun shortly after her registration, was from Spencer's Island to Windsor—a port further up in Minas Basin—for a load of plaster for New York. Soon after leaving Spencer's Island, Robert McLellan, her captain and part owner, was taken sick. On her way down the bay, she stopped at Spencer's Island and landed the captain, who died a few days later, on 19 June 1861. "After Captain McLellan died, Captain Jack Parker[9] took command and sailed her for two years. During this time, he made money every trip for the owners. At the end of two years, he left the *Amazon* in New York and came home to take command of the brig *W. H. Bigelow*. That would be 1863. During these two years, the *Amazon* was in the coast or West India trade, and once to France."[10] While at Marseille, a painting of her was made. This painting, the property of Mr. R. Lester Dewis of West Advocate, Nova Scotia, grandson of Joshua Dewis the boss-

9. John Nutting Parker.
10. Letter from R. Lester Dewis to the author.

builder, is on exhibition at the Museum of Fort Beauséjour Historic Site, Aulac, New Brunswick, Canada. It bears
the following inscription: "*Amazon* of Parrsboro, J. N.
Parker, Commander, entering Marseilles Nov'b'r. 1861."
The accompanying illustration (Plate XI) is from a photograph of the painting.

"Sometime in the latter part of 1863, Captain William
Thompson took the *Amazon* and for the first year or two
made good for the owners. Later, as the result of some dissatisfaction with his management, the owners decided to
make a change, and sent a new master to Halifax where
the vessel was lying at that time. Before his arrival, however, Captain Thompson put to sea, and shortly thereafter, the vessel was ashore at Cow Bay [at one time called
Big Glace Bay, but now Port Morien] Cape Breton Island.
This occurred in 1867, sometime after 1 November."

3. *Transfers of Ownership*

Robert McLellan, first master of the vessel, having died
intestate, letters of administration of his estate were grant-
ed on 29 October 1862, by the Probate Court of the County
of Colchester, to Mary Ann McLellan, his widow.

According to the registry, on 11 January 1864, the four
sixty-fourths interest owned in the vessel by Robert Mc-
Lellan was transferred to his widow, Mary Ann McLellan.

On 12 January 1864 the same interest was transferred
by Mary Ann McLellan to W. H. Payzant, Daniel Cox,
and William H. Bigelow. It will be noted that these three
were originally the joint owners of twelve sixty-fourths
interest, now increased to sixteen sixty-fourths.

On the same record appears the notation "The above
named ship was wreck [*sic*] at Big Glace Bay, C. B. and registered at the Port of Sydney on 9th November, 1867. Old

certificate cancelled and returned to this office. Registry closed 18th November 1867—See letter from C. E. Leonard dated Sydney 11 Nov. 1867—Certificate sent to London 6 Dec. 1867."

A new register dated 9 November 1867,[11] indicates a change in ownership. One Alex. McBean "of Big Glace Bay in the Island of Cape Breton, Gentleman," apparently sole owner, transfers his sixty-four shares, according to a bill of sale dated 9 November 1867, to "John Howard Beatty, at present of Big Glace Bay, aforesaid formerly of Moncton, Westmoreland County, New Brunswick, Gentleman." The record bears the notation: "Registered by order of the Lieutenant Governor of Nova Scotia." The document is signed "C. S. Leonard, Jr. Registrar." The vessel's official number is given as 37,671.

From the foregoing, it would appear that the original owners abandoned their interest in the vessel, which had gone ashore; that the wreck was sold to Alex. McBean; and that, in the circumstances, the assent of the Lieutenant-Governor was deemed necessary in order to legalize the transfer from McBean to Beatty.

11. See Appendix E for copy of register of 9 November 1867.

Atlantic Mutual Insurance Company's Vessel Record of the Mary Celeste

CHAPTER VII

British *Amazon* becomes American *Mary Celeste*

AFTER the transfer of the *Amazon* in November 1867 from McBean to Beatty, there is a period of about twelve months during which very little information concerning the vessel is available.

In the latter part of 1868, we find, by a strange coincidence, two vessels named *Amazon,* one a schooner and one a brigantine, both applying for American registry. Both were Nova Scotian built; both had sailed under the British flag; both had been in disaster; and both were sold to New Yorkers. After applying for registry in October the schooner *Amazon,* a vessel of 92 tons, was purchased by O. J. Eggers in 1869, and re-named *Porto Plata,* port of hail, New York.

A letter dated 22 December 1868 from the Secretary of the Treasury to the Collector of Customs at New York, authorized the latter to grant American registry "to a foreign built brig *Amazon.*" This vessel had been wrecked in the waters of the United States and sold to the applicant for the register, Richard W. Haines, an American citizen, for $1,750.00 and repaired at a cost of $8,825.03. On 31 December 1868[1] the brigantine *Amazon* was formally transferred to American registry and her name changed to *Mary Celeste.* This register No. 485 was issued at New York to Richard W. Haines of New York who is described therein as "the only owner of the ship or vessel called the *Mary*

1. The records of the Atlantic Mutual Insurance Company show that their first inspection of the vessel (see reproduction of inspection record on page 52) was in December 1868. The various registers issued to the *Mary Celeste* throughout her career as an American vessel are summarized in Appendix H.

Celeste which said ship or vessel was formerly the Brg. *Amazon.*" (Appendix F.)

The register states that she has one deck; two masts; and her measurements are as follows: length, 98.5 feet; breadth, 25 feet; depth, 11.6 feet; tonnage under deck, 177.42; enclosures on upper deck, 28.86; total tons 206.28.

On the same day, 31 December 1868, register No. 485 was cancelled and a new register No. 486 was issued, due, apparently, to a change in the vessel's ownership. Richard W. Haines, originally sole owner, now appears as owning only seven-eighths, having sold a one-eighth interest to Sylvester Goodwin of New York. In this register, Richard W. Haines is stated to be master of the vessel. In other respects it is the same as register No. 485.

According to register No. 339, dated 13 October 1869 (and issued in place of 486), another change took place in the ownership, which is stated as follows: James H. Winchester, six-eighths; Sylvester Goodwin, one-eighth; and Daniel T. Samson, one-eighth; all described as of "the City of New York." The name of the master is now Walter S. Johnson. The total tonnage is given as 206.29 tons.

On 11 January 1870, register No. 16 was issued at New York in place of 339 cancelled. While the measurements and tonnage remain the same, another change in ownership has occurred. The shares are now split up as follows: James H. Winchester, four-eighths; Sylvester Goodman [*sic*], one-eighth; Daniel T. Samson, one-eighth; Rufus W. Fowler of Searsport (designated as master), two-eighths.

On 29 October 1872, less than two weeks before the departure of the *Mary Celeste* on her fateful passage, a new register No. 122 was issued at New York in place of No. 16 —cancelled. This register discloses not only a number of changes in the ownership, but also in the construction of the vessel. The ownership is now divided as follows: James H. Winchester, twelve twenty-fourths; Sylvester Goodwin, two twenty-fourths; Daniel T. Samson, two twenty-fourths; Benjamin S. Briggs of Marion, State of Maine,[2] eight twenty-fourths. The vessel now has two decks, instead of one as before; two masts as before, but her length has been increased to 103 feet; her breadth to 25.7 feet; her depth to 16.2 feet; her capacity under tonnage deck to 271.79, which, added to 3.69 for head-room and 6.80 for the deck-house, make a total tonnage of 282.28. According to Atlantic Mutual inspection record, under date of October 1872, the following changes and repairs were noted by the company's inspector: three-quarter poop extended over all; several new timbers; new transoms; part new knightheads, stern and stem; new bends and topsides and stern; patched with yellow metal. It was probably at this time that her topsail was divided, for the sake of easier handling, into an upper and a lower topsail, as she was so rigged when she was found by the *Dei Gratia*.

All of these registers refer to the former name of the vessel as the British brig *Amazon*, and describe her as having a billet-head and a square stern. Over a considerable period of years, the terms "half-brig" and "brigantine" appear to have been used interchangeably as though they were synonymous terms, although they are actually two different types of vessels. As previously indicated, the *Mary Celeste*, with a square-rig on her foremast, and a fore-and-aft or schooner-rig on her mainmast, was clearly a half-, or hermaphrodite brig, or brigantine of modern type.[3] In the

2. "Maine" obviously should have read "Massachusetts." The text of this register is reproduced as Appendix G.

3. "In olden times, a brigantine was a two-masted vessel, square-rigged on the fore, and schooner-rigged on the main, with this addition, that she carried a light square topsail on the mainmast. In these days, a brigantine

American Record of Shipping and on the vessel record of the Atlantic Mutual Insurance Company she is described as a "half-brig."

dispenses with the square main topsail, so that no difference exists between the rigs of a brigantine and a hermaphrodite brig." *Patterson's Illustrated Nautical Encyclopedia.*

Hermaphrodite Brig: "A vessel with a brig's foremast and a schooner's mainmast having the complicated square-sail rig on only one mast, the hermaphrodite rig permitted a reduction in the number of men necessary for a crew to man her. This economical phase of the situation caused the construction of a great fleet of 'half-brigs,' as sailors used to call them, because it was a more euphonious name than that given by the dictionary. So where history refers to brigs, it is just as likely to have been a hermaphrodite brig as a true brig." Charles G. Davis, *Silhouettes of Shipping and Craft* (Salem: Marine Research Society, 1929).

CHAPTER VIII

Difficulties over Vessel's Registry

FROM the following article in the *New York Sun* of 12 March 1873, it appears that some question touching the regularity of the transfer to American registry arose at this time.

The Abandoned Ship. No Mutiny but a Scheme to Defraud the Insurance Company

The stories in regard to the desertion of the Brig *Mary Celeste,* which another ship recently found abandoned in mid-ocean, are not credited in Custom House circles. Mention is made of several suspicious circumstances to show that more selfish motives than the revolting of sailors and the slaying of their officers might have prompted the abandonment of the vessel. A *Sun* reporter was informed that the *Mary Celeste* had been improperly cleared and sailed under false colors after going out of this port. It was charged that deception was resorted to for the purpose of getting her registered as an American vessel. She was built at Parrsboro,[1] Nova Scotia in 1861 and formerly sailed under the British flag, being known as the *Amazon.*

In 1870[2] she took her present name, and was afterward registered as American built. Deputy Surveyor Abeel discovered the deception a few months ago, and took measures to seize the brig on her next arrival in port.

Contrary to expectations, she failed to appear here, and the Deputy Surveyor threatened that, unless she returned to American waters, he would have her seized in whatever foreign port she might enter.

Subsequently, the brig reappeared at Boston, and she was attached by the Collector of the Port. She was appraised at $2,600.00

1. Error. Read Spencer's Island, Nova Scotia.

2. Error. See first American register No. 485, 31 December 1868 issued in name of *Mary Celeste,* formerly the British Brig *Amazon.* (Appendix F.)

57

and was bonded by the owners in that amount. When she sailed on her last voyage she was insured at the rate of $16,000. or at $13,400.00 over the Boston appraisement. This discrepancy furnishes a clue upon which the insurance companies will probably act.

Yesterday, Mr. J. H. Winchester, who had been to Gibraltar at the request of the underwriters to inquire into the condition of the brig, was informed by telegraph that she had started from Gibraltar with new officers and crew for Genoa, her original port of destination.

Naturally, this article stirred the resentment of J. H. Winchester & Co., whose reply appeared in the *New York Herald,* under date of 15 March 1873.

Having read an article in the *Sun* of the 12th, headed *The Abandoned Ship* and setting forth the Brig *Mary Celeste* was not properly cleared at the Custom House, when she sailed on her last voyage, and that she sailed under false colors, this is an atrocious falsehood, as the records of the Custom House will show, and we are informed that the "Custom House Circles" mentioned in that article is one Mr. Abeel, a Deputy Surveyor. We now propose to give the true history of the vessel, as far as we know, together with Mr. Abeel's connection with said vessel.

The Brig *Mary Celeste* which was picked up derelict on the 4th. of December and taken to Gibraltar, was formerly a single-deck brig called the *Amazon,* of Parrsboro, Nova Scotia, and in November 1868, arrived at this port a wreck and was sold at public auction by Messrs. Burdett & Dennis to Richard W. Haines, who repaired the vessel by putting in a new keel, stern, sternpost, bottom, and mostly new spars rigging, sails etc. at an expense of $16,000.00 and believing he was entitled to put his vessel under the American flag, he at that time applied, through a Custom House broker, for an American register, and obtained it in October 1869.[3] Ten months after she had received her register, she was again sold at auction for debt, and bought by her present own-

3. Error. See first American register dated 31 December 1868, issued to Richard W. Haines.

ers, who ran her until April, 1872, without knowing there was any trouble with her register; but at this time, the aforesaid Abeel came to our office and stated that the *Mary Celeste* had a fraudulent register.

We told him we were not aware of it. He said it was the case, and, after considerable talk and quibbling, he said he knew we were innocent parties and did not want to be hard on us, and that we could settle the matter. This looked so much like blackmail that Mr. Winchester told him if the vessel belonged to the United States Government, they would have to take her, as we had no money to settle with him or anybody else. He then "sloped." We then telegraphed the Captain at St. Thomas to take the best freight he could and bring the vessel home, knowing that she would be seized. The brig came to Boston, was there seized on account of her register, appraised by parties appointed by the Government and bonded for $2,600.00, which suit is still pending. She went from Boston to Cow Bay and back to New York, and was then torn down to her copper and rebuilt and made a double-decked vessel at an expense of $11,500.00. She then loaded on her present unfortunate voyage, and when she sailed from New York was insured for $14,000.00[4] valued at $16,000.00; and we now would ask if an attempt has been made to defraud the underwriters? What has become of the Captain, his wife and child, officers and crew?

We would also refer all parties for further information to the officers of the following insurance companies, where the vessel was insured: Atlantic Mutual, Mercantile Mutual, Orient Mutual, and Maine Lloyds.

[Signed] J. H. WINCHESTER & Co., Ship Owners &
Commission Merchants, 52 South Street.

Elsewhere, in the *Herald* of the same date, appears an article containing substantially the same facts as mentioned in the foregoing statement made by J. H. Winchester & Co. The following is a quotation, in part, from Captain Winchester's statement to the *Herald* reporter:

4. This did not include the Atlantic Mutual's insurance of $3,400 on freight on charter.

She was bound for Genoa with a cargo of alcohol valued at $37,000.00 belonging to Messrs. Ackerman & Co.[5] who, I learn, are partially insured, in Hamburg companies. The *Mary Celeste* is insured for $14,000.00 and is appraised at $16,000.00. She is insured in the Mercantile Mutual for $2,500.00; the Orient Mutual for $4,000.00; The Maine Lloyds for $6,000.00 and the New England of Boston for $1,500.00. Total $14,000.00.[6] A despatch received from Gibraltar from the American Consul states that she sailed from that port for Genoa on the 10th instant. This is all I know of the vessel; but permit me to say that published reports about the vessel being illegally cleared and sailing under a false flag, which originated with the Custom House official, are base fabrications, as anyone interested in the matter can discover by referring to the record of the Custom House and the officers of the companies in which we are insured.

The precise nature of the difficulty over the vessel's registry is not known. Inquiries addressed to several government departments have failed to elicit any information on this point. Whatever the difficulty may have been, it can be accepted as beyond question that there was no irregularity on the part of J. H. Winchester & Co., a firm of excellent repute which has continued through the years to hold, as it does today, an honored place in the commercial life of New York City.

5. Meissner, Ackerman & Co.

6. This manifestly refers to hull insurance only, and does not include the Atlantic Mutual's insurance on freight on charter.

CHAPTER IX

Proceedings at Gibraltar

1. *Salvage Claim before Vice-Admiralty Court*

O<small>N</small> Wednesday, 18 December 1872, five days after the arrival of the *Mary Celeste* "The Queen, in her office of Admiralty Against the Ship or Vessel supposed to be called *Mary Celeste* and her cargo proceeded against as derelict," held the first session of the Court. The Queen was represented by Sir James Cochrane, Knight, and Commissary of the Vice-Admiralty Court of Gibraltar, and the purpose of the session was to hear testimony in connection with the claim for salvage, of the owners, officers and crew of the British brigantine *Dei Gratia*.[1]

The persons recorded as taking part in the proceedings were: Edward Joscelyn Baumgartner, Registrar; Frederick Solly Flood, Esq., Advocate and Proctor for the Queen in her office of Admiralty; Henry Peter Pisani, Advocate and Proctor for David Reed Morehouse, master of the

---

1. In the latter part of the year 1930, Mr. J. C. Anakin of 181 Boaler Street, Liverpool, England, noticed in *The Times* a letter from Harold T. Wilkins, a writer, then living at Bexley Heath, London. Mr. Wilkins deplored the government's practice of destroying documents relating to very important and interesting subjects, after a lapse of years, when the documents were supposed to be of no further use. Among the documents mentioned by Mr. Wilkins in his letter were some relating to the case of the *Mary Celeste*. Mr. Anakin communicated at once with Mr. Wilkins and effected an arrangement whereby they would share the cost of having photostatic copies made of these documents, including the testimony of the *Dei Gratia* salvors before the Vice-Admiralty Court at Gibraltar. A typewritten copy of this testimony was sent by Mr. Anakin to Dr. Oliver W. Cobb in December 1930, and soon thereafter this copy was loaned to Charles Edey Fay, then Vice-President of the Atlantic Mutual Insurance Company, who was making a study of the case in connection with his book *Ninety Years of Marine Insurance* published in 1932.

British brigantine, *Dei Gratia,* and for the owners, officers and crew of the said brigantine, claiming as salvors. Other participants in the proceedings were George F. Cornwell "of Lincoln's Inn, London, Eng., practising in Gibraltar," Proctor for the claimants of the *Mary Celeste,* and Martin W. Stokes, Proctor for the claimants of the cargo.

Oliver Deveau was the first witness called. After being duly sworn he deposed as follows:

"I am Chief Mate of the British Vessel *Dei Gratia.* I left New York on the 15th November, bound for Gibraltar 'for orders.' Captain Morehouse, Master. On the 5th December Sea Time,[2] being my watch below, the Captain called me and said there was a strange sail on the windward bow, apparently in distress, requiring assistance. That was probably about 1:00 P.M.[3] Sea Time. I came on deck and saw a vessel through the glass,—she appeared about 4 or 5 miles off.

"The Master proposed to speak the vessel in order to render assistance if necessary, and to haul wind for the purpose, we did. By my reckoning, we were 38° 20′ North Latitude and 17° 15′ West Longitude by dead reckoning of our own ship. We hauled up, hailed the vessel,—found no one on board. I cannot say whether the Master or I proposed to lower the boat, but one of us did so, and a boat was launched, and I and two men with me went in her to board the vessel. The sea was running high, the weather having been stormy, though then the wind was moderating. I boarded the vessel and the first thing I did was to sound the pumps, which were in good order.

2. Sea-time. At sea, in those days, the date changed every day at noon. Inasmuch as the *Dei Gratia* sighted the *Mary Celeste* between 1:00 and 2:00 P.M. on Wednesday 4 December the entry of the event on the log or log slate would be dated 5 December.

3. The witness later amended this statement, saying that the time when he was called was 1:30 P.M.

"I found no one on board the vessel. I found three feet and a half of water in the pumps on sounding them. The pump gear was good, but one of the pumps was drawn to let the sounding-rod down. There was no place to let the rod down without drawing the box, as is often the case in a small vessel. I cannot say how long it would take to draw the pump—it depends upon circumstances. I only used the other pump on my way here, and the other pump I left in the same state as I found it.

"I found the fore-hatch and the lazarette-hatch[4] both off,—the binnacle stove in, a great deal of water between decks,—the forward-house full of water up to the coaming. The forward-house is on the upper deck. I found everything wet in the cabin in which there had been a great deal of water,—the clock was spoilt by the water,—the skylight of the cabin was open and raised,—the compass in the binnacle was destroyed. I found all the Captain's effects had been left,—I mean his clothing, furniture, etc.—the bed was just as they had left it,—the bed and the other clothes were wet. I judged that there had been a woman on board. I found the Captain's charts and books, a number of them,—in the Cabin,—some were in two bags under the bed, and some (two or three) loose charts over the bed. I found no charts on the table. I found the Log Book in the Mate's cabin on his desk,—the Log Slate I found on the cabin table. I found an entry in the Log Book up to 24th November, and an entry on the Log Slate dated 25th November showing that they had made the Island of Saint Mary. I did not observe the entry on the slate the first day, and made some entries of my own on it, and so, unintentionally rubbed out the entry when I came to use the slate; at least, I thought I did.

4. The lazarette was a low, head-room space below the main deck on the after part of the vessel, where provisions and spare gear were stowed.

"I did not find the ship's register or other papers concerning the ship, but only some letters and account books. I found the Mate's note book in which were entered receipts for cargo, etc.—The book now shown to me is the book I found, also the Mate's Chart.

"In his cabin hanging over the mate's bed showing the track of the vessel up to the 24th there were two charts,—one under the mate's bed and one, as I have said, hanging over it. I am not positive whether the chart with the ship's track marked on it was found above or below the mate's bed. There seemed to be everything left behind in the cabin as if left in a hurry, but everything in its place. I noticed the impression in the Captain's bed as of a child having lain there. The hull of the vessel appeared in good condition and nearly new. There were a great many other things in the cabin, but impossible for me to mention all,—the things were all wet,—the sky-light was not off but open,—the hatches were off—the cabin was wet, but had no water in it,—the water had naturally run out of it,—the hull of the ship was apparently new,—the masts were good,—the spars all right,—the rigging in very bad order,—some of the running rigging carried away,—gone,—the standing rigging was all right,—the upper fore-topsail and foresail gone,—apparently blown away from the yards. Lower fore-topsail hanging by the four corners. Main staysail hauled down and lying on the forward-house, loose, as if it had been let run down. Jib and foretop staysail set. All [the] rest of the sails being furled. The vessel is a brigantine-rigged, I should say, of over 200 tons. The vessel I should say was seaworthy, and almost a new vessel. Anchors and chains all right; there were no boats,—and no davits at the side. I don't think she used davits. It appeared as if she carried her boat on deck. There was a spar lashed across the stern davits, so that no boat had been there.

"I went back to my vessel and reported the state of the brigantine to the Captain. I proposed taking her in, he told me well to consider the matter, as there was great risk and danger to our lives and also to our own vessel. We consulted amongst ourselves and crew and resolved to bring her in. A distance, I estimate, at six to seven hundred miles,[5] but have not made out the exact distance.

"The Captain gave me two men, the small boat, a barometer, compass and watch. I took with me my own nautical instruments and whatever food our steward had prepared. I went on board the same afternoon, the 5th[6] about an hour afterwards, perhaps, hoisted the boat on deck,—pumped her out and took charge of the vessel. Augustus Anderson and Charles Lund are the names of the two men I took with me. They were not the same men as I took with me when I first boarded the brigantine. Their names are John Wright and John Johnson. We arrived in Gibraltar on the morning of the 13th December. When first we went on board, we had a good deal to do to get the ship into order. I found a spare trysail which I used as a foresail. It took me two days to set things to rights so as to proceed on voyage to make any headway. We had fine weather at first and until we got into the Straits, when it came on a storm, so that I dare not make the Bay, but laid to under Ceuta and afterwards on the Spanish Coast to the East. When I arrived at Gibraltar, I found the *Dei Gratia* already there. I had seen her almost every day during the voyage and spoke her three or four times. We kept company with her until the night of the storm when I lost sight of her. I saw between decks the nature of the cargo,—barrels marked 'alcohol,'—on the head of them,—and like-

5. Estimated at about six hundred miles by Navy Department, Washington. Letter of 7 December 1940 to the author.

6. According to sea-time, but actually 4 December.

wise in the note-book of the Mate of the *Celeste,* whereby it appeared he had given receipts for so many barrels of alcohol at a time. I forgot to state that the cabin, which was a deck cabin, had all its windows battened up. I also found the sounding-rod on deck alongside the pump."

Cross-examined by the Queen's Advocate and Proctor: "I left New York on the 15th November. I examined the Log of the vessel found, to see when she left New York, and believe she left 8 days before us or 11 days before us, or more or less. I cannot say what number of days she left before us. I found the vessel a fair sailer. I could not call her more than a fair sailer—I call the *Dei Gratia* a fair sailer. Supposing both vessels to have been equally well-found, manned and sailed, she would have been faster than our own ship. We spoke one other brigantine on our voyage, bound for Boston, but did not pass nor see any other vessel of a similar class on our outward voyage. Therefore, the first time we could have seen this vessel was the day we found her as we did—deserted. I cannot say, without referring to my Log, where our ship was on the 24th. or 25th.—I do know we were to the North of the other vessel. I know that we were between Latitude 40° and 42°. I only know that we were North of the vessel from seeing her track traced on her chart.

"We did not sight St. Mary's Isle during any part of our voyage. I do not know the Latitude or Longitude of St. Mary without seeing a chart. I have made only one voyage from New York to Gibraltar before, and did not sight St. Mary's then. I never was at St. Mary's—never saw it. I think I could enter St. Mary's by help of charts and sailing directions as well as any other port to which I have not been. Without reference to a [*word omitted*] or sailing directions, I do not know what sort of harbour St. Mary was. From 15th. November to 24th. November, we had stormy weather most of the time of our passage,—most time very heavy weather. During that time we never took off our fore-hatch since we sailed—the Main-hatch was off for one hour, perhaps. We have four hatches: fore, main, aft and lazaret. The *Mary Celeste* has only two hatches, fore and main besides the lazareto. The cabin of the *Mary Celeste* is slightly raised above the upper deck—about two feet above—and the windows are in those two feet—there were six windows, 2 in Captain's, 1 in Mate's, 1 in W.C., 1 in Pantry, and 1 facing the bow of the ship. They were all battened up with canvas and boards—I knocked one off in the Mate's room; all the others remained the same as I found them. The topgallant masts and topmasts were all up. She had four[7] yards, two topgallant and fore-yards and topgallant royal yards—the royal and topgallant sails were furled—the running rigging of those sails were all in proper place. The rigging out of order was: fore-braces on port side broken; starboard lower-topsail brace broken; main peak halyards broken; the gear of the foresail all broken; clew-lines and buntings [*sic*] gone.

"Her head was westward when we first saw her—she was on starboard tack; the wheel was not lashed—the wheel gear was good. With her foresails set, she would not come up to the wind and fall off again. With sails she had when I first saw her, she might come up and fall away a little, but not much. She would always keep those sails full. The wind was North: not much then, though blowing heavily in the morning. I am not acquainted with the currents, but we allow for a current running easterly; the currents there depend very much on the winds. The first point I made when I could take my bearings by sight was

7. Deveau's reference to four yards is not clear, inasmuch as she had five yards, all on her foremast, viz: fore-yard, lower topsail-yard, upper topsail-yard, topgallant-yard and royal-yard.

Cape St. Vincent which I knew from my Latitude. I compared my dead reckoning with the place I supposed St. Vincent, and, of course, found myself out of my reckoning, but I cannot say how much I was out—perhaps ten miles or so. I was in advance of my reckoning, but I cannot say how much. The sheet was fast on the port side. She was found on starboard tack. The wind would entirely govern the tack on which she was at the time. Both vessels going one way, one might be on port tack, the other on starboard tack on the same day.

"There were no spare spars on the decks of the *Mary Celeste* whatever. When there is no boat on the davits in the stern, there is often a spar lashed to keep the davits steady. In this case, the spar was lashed through the sheave-holes,[8] which showed there had been no boat there. Wind would be blowing from S. E. if the vessel was bound to Gibraltar. We had two boats. The *Celeste* had not accommodation on deck for two boats. One could see where the boat had been lashed across the main hatch, but that was not the right place for her. There were no lashings visible, therefore, I cannot swear that the *Mary Celeste* had any boat at all, but there were two fenders where the boat would be lashed. Assuming that there was a boat, there was nothing to show how the boat was launched—there were no signs of any tackles to launch her. We launched our boat that way from the rail of the vessel without tackle or hoisting her up with a tow rope only to secure her. The way down into the hold is through the hatchways, which is quite different from the cabin. Into the Cabin, the entrance is through the companionway, down steps. I went into the cabin within a few minutes of sounding the pumps. On the table there was the Log Slate, but I cannot state what else there might be on the table. I do not know whether

8. Sheave-holes. The spaces between the cheeks of a block.

there were any knives. I saw no preparations made for eating in the cabin; there was plenty to eat, but all the knives and forks were in the pantry. The rack[9] was on the table, but no eatables; there was nothing to eat or drink in the cabin on the table, but preserved meats in the pantry. I examined the state of the ship's galley. It was in the corner of the forward-house, and all the things: pots, kettles, etc. were washed up—water in the house a foot or so deep; I cannot say how the water got in, but the door was open, and the scuttle-hatch[10] off; the windows were shut. There were no cooked provisions in the galley. I never saw the water come over the top of the mast of a vessel. There was a barrel of flour in the galley, one third gone. We used the provisions found on board the *Mary Celeste*. We used potatoes and meat. She had, I should say, six months provisions on board. The binnacle was injured when I went on board. I fixed it and used it on our way here. The glass was broken. The binnacle was washed away from its place and I set it back again. It is lashed on the top of the cabin above the deck; being a wooden one, the lashings had given way—one of the cleats was gone. I found a compass on board afterwards—the Cabin compass—in the Mate's room. I did not find [it] until I went on board the second time. It is usual for a vessel to carry two or three compasses. I found two quadrants—one in Second Mate's room. I made no further examination of the cargo than what I have already stated. The cargo seemed to be in good condition and well-stowed, and had not shifted. As far as I could judge, the cargo was not injured. I found no wine, beer or spirits whatever in the ship.''

9. Rack or fiddle-rack, a framework fastened to the table to prevent dishes from sliding off when in a seaway.

10. Scuttle-hatch. There is a scuttle in the roof of the galley for ventilation, and the scuttle-hatch would be the cover.

Cross-examined by Judge. "The vessel was perfectly upright whilst I was on board, and I saw no signs whatever to induce me to believe that she had been on her beam ends at any time. If she had been thrown on her beam ends, her hatches would have been washed off. Suppose the vessel had been thrown on her beam ends, and her hatches had been all closed, she might have righted again without her cargo shifting or without showing any indication. My idea is, that the crew got alarmed, and by sounding-rod being found lying alongside the pumps, that they had sounded the pumps and found perhaps a quantity of water in the pumps at the moment, and thinking she would go down, abandoned her. The pumps would be sounded, perhaps, every two hours or four hours. In order to make entry in the Log of 'pumps carefully attended to,' the pumps should be sounded every watch, or every four hours. If the vessel were leaky, more often. The fact of finding the vessel with only four feet of water when I boarded her, shows that she made little or no water—about one inch in 24 hours, and therefore, I conclude that all the water found in her, went down her hatches and through the cabin."

Exhibit. "The Log now produced is the one I found on board the *Mary Celeste,* and which I continued in my journey to Gibraltar. It is in my handwriting from the 5th[11] day of December to the 13th day of December, day of arrival, including the marginal notes of Latitude and Longitude. The figures showing the figure of speed are only guess. I had no log on board to heave, and no log-line. When I made the land, I omitted the entry of supposed speed. The weather came on to blow hard after we had made Cape Spartel on the 11th—Ceuta Light.

11. 5 December, sea-time; actually 4 December, civil time.

"I say that we must have run up the Spanish Coast 30 miles after leaving Cape Ceuta, or 40 miles: that was after leaving Ceuta at 6 A.M. in sight of land."

Exhibit. The Slate. The Attorney-General reads the entry on the slate log 26[12] November, "I never used the side of the slate upon which this entry now appears. I left the charts on board the *Mary Celeste*." To Judge. "I have been master of a brig, myself. I kept the Log on board the *Dei Gratia*. I have no Master's ticket but a Mate's certificate."

The Judge adjourned the Vice-Admiralty Court to Friday next.

Friday 20 December 1872

The further examination of the witnesses was proceeded with this day.

The witness Oliver Deveau recalled. "I wish to correct a statement I made on Wednesday, namely, that the hour at which the Captain called me was half past one, and not three P.M. as I have stated. It was 3 P.M. when I boarded the vessel we found abandoned."

To the Judge: "The tonnage of my ship is about 295 tons. Our crew numbers eight hands, all told. The *Dei Gratia* is also a Brigantine."

To the Queen's Proctor and Advocate. "We passed North of the whole group of the Azores. Some vessels go to the South and some to the North. I have myself only passed to the North of the Group of the Azores. I have said that there

12. In the light of other testimony, the reference to 26 November seems to be an error. It is, however, barely possible that, in preparation for the new day which, according to sea-time, would begin at noon (only four hours after the entry made at 8 A.M.) one of the mates may have prepared the other side of the slate for the entries pertaining to the new day, and therefore wrote down the date "26 November" on the unused side of the slate, as above mentioned.

was the appearance on the bed in the Captain's cabin as if a child had slept in it. There was room in the berth for a child and a woman and also for the Captain. I saw articles of child's wearing apparel; also child's toys. The bed was as it had been left after being slept in—not made. I noticed female clothing—an old dress hanging near the bed; also india-rubber over-shoes. The dress was dirty, as if worn; it was not wet. The bedding was wet. I should say that the water had got through the windows near the bed, or, probably, it might have got through the skylight. The windows were battened up. There had been rain and squalls the morning we found the *Mary Celeste* but I don't think it was that which wetted the bed. There were two boxes of clothing—in one box, male and female clothing mixed together. The box was shut but not locked. The clothing was not wet. The other box had only remnants of cloth in it. Both boxes were open. I afterwards found some clothing in two drawers under the bed, which also I afterwards took out and put into the second box which was nearly empty. The clothing found under the bed place was mostly men's clothing, and some of it was wet—that found in the lower drawer. The clothing was of the usual sort worn by men and women. There were also work-bags, with needles, threads, buttons, hooks and a case of instruments —a dressing case and other things in the drawers. The two boxes were in the cabin. There was also a valise-case which I could not nor did not open. There was also a writing-desk. There was a bag of dirty clothing—man's, woman's and child's—hanging up in the water-closet. They were damp. I cannot say how they got damp. There was a stove in the fore-cabin, but I made no fire in it. There were a few old coats and a pair of sea-boots also. The clothes were not those of a passenger, but of a sea-faring man. The stove was in the fore-cabin—not in the Captain's cabin. There was a swinging lamp on the side of the Cabin — one in each cabin. They were parafine lamps. There was no appearance of damage by fire nor any appearance of fire or smoke in any part of the ship. The staysail which had fallen down was on the stove-pipe of the galley. There were plenty of provisions and plenty of water on board the vessel. There was a harmonium or melodeon in the cabin."

Chart Exhibit C. "The chart now produced is the chart I found on board the *Mary Celeste* with the ship's course marked on it. I used it afterwards myself, for our track here. The words written: '*Mary Celeste,* abandoned 5th.[13] December 1872' are in my writing. I put it down merely by guess as the place where I supposed we found the vessel as nearly as I could. The arrows shown on the chart show the way the currents are supposed to run, but they often practically run just in a contrary direction. That chart is the chart found in the Mate's cabin."

To Judge. "We passed to the North of the Group — the *Mary Celeste* passed to the South. I should say that, from the spot marked on the chart as the last position of the *Mary Celeste* on the 24th up to the place where we found her, I should say would be from five to six hundred miles. The wind was blowing from the N. to S.W. in the interval between 24th November and 5th December[14] as near as I can tell, which will more correctly appear in the Log of the *Dei Gratia*. The only explanation of the abandonment which I can give, is that there was a panic from the belief that the vessel had more water in her than she had, as afterwards proved. I cannot give an opinion as to whether the derelict could have run the distance where we found her, in the interval, with the sails she had set.

13. 5 December (sea-time) but actually 4 December, was the date on which the derelict was found.

14. 5 December, sea-time.

She was going steadily from 1½ to 2 knots when we saw her, with the wind on her beam. She might have had more sails set at first. She would not run steadily before the wind with her rudder unlashed. She had two head-sails set—jib and foretop staysail set on starboard tack; her yards were square; her lower fore topsail was hanging by the four corners. The wind was to the Northward; her head to the westward. She was then going in opposite direction to ourselves. We met her. She probably had changed her course more than once. She was going[15] backwards. It is impossible to say, therefore, how long or how often she had changed her course. There were four berths in the forecastle with bedding, in the *Celeste*, but only three sea-chests.

"Often, two sailors chum for one chest. The bedding was damp and as if it had not been used. There was one berth in the Mate's cabin, and one berth in the galley; also a berth in the second Mate's room or boatswain's room; all apparently had been occupied, with the Captain, making eight, all told, besides the woman and child. She was sheeted on the starboard tack when we found her. The wind during last four days before we found the vessel was Northwesterly. The men's clothing was all left behind: their oilskins, boots, and even their pipes, as if they had left in a great hurry or haste. My reason for saying that they left in haste is that a sailor would generally take such things, especially his pipe, if not in great haste. The Chronometer, Sextant, Navigation Book were all absent. The Ship's Register and Papers were also not found. There was no Logline ready for use. The carpenter's tools were in the Mate's room. The water casks were on chocks. The chocks had been moved as if struck by a heavy sea. The provision casks

15. Meaning, no doubt, back toward the place she had sailed from, as she was headed "westward."

Brigantine Dei Gratia, from a painting made at Messina, Sicily in April 1873 by Giuseppe Coli

PLATE VIII

Captain David Reed Morehouse, Master of the Dei Gratia
from a photograph taken at Gibraltar about 1873

PLATE IX

were below in their proper place; they were not thrown over. If the vessel had been capsized, they would have been thrown over."

"The evidence having been read to the witness by the Registrar in open Court, and corrected as it now appears, he stated that it was all correct, to the best of his belief.

[signed] EDWARD J. BAUMGARTNER, *Registrar.*

20th December 1872."

At the conclusion of the testimony given by Deveau on 20 December, he was followed by John Wright, second mate of the *Dei Gratia* whose account agrees, substantially, with that previously given. Inasmuch as Wright went with Deveau to the derelict on the first trip only, and did not accompany him to Gibraltar, his opportunities for observation were limited to the half-hour, which, according to his own statement, he spent on board the *Mary Celeste.*

The 20 December session of the Court concluded with the testimony of Seaman Charles Lund. On the following day, Seamen Anderson and Johnson were heard. The accounts given by Lund and Anderson are more significant, for the reason that they assisted Deveau in bringing the derelict to Gibraltar. Johnson's statement was very brief and comparatively unimportant, for the reason that he had not boarded the vessel at all, but remained in the small boat alongside, while Deveau and Wright were making their examination. The Queen's Proctor declined to cross-examine Johnson, on the ground that the latter understood very little English. The testimony given by Wright, Lund and Anderson (published in Appendix N) will be commented upon in a later chapter.

2. *Derelict Surveyed.* Dei Gratia *Sails.* Captain Winchester Arrives

The statements made by these witnesses presented so extraordinary a picture, that it is not surprising to find the suspicions of the Queen's Proctor fully aroused, as evidenced by his subsequent action. On Monday, 23 December, following the Saturday session of the Court, he ordered a special survey of the vessel. Accordingly, John Austin, Surveyor of Shipping, and Ricardo Portunato, a diver, accompanied by Thomas J. Vecchio, Marshal of the Court and Mr. Flood, Queen's Proctor, made a thorough survey of the vessel, internally and externally, lasting several hours. (Copies of these reports will be found in the Appendix.) On the same day, the *Dei Gratia*, which had been waiting since her arrival on 12 December, sailed with her cargo of petroleum for Genoa, arriving there on 16 January 1873. She was then under the command of Oliver Deveau, while Captain Morehouse remained at Gibraltar. This division of responsibility elicited some sharp comment from Justice Cochrane at the conclusion of the 31 January session of the Court, reference to which will later be made.

The results of the surveys above mentioned apparently did not satisfy Mr. Flood, who ordered a still further examination of the vessel. This was held on 7 January.[16]

On 15 January 1873, Captain James H. Winchester, owner of a twelve twenty-fourths interest in the *Mary Celeste,* arrived at Gibraltar, as will be attested by the following excerpt from Consul Sprague's letter of 20 January (No. 130) to the Department of State: "I have now to inform you that her [*Mary Celeste's*] principal owner, Mr.

16. Letter on 22 January 1873 from Frederick Solly Flood to Board of Trade, London, England.

James H. Winchester, arrived here on the 15th instant from New York for the purpose of claiming the Brig and attending to the interests of all those concerned in her case, including the New York underwriters who have also empowered him to that effect. Mr. Winchester is now about entering his claim in the Vice Admiralty Court, with the assistance of a Proctor[17] as required by British law in such cases. A claim for the cargo has already been entered by the holders of the Bill of Lading through their proctor;[18] in the meanwhile, nothing is heard from the missing crew of the *Mary Celeste*, and in face of the apparently seaworthy condition of this vessel, it is difficult to account for her abandonment, particularly as her Master, who was well-known, bore the highest character for seamanship and correctness; besides, he had his wife and young child with him and was part owner of the *Mary Celeste*.

"The Queen's Proctor in the Vice Admiralty Court of this City, who is also the Attorney General, seems to take the greatest interest in the case and rather entertains the apprehension of some foul play having occurred. Quite a quantity of clothes belonging to the Master, his family and crew has been found on board, but the Chronometer of the Brig, her papers and boat are missing: in fact, so far, the matter is wrapped up in mystery."

3. *Queen's Proctor informs London Board of Trade*

On 22 January 1873, Mr. Flood addressed the following letter to the Board of Trade, Marine Department, London.

17. George F. Cornwell of Lincoln's Inn, London, practising at Gibraltar.

18. Martin W. Stokes.

Sir: *Gibraltar, 22nd Jan'y* 1873

I have the honour to acquaint you, for the information of the Committee of the Privy Council for Trade, that early on the morning of the 13th Dec. part of the Crew of the Brit. Vessel *Dei Gratia* bound fr: New York to Gibraltar for orders brought into this port a brigantine wh: they stated they had found on the 5th of the month in latitude 38.20 N. Longitude 17.15 W 3 P.M. Sea time totally abandoned and derelict and which they supposed from the log to be the American brigantine *Mary Celeste* bound fr: New York to Genoa.

They stated that the wind being from the north and the *Dei Gratia* consequently on the Port tack they met the derelict with her jib and foremast stay sail set on the Starboard tack.

I caused the derelict to be arrested in the customary manner upon her arrival whereupon the Master of the *Dei Gratia* which had arrived on the evening of the 12th of November[19] made his claim for salvage.

The second Mate of the *Dei Gratia* and those of her Crew who had boarded the derelict were examined in support of the claim to salvage on the 20th and 21st ultimo.[20]

But the account which they gave of the soundness and good condition of the derelict was so extraordinary that I found it necessary to apply for a survey wh: was held in my presence on the 23rd of the same month and the result of which is embodied in the affidavit of Mr. Ricardo Fortunato,[21] a diver sworn on the 7th inst; of Mr. John Austin, Surveyor of shipping, sworn on the 8th inst; and Mr. F. I. Vecchio[22] sworn on the 9th inst.

From the survey it appears that both bows of the derelict had been recently cut by a sharp instrument but that she was thoroughly sound staunch strong and every way seaworthy and well found, that she was well provisioned and that she had encountered no seriously heavy weather and that no appearance of fire or of explosion or of alarm of fire or of explosion or any other assignable

19. Obviously intended to read "December" as the *Dei Gratia* did not sail from New York until 15 November.

20. For their testimony, see Appendix N.

21. Portunato.

22. T. J. Vecchio.

cause for abandonment was discoverable. A Sword however was found wh: appeared to me to exhibit traces of blood and to have been wiped before being returned into the scabbard.

My opinion in this respect having been corroborated by others I Proceeded on the 7th inst. to make with the assistance of the Marshal of the Vice Admiralty Court a still more minute examination for marks of violence, and had the honor of being accompanied and greatly assisted by Capt. Fitzroy, R. N., H. M. S. *Minotaur;* Capt. Adeane, R. N., H. M. S. *Agincourt;* Capt. Dowell, C. B., R. N., H. M. S. *Hercules;* Capt. Vansittart, R. N., H. M. S. *Sultan,* and by Col. Laffan, R. E. all of whom agreed with me in opinion that the injury to the bows had been effected intentionally by a sharp instrument.

On examining the Starboard top gallant sail[23] marks were discovered apparently of blood and a mark of a blow apparently of a sharp axe.

On descending through the forehatch a barrel ostensibly of Alcohol appeared to have been tampered with.

The Vessel's Register Manifest and Bills of lading have not been found neither has any sextant or Chronometer been found. On the other hand almost the whole personal effects of the Master and so I believe of his wife and child and of the Crew have been found in good order & condition.

They are of considerable value. In the Cap't's Cabin were a Harmonium in a Rosewood case books of music and others mostly of a religious tendency. Gold Lockets and other Trinkets and jewellery, and female attire of a superior description were in the lady's boxes. The working Chart and ships log were also found on the arrest of the Vessel both are complete up to noon of the 24th of Novbr. I transmit copy of the last days work and the deck or slate log is continued, a copy of wh. is enclosed up to 8 A.M. on the following day at wh. hour the eastern point of St. Mary's (Azores) bore S.S.W. distant 6 miles — she had therefore run considerably less number of knots since the previous noon than that entered in the Slate, the Longitude of St. Mary's being 25.9 W. Since then eight weeks have elapsed and nothing whatsoever has been heard of the Master or Crew or of the unhappy Lady and Child.

23. Rail.

The Ships log wh. was found on board shows the last day's work of the Ship up to noon on the 24th Novbr. when the weather was sufficiently fine to enable an observation to be taken; The position then was by observation Lat. 36.56 N. Longitude 27.20 W. Entries on the Slate log are carried up to 8 A.M. on the 25th wh. is the last and at wh. time she had passed from W. to E. to the north of the Island of St. Mary's, the eastern point of which bore S.S.W. 6 miles distant. The distance of the longitude of the place where she was found from that of the Island of St. Mary's is 10 N.E. and the corrected distance of the lat. of the place when she was found from that last mentioned on the log is 1.18 N so that she must actually have held her due course for 10 days after the 25th Novbr. the wheel being loose all that time.

My object is to move the Bd. of Trade to take such action as they may think fit to discover if possible the fate of the Master his wife and Child, and the crew of the derelict. My own theory or guess is that the Crew got at the alcohol and in the fury of drunkenness murdered the Master whose name was Briggs and wife and Child and the Chief Mate — that they then damaged the bows of the Vessel with the view of giving it the appearance of having struck on rocks or suffered from a collision so as to induce the Master of any Vessel wh. might pick them up if they saw her at some distance to think her not worth attempting to save and that they did sometime between the 25th Novbr. and the 5th Decbr. escape on board some vessel bound for some north or South American port or the West Indies.

I shall however be thankful for any information and have etc

[Signed] Fredk. Solly Flood

H. M. S. Advocate Genl. and Proctor for the Queen in Her Office of Admiralty & Attorney Genl. for Gibraltar.

To the Board of Trade, Marine Depm't. London

This letter was supplemented by a further communication dated the day following:

4. *His Theory of Abandonment*

Copy M. 1803

SIR,   *Gibraltar, 23 January* 1873

I beg leave to supplement my letter of the 22*nd* Inst by inclos-
ing an extract[24] from so much of the log, of the *Dei Gratia* as is
necessary to show the position of that vessel on & from the 24th
of November to the day when she met the *Mary Celeste* on the 5*th*
of December from which it will appear that the wind during the
whole of that time was more or less from the North, that she[25] was
during the whole of that time on the Port tack, & that consequently
it seems incredible that the *Mary Celeste* should have run during
the same period a distance of 7'.54 E at least upon the starboard
tack, upon which tack she was when *met* by the *Dei Gratia*.

These circumstances seem to me to lead to the conclusion that—
although no entry either in the Log or on the slate of the *Mary
Celeste* later than 8 a.m. on the 25*th* of November is to be found,
she had in fact not been abandoned till several days afterwards,
and probably also that she was abandoned much further to the
Eastward than the spot where she was found.

I have &.

SD   FREDK. SOLLY FLOOD,

HMS Advocate General & Proctor for The Queen in Her
Office of Admiralty & Attorney General for Gibraltar.

To the Secretary, Board of Trade

5. *Supposed Blood-stains Analyzed. New Master Arrives*

It was during the week beginning Monday, 27 January
1873, that at the direction of the Queen's Advocate Frederick Solly Flood, whose apprehensions of foul play had
been strengthened by the Court testimony, a careful and
minute inspection of the vessel was made by Dr. J. Patron.

24. Copy of extracts from the *Dei Gratia's* Log, mentioned in Mr. Flood's
letter, will be found in Appendix L.

25. i.e., the *Dei Gratia*.

This examination included the deck of the vessel, the top-gallant-rail, the cabin floor, the sides of the berths, the mattresses, and a certain piece of the vessel's timber which had been kept in the Attorney-General's chambers. The examination also included the sword found by the Marshal on the cabin floor, and which had stains supposed to be blood. According to the voluminous report dated 30 January 1873,[26] Dr. Patron acknowledges having received from the Marshal five papers, numbered consecutively one to five, containing powder-like scrapings from various parts of the vessel and also from the sword with its sheath. The report concludes with the following statement: "From the preceding negative experiments, I feel myself authorized to conclude that, according to our present scientifical knowledge, there is no blood, either in the stains observed on the deck of the *Mary Celeste,* or on those found on the blade of the sword that I have examined."

Although the result of this report was well known at the time, it is a curious fact that for fourteen years it slumbered in the official archives of the Attorney-General's office under an unbroken seal. Further reference to this rather singular phase of the matter will be made in a subsequent chapter.

An excerpt from Consul Sprague's letter (No. 131) dated 1 February 1873 informed the Department of State that: "This Court is now setting[*sic*] since the beginning of the week, and matters are progressing for the early release of both vessel and cargo on bail being given, which will enable the *Mary Celeste* to proceed on her voyage to Genoa, and earn her freight. A new Master, brought out from New York, will take charge of the Brig, a new crew put on board, and the vessel be refitted with all possible despatch. I have notified the Court that I am ready to take charge of

26. See Appendix Q.

Oliver Deveau, First Mate of the Dei Gratia;
in command of the Mary Celeste *while she was being
sailed from Latitude* 38° 20′ *North, Longitude*
17° 15′ *West to Gibraltar*

PLATE X

Half-brig Amazon (later renamed Mary Celeste) from an unsigned painting, made at Marseille in November 1861, possibly by Honoré Pellegrin, owned by Mr. R. Lester Dewis and now exhibited at Fort Beauséjour Historic Site, Aulac, New Brunswick

PLATE XI

the effects of the missing Master and family and also of the crew, whenever the Judge should feel disposed to deliver them over. I have examined the sword to which the article in the 'Gibraltar Chronicle'[27] refers. It was found on the floor in the cabin of the *Mary Celeste* by the Marshal of the Court. It is evidently of Italian make, and bears a cross of Savoy on the hilt; it remains in the custody of the Court. The chronometer and ship's papers cannot be found. I am Sir, Your obedient serv't., Horatio J. Sprague, U.S. Consul."

6. *Court Refuses to Release* Mary Celeste. *Criticizes Conduct of Salvors*

In confirmation of Consul Sprague's report to Washington that the Court had been in session, we find from the record of its proceedings on Friday, 31 January, that this was the day assigned to George F. Cornwell, Proctor for claimant of the vessel, to bring in the proofs of his parties claiming to be the owners of the *Mary Celeste*. Cornwell "prayed the Judges to admit the claim of his party, James H. Winchester, as the lawful owner of the said Brig *Mary Celeste* and to decree restitution thereof to him upon payment of salvage and salvage expenses, and upon finding sureties to answer all latent claims, the Queen's Advocate being present and consenting thereto, as also Pisani, Proctor for the Salvors."

Apparently, Judge Cochrane was of the opinion that there were some matters which had not been wholly satisfactorily explained. He seems to have shared the opinion of the Queen's Advocate that foul play had been committed. We find him, therefore, replying to Mr. Cornwell's petition as follows: "There are certain matters which

27. Consul Sprague enclosed an article from this paper, dated 31 January 1873.

have been brought to my notice respecting this vessel, my opinion about which I have already very decidedly expressed and which make it desirable, and even necessary, that further investigation should take place before the release of the vessel can be sanctioned, or before she can quit this port.

"The conduct of the Salvors in going away, as they have done, has, in my opinion, been most reprehensible and may probably influence the decision as to their claim for remuneration for their services, and it appears very strange why the Captain of the *Dei Gratia* who knows little or nothing to help the investigation, should have remained here, whilst the First Mate and the crew who boarded the *Celeste* and brought her here should have been allowed to go away as they have done. The Court will take time to consider the decree for restitution."

The *Dei Gratia* had been waiting with her cargo of petroleum from 12 December until 23 December when she sailed for Genoa. It was costing the *Dei Gratia* something to maintain a crew of eight in addition to the usual port charges. In the circumstances, the strictures of the presiding judge upon the master and crew of the *Dei Gratia* seem somewhat severe. His comment, however, makes clear the fact that, contrary to previous reports, Captain Morehouse himself did not bring the *Mary Celeste* in to Gibraltar. Like a prudent mariner, mindful of his obligation to the owners of the *Dei Gratia,* he remained at all times on board of his own ship, and committed to his subordinates the task of examining the derelict when she was first discovered, and of sailing her into port.

Captain Morehouse may have had good reason for remaining at Gibraltar, and sending his vessel on to Genoa under the command of Oliver Deveau. As previously pointed out, he was the representative of the owners of the vessel, and as such, was empowered to receive the salvage money when it should be awarded by the Court. It is possible that he was acting under instructions from the owners.

Captain Morehouse was born at Sandy Cove, Nova Scotia, on 22 March 1838; went to sea when he was sixteen years old, and became a captain at the age of twenty-one. A correspondent in a recent letter to the author, states that Captain Morehouse "was admired by sea-faring men for his knowledge of navigation." An old resident of Bear Island, Nova Scotia, the home town of Captain Morehouse, writes: "He was very honourable in his dealings and a good citizen." Charges circulated by a certain writer that Captain Morehouse and Captain Briggs entered into an illicit bargain with respect to their two vessels, appear to be entirely without foundation in fact, and have aroused the just indignation of their relatives and friends.

7. Captain Shufeldt, U.S.N., Surveys Derelict. Rejects Theory of Mutiny

During the week following Judge Cochrane's pronouncement, the U. S. S. *Plymouth,* under command of Captain R. W. Shufeldt, arrived at Gibraltar, on 5 February. At the request of Consul Sprague, he made an examination of the *Mary Celeste* and, under date of 6 February, made written report to Consul Sprague. On the following day, 7 February, Captain Shufeldt sailed in the *Plymouth* from Gibraltar.

On 7 February (Letter No. 132) Consul Sprague addressed the Department of State as follows:

"In continuation to [*sic*] my last communication, dated 1st instant, on the subject of the derelict *Mary Celeste,* I have to report that, by direction of the Vice Admiralty

Court, the marks or stains which appeared on the sword found on board the vessel, as well as on some of the woodwork on board, have undergone an analysis, the result of which is considered to negative anything like blood existing thereon.

"I now have much pleasure in forwarding the report of Captain Shufeldt of our Navy on the subject of the *Mary Celeste's* situation, the perusal of which may prove interesting to your Department. Captain Shufeldt arrived at this port in command of the U. S. Ship *Plymouth* on the 5th instant from Villefranche, homeward bound via Lisbon, and the Coast of Africa. The *Plymouth* left this morning for her destination."

Captain Shufeldt's report reads as follows:

U. S. S. PLYMOUTH
Gibraltar Feb'y. 6, 1873

HORATIO SPRAGUE, ESQ., U. S. Consul
My dear Sir:

At your request, I visited the American Brig *Mary Celeste* found derelict at sea, Dec. 5, 1872 and brought into this port. After a cursory examination of the vessel and a somewhat imperfect knowledge of the circumstances, I am of the opinion that she was abandoned by the master & crew in a moment of panic & for no sufficient reason. She may have strained in the gale through which she was passing & for the time leaked so much as to alarm the Master, and it is possible that, at this moment, another vessel in sight, induced him (having his wife and child on board,) to abandon thus hastily. In this event, he may not be heard from for some time to come, as the ship which rescued him may have been bound to a distant port.

I reject the idea of mutiny, from the fact that there is no evidence of violence about the decks or in the cabins; besides the force aft and forward was so equally divided, that a mutiny could hardly have had such a result.

The damage about the bows of the Brig appears to me to amount to nothing more than splinters made in the bending of the planks

—which were afterwards forced off by the action of the sea, without hurting the ship, *nor by any possible chance, the result of an intention to do so.* [The italics are the author's.]

The vessel at the present moment appears staunch and seaworthy—Some day, I hope & expect to hear from her crew. If surviving, the Master will regret his hasty action. But if we should never hear of them again, I shall nevertheless think they were lost in the boat in which both Master & crew abandoned the *Mary Celeste* & shall remember with interest this sad and silent mystery of the sea.

I am very faithfully, Your friend & obdt. servt.

R. W. SHUFELDT, *Captain.*

Inasmuch as there is a sharp divergence between the views of Captain Shufeldt and those of John Austin, Surveyor of Shipping, in regard to the alleged damage to the vessel's bows, the reader is referred to the latter's voluminous report to be found in the Appendix.[28]

8. *Captain Winchester leaves Gibraltar. Meets Captain Appleby at Cadiz*

Captain Winchester had arrived at Gibraltar on 15 January 1873 and several weeks had passed with little or nothing accomplished. Thus far, he had been unable to satisfy the demands of the Court authorities who required certain guarantees which he was either unwilling or unable to give. His departure from New York had been so suddenly decided upon, that he had not provided himself with all the necessary papers. During the first week in February, we find him at Cadiz about seventy-five miles from Gibraltar. There he had hoped to find a ship-broker named Bensusan with whom he was acquainted, but on arrival at Cadiz, it was found that his friend had died some time before. The trip to Cadiz, however, proved not unreward-

28. Published in part in *Shipping Gazette* (London) 5 February 1873.

ing as there Captain Winchester found his friend, young Captain Henry O. Appleby, master of the brigantine *Daisy Boynton* which had arrived at Cadiz on 28 January, discharged her cargo and received her freight money. To him Captain Winchester explained the situation and spoke of his intention to go to London to lay the matter before the American minister. This, however, proved unnecessary, as sympathetic Captain Appleby (whose father, Captain Lemuel Appleby, was part owner of the *Daisy Boynton*) agreed to let Captain Winchester borrow the vessel's freight money just received.

According to Captain Appleby,[29] Captain Winchester was worried. The *Mary Celeste* had been detained at Gibraltar for more than seven weeks, with no immediate prospect of release; the vessel was not only out of circulation, but was undoubtedly running up expense. The necessity for hiring a new captain and a new crew was, of course, imminent. It is not known when the new crew was engaged—whether before or after the vessel's release—but in view of Captain Winchester's eagerness to get his vessel out of Gibraltar at the earliest opportunity, it is possible that a crew was engaged considerably in advance.[30] Bringing Captain George W. Blatchford from Wrentham, Massachusetts, to Gibraltar to take charge of the *Mary Celeste* and sail her to Genoa, had to be arranged for without delay and was not accomplished without extra cost. It is not known precisely when Captain Blatchford reached Gibral-

29. In the summer of 1930, Captain Appleby called upon the author at the Atlantic Mutual Office and told of his conversation at Cadiz with Captain Winchester. He recalled having been at Cadiz on 11 February when King Amadeus resigned the Spanish throne and a Republic was declared. The *Daisy Boynton* is reported as having sailed from Cadiz on 21 February 1873 (*Maritime Register*).

30. The author has on file a photostatic copy of the record showing the names of the master, first and second mates and the seamen, who sailed the *Mary Celeste* from Gibraltar to Genoa.

tar, but it must have been at some time prior to 6 March as on that day we find his name signed to the receipt for a long list of articles belonging to the master and crew of the *Mary Celeste,* including articles manifestly the property of Mrs. Briggs and little Sophia, and which were to be shipped to the United States. Besides all this, Captain Winchester must have had in mind the *Mary Celeste's* return-charter, presumably of fruit, from Messina, Sicily. The fruit market was seasonal, and the charter-party in all probability contained some stipulations as to the time for loading there. Naturally, the Messina shippers could not wait indefinitely for the *Mary Celeste* to fulfill her charter obligations, and the record of subsequent events proved that they did not wait.[31] Captain Winchester's problem was indeed a difficult one, as he could not take measures to prevent delays without incurring additional expense, and expenses were mounting.

A letter[32] from Mrs. Thomas J. Port of Stapleton, Staten Island, New York, daughter of the late Captain Appleby,[33] tells of the incident:

"The brigantine *Daisy Boynton* was my father's first command, and he was only 22 when he was in Cadiz at the time Captain Winchester came to him because he (Capt. W) was a stranger over there at the time the *Mary Celeste* was brought in to Gibraltar. Captain Winchester came to my father because he needed cash, as the authorities over there

31. The *Maritime Register* of 14 May 1873 reports the vessel hove down at Genoa in order to have her bottom surveyed, and states "this vessel was laying [*sic*] there waiting the settlement of damages, *the charterers having cancelled her charter party.*" [The italics are the author's.] As the *Dei Gratia* arrived at Messina on 29 March and sailed from there on 27 April, it is not improbable that she got the cargo originally intended for the *Mary Celeste.*

32. 16 January 1941 to the author.

33. Captain Henry O. Appleby died in 1931 at the age of eighty. He was at that time a member of the Marine Society of New York and a member of the New York State Commissioners of Pilots.

would not accept his note, being a stranger. My father had gone to school with Captain Winchester's daughter—therefore he knew him well and gave him the freight money of the Brig *Daisy Boynton* so that Captain Winchester might release the *Mary Celeste*—therefore father indirectly helped to release the *Mary Celeste*."

In a subsequent letter[34] Mrs. Port says: "I do know my father loaned Captain Winchester the money because he spoke of it to me every time as something daring on his part, as it was his first command, and he was so young. . . . My father put up cash and took his note. Naturally, he would have to have that money as soon as he could. I know Captain Winchester had a great deal of trouble in Gibraltar. It was not so easy to release the *Mary Celeste* as he had anticipated. Of course, time is a great factor; the longer a vessel remains in port, the more it costs."

In Captain Winchester's departure from Gibraltar, there appears to have been the element of the unexpected. In Consul Sprague's letter (No. 133) of 12 February 1873 to the Department of State, from which we quote, he wrote: "I have now to report the return to the United States, of her (i.e. the *Mary Celeste's*) principal owner, Mr. Winchester, who had come out to represent his interests and those of underwriters before the Vice Admiralty Court of this city. He never announced his intention to the Court, and at the time of leaving this[35] . . . he gave parties here to understand that he was merely going on a short pleasure trip to Cadiz. I have since received a letter from him dated, Lisbon the 6th.[36] instant, announcing his determination to return to New York by the Anchor Line Steamer *Caledonia* then about leaving that port."

34. Letter of 19 February 1941 to the author.
35. Word omitted.
36. 6 February 1873.

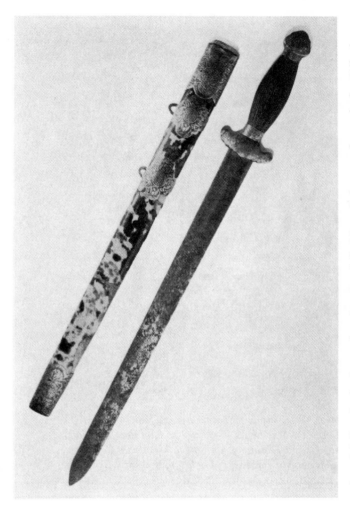

Sword, believed to be the one found on board the Mary Celeste *on her arrival at Gibraltar and later shipped by Consul Horatio J. Sprague to Mr. James C. Briggs, New Bedford, Massachusetts, brother of Captain Benjamin Spooner Briggs*

PLATE XII

Melodeon of Mrs. Benjamin Spooner Briggs, found on board the
Mary Celeste *when the vessel arrived at Gibraltar, and later
shipped by Consul Horatio J. Sprague to Mr. James C. Briggs,
New Bedford, Massachusetts, brother of Captain Benjamin
Spooner Briggs*

PLATE XIII

9. *Consul Sprague Informs Department of State of Court's Refusal*

Consul Sprague's letter (No. 133) of 12 February 1873 previously mentioned contained also the following information regarding the attitude of the Court:

"For the information of your Department, I beg to state that, yesterday, the Vice Admiralty Court sat, and the Queen's Proctor declines to allow any restitution of the *Mary Celeste* to her owners, unless they are prepared to give bail to the Court, to answer for any claims that may be set up either by Captain Briggs (the missing master who is part owner of the vessel) or his representatives, or by the mortgagee, a Mr. Hart,[37] or any other latent demands on the vessel of which there is now no notice. The Court would call for two sureties in double the value of the vessel (probably some 15,000 dollars) to answer these claims, as also the salvage claim and expenses; but Mr. Winchester's agent here has cabled to New York not only Mr. Winchester's return to the United States, but also his unwillingness to stand security for the parties interested. The Queen's Proctor also intimated that the signature of Mr. Winchester to this bail-bond would be desirable. The suggested course now, is to take out and send on the cargo to its destination and allow the vessel to remain as she is, until the above bail is duly given."

10. Mary Celeste *finally Released*

Within the two-week period following Consul Sprague's letter of 12 February to the Department, the disposition of the Court toward the matter of releasing the *Mary Celeste*

37. Simpson Hart of New Bedford, Massachusetts, who, it is believed, loaned Captain Briggs money for the purchase of the latter's shares in the *Mary Celeste.*

appears to have changed, for we find the Consul addressing the Department under date of 25 February (No. 134) as follows:

"Since my last communication dated the 12th. instant, on the subject of the *Mary Celeste* case, I have conferred with the Queen's Proctor in the Vice Admiralty Court regarding the formalities required by him for the restitution of the vessel to her original owners, and I am happy to add that I have succeeded in prevailing upon this law officer of the Crown, [*sic*] the abandonment of his pretensions to have the said vessel bailed against any latent or other demands, beyond those of meeting the salvage claims and Court expenses. This formality has just been gone through, and the *Mary Celeste* has this evening been restored to her original owners, and she will now be in position to proceed on her voyage to Genoa with her cargo of alcohol taken in at New York, thereby enabling her to earn her freight, and spare to the parties concerned much time and extra expenses. Of the missing Master and crew, nothing continues to be heard of them."

It is not improbable that, in the interim, the underwriters who had insured the vessel, freight and cargo, as well as the various owners, were anxious to have the voyage performed, and had been making strong representations to Mr. Sprague on the subject.

Horatio Jones Sprague (succeeding his father in the American Consulship at Gibraltar) had been appointed Consul by President Polk in May 1848, and was held in high esteem by the authorities at Gibraltar as well as at Washington. It is not unlikely that the release of the *Mary Celeste* from official custody was in some measure due to the influence of Consul Sprague, as well as to the financial assistance rendered by Captain Appleby.

11. *Oliver Deveau Recalled to Testify*

On 4 March 1873 the record discloses the fact that Oliver Deveau was again testifying before the Vice-Admiralty Court at Gibraltar. It will be recalled that he left that port on 23 December 1872 in command of the *Dei Gratia,* leaving Captain Morehouse at Gibraltar. According to the *Maritime Register,* this vessel arrived at Genoa on 16 January 1873 and remained there until 17 March when she sailed for Messina. It was, therefore, during the *Dei Gratia's* stay at Genoa, that Deveau was summoned to appear at Gibraltar. In order to make the trip there and back, it must have been necessary to take passage by steamer. From the nature of the testimony, it is evident that the Court still entertained the idea of some act of violence having been responsible for the *Mary Celeste's* abandonment.

The record of his final Court appearance on 4 March 1873 reads as follows:

"Oliver Deveau cross-examined by the Queen's Advocate and Proctor in Her Office of Admiralty:

'I saw no remains of a painter or boat's rope fastened to the rail. I did not notice any mark of an axe on the rail or cut. I did not see this cut in the rail now shown me, to notice it. I cannot say how the cut came in rail—it appears to have been done with a sharp axe, and I do not think it could have been done by my men whilst we were in possession of the vessel. I did not see any new axes on board the *Celeste;* there was an old axe we found on board. I did not replace the rails of the ship found on the deck before I returned to the *Dei Gratia* the first time.[38]

38. This is the first mention of a section of rail having been removed by the crew of the *Mary Celeste* when they got out the boat to leave the vessel. The *Mary Celeste* had no bulwarks, but was a flush-deck vessel with open rails fore and aft. It is amazing that Deveau did not mention this in his previous testimony.

'I can form no opinion about the cause of the axe cut on the rail.

'I observed no marks of blood on deck. I noticed no marks or traces of blood upon the deck. I cannot say whether there were any or not; we never washed the decks of the *Mary Celeste* nor scraped them. We had not men enough for that. The sea washed over the decks.'

'(The Queen's Proctor explains that salt water contains chloric acid which dissolves the particles of the blood.)'

'If there are some parts of the deck or rail scraped, I did not notice them, and they were not done whilst we were on board.

'I saw a sword on board the *Mary Celeste*. I found that sword under the Captain's berth. I took it out from there. I looked at it—drew it from its sheath; there was nothing remarkable on it. I do not think there is anything remarkable about it now—it seems rusty. I think I put it back where I found it or somewhere near there. I did not see it at the foot of the ladder—perhaps some of my men may have put it there. I was not on board the *Celeste* when the Marshal came on the *Celeste* to arrest the vessel, and therefore I did not see him find the sword.'

[The Queen's Proctor goes on to explain that the sword has been cleaned with lemon which has covered it with citrate of iron which has destroyed the marks of the supposed blood, which therefore, is not blood at all, as at first supposed, but another substance put there to destroy and disguise the original marks of the blood which were once there.]

'It did not occur to me,' [Deveau answered] 'that there had been any act of violence—there was nothing to induce one to believe or to show that there had been any violence.' "

CHAPTER X

Interesting Side-lights Disclosed by Correspondence

1. *Consul Sprague Reports Vessel's Release to Department of State*

THE final testimony of Deveau, given in the previous chapter, concludes the record of the proceedings before the Vice-Admiralty Court. As reported by Consul Sprague, the vessel had been restored to her owners on 25 February 1873.[1] Accordingly, we find Consul Sprague, under date of 10 March, addressing the Department of State (Letter No. 135), from which we quote:

"The *Mary Celeste* has just cleared for Genoa with her original cargo taken in at New York, and in charge of Captain George W. Blatchford sent out to this port, for that purpose, by her owners in New York. It is expected that the Vice Admiralty Court will very shortly adjudicate in the *Mary Celeste's* case, of salvage to be awarded to the salvors ex: British Brig *Dei Gratia*."

The *Mary Celeste,* therefore, having lain at Gibraltar from 13 December 1872 until 10 March 1873—a period of eighty-seven days—finally proceeded with new master and crew to Genoa, at which port she arrived on 21 March.[2] She discharged her cargo in good order, having made the passage in eleven days, as against twenty-four days required by the *Dei Gratia* to perform a similar journey two months previously.

1. According to the *Maritime Register* of 19 March 1873, she was released by the Court as of date of 28 February, after bond had been given for ship and cargo.

2. *Maritime Register,* 9 April 1873.

2. *Court Officials Secretive about Analysis of supposed Blood-stains*

It was on 14 March, a few days after the *Mary Celeste's* departure, that Dr. Patron's analysis of the supposed blood-stains found on the sword and on the woodwork of the vessel was brought into Court, under seal. It is a strange circumstance that this document remained under unbroken seal for fourteen years and that the Court was secretive about it. Consul Sprague became aware of this attitude, and made mention of it in his official communication of 4 April 1873 (No. 142) to the Department of State, from which we quote: "I am confidentially informed that the Judge of the Vice Admiralty Court has refused to permit the analysis made on the spots found on the sword and wood-work of the *Mary Celeste* to be opened for the present, *even for the purpose of furnishing a copy to the Governor of this Fortress.*"[3] The motivation for the Court's refusal of the Governor's request was not disclosed until twelve years later when the Queen's Proctor, in his letter of 9 January 1885 to Consul Sprague,[4] reveals the reason for official reticence on the subject. Two years after that, namely on 25 July 1887, the seal was finally broken by the Registrar of the Court in Consul Sprague's presence, and a certified copy was given to him on 28 July for transmission to the Department of State.

3. *Captain Winchester's Reasons for Returning Home*

An interesting side-light on the activities of the Queen's Advocate is furnished by a letter from Captain Winchester written 10 March 1873 (which was shortly after his return

3. The italics are the author's.
4. See Chapter XVII.

to the United States) and addressed to Consul Sprague at Gibraltar. Captain Winchester encloses a power of attorney, duly legalized by the English Consul, from Simpson Hart who had acquired an interest in the *Mary Celeste,* presumably through his loans to Captain Briggs. Captain Winchester states that, on arrival home, he found his wife's condition of health had grown more serious. He explains that his anxiety concerning her was one of the contributory causes of his unexpected departure from Gibraltar. Moreover, he states that his presence there was accomplishing very little; that he was under considerable expense, and that his business at home was suffering through his absence. The letter goes on to say that a gentleman came to him at Gibraltar and told him that after the Judge and the Attorney General had used up every other pretense to cause delay and expense, they were going to arrest him for hiring the crew to make away with the officers. This idea, writes Captain Winchester, was very ridiculous, but, he adds, "from what you and everybody else in Gibraltar had told me about the attorney general, I did not know but he might do it as they seam [*sic*] to do just as they like." The letter also states that when he left Gibraltar, he expected to go back, but after talking with the Consul at Cadiz, he decided to come home.

The idea of Captain Winchester conspiring with the crew of the *Mary Celeste* to murder its officers was, indeed, ridiculous. Captain Winchester was well known and highly respected in maritime circles. For years, a warm friendship had existed between him and the Briggs family. Captain Nathan Briggs, father of Captain Ben, had commanded, from 1851 to 1853, the fine ship *Winchester*[5] owned by

5. The *Winchester* was a large new ship. Her first cargo of cotton, loaded at New Orleans for Liverpool, was the largest cotton cargo ever loaded at that port up to that time.

J. H. Winchester and Co. Mate Richardson, of the *Mary Celeste,* had married Frances Spates, the niece of Captain Winchester's wife.

Captain Winchester's impatience over the delay in obtaining the release of his vessel; his anxiety concerning his wife's health, and his indignation over the suggestion of criminal intent were quite sufficient to bring about his decision to return home.

4. *Consul Sprague Answers Query of German Official Regarding Missing Seamen*

U. S. CONSULATE
Gibraltar 4th April 1873

DEAR SIR,

I am this day in receipt of your communication of the 24th ulto: asking for information regarding the missing Master and Crew of the American Brig *Mary Celeste.* I regret to say that up to this moment, we continue without any tidings of them, and the general impression is, that they must have been drowned in the Ship's boat, no boat having been found with the Brig when she was met at Sea, it being missing, also the Chronometer and the Ship's papers—The Logbook I possess, and keep it subject to the orders of my Government, also the clothes found on board, which however, are of very little value. The last entry of the Log was the 24th November then a few miles from St. Mary's (Azores). The general opinion is, that no violence took place on board, as no signs were found to that effect. I inclose copy of a report made to me by one of our Naval Commanders, and which partakes of the general impressions elicited in the case—and which has met the full attention of the Vice Admiralty Court in Gibraltar, and also of this Consulate. The Brig *Mary Celeste,* after being liberated by the Court under the usual legal forms, proceeded on her voyage to Genoa, under the command of a newly appointed Master and Crew, where she arrived after a short passage from this port.

As the Clothes of the missing Crew of the *Mary Celeste* remain here subject to the orders of the American Government, I would suggest your addressing yourself to the Secretary of State at Washington, should the relatives of the missing crew have any desire to obtain them—I believe the names of the four Seamen that shipped by the *Mary Celeste* at New York, were: Walkert Lorenzen,[6] Boz Lorenzen, Aran Hardens,[6] and Gallbit Goudschatt.[6]

Should I ever learn anything about the missing crew or any other information, relating to this mysterious affair, I shall not fail to address you on the subject.

I am truly yours

H. J. S., Am. C.

W. T. A. Nickelsen, Uettersum auf Foke,[7] Prussia.

6. These three names are incorrectly stated. See correct names under "Common Errors and Misconceptions," in Appendix C.

7. This should read "Föhr."

CHAPTER XI

Theory of the Cause of Abandonment and
Fate of Ship's Company

FROM the testimony given before the Vice-Admiralty Court and from other trustworthy sources, it is possible to trace, with some degree of precision, the movements of the *Mary Celeste* from noon on Sunday, 24 November, until eight o'clock in the morning of the day following. In view of the special significance of the events of these last two days, it seems desirable to consider separately, and somewhat minutely, the available records relating to each day, with a view to reaching just conclusions as to the probable causes of the known effects.

Sunday, 24 November 1872

It is noon, and according to the observation taken at this time and noted on the vessel's log, the *Mary Celeste* is in latitude 36° 56′ N, and longitude 27° 20′ W. All of the Azores group are now astern except San Miguel [St. Michael's] off to the northeast about 100 miles distant, and Santa Maria [St. Mary's] about 110 miles directly east and therefore practically dead-ahead of the *Mary Celeste*. She is making 8 knots, at which rate she continues until 7 P.M. when, with freshening wind, her speed increases to 9 knots.

The night promises to be a stormy one, and at eight o'clock when the first watch comes on duty, they take in her royal and topgallant sails. By 9 P.M. her speed drops back to 8 knots, at which rate she continues up to midnight. At this time—twelve o'clock, midnight—the log reads: "Knots, 8: Course, E. by S: Wind, west: M.P. rainy."

It is probable that, by this time, at the speed the vessel has been making since noon of the previous day, she has travelled about ninety miles, and must be nearing the western end of Santa Maria [St. Mary's] Island. It is a matter of official record that "stormy conditions prevailed over the Azores on November 24 and November 25." It is therefore more than likely that the little brigantine is getting her share of the bad weather, and that her men who have the watch from eight until midnight are having an uncomfortable time of it. Presumably for them, and for the other members of the ship's company, asleep in their berths below, there is no foreshadowing of the direful events awaiting them with the new day about to dawn.

Monday, 25 November 1872

Midnight is passed and a new and eventful day is beginning. The speed of the vessel continues steadily. One o'clock, two o'clock, three o'clock, four o'clock, the entry against each hour reads the same—8 knots. Soon the first streaks of dawn will be visible, and now there is land ahead, for the log-slate entry reads: "At 5, made the island of S. Mary's, bearing ESE" and a similar entry appears against the sixth hour. With this bearing, it seems that the point of land observed by the vessel's watch must be Ponta Cabraestante which is the *northwestern* extremity of Saint Mary's. The vessel is now, approximately, in latitude 37° 0′, which is slightly further *north* than her position on the previous day, at noon, when she was in latitude 36° 56′. But why, we inquire, is Captain Briggs, or whoever is directing the vessel's course, taking her to the *north* of St. Mary's,[1]

1. Lieutenant-Colonel J. Agostinho, Director of the Servico Meteorologico dos Açores, writing from Angra do Heroismo, Azores, under date of 17 October 1941, states that Captain Briggs probably feared "to fall to the

when it must be known by all hands that, in order to reach Genoa, they must pass through the Strait of Gibraltar, which lies off to the *southeast* in the lower latitude of 35° 57′? Surely, he is not planning to land along the island's north shore, as it is well known to all navigators that neither here nor elsewhere on this island are there any harbors where vessels can find safe accommodation. Moreover, he must also know that about twenty-one miles to the northeast of the island's northeast extremity, lies the dangerous Dollabarat Shoal on which the sea breaks with great violence in stormy weather, but whose barely hidden rocks are not visible when the sea is calm. His present course, if continued, will take him between this shoal and the northeast end of the island. With a shifting wind—not an unusual occurrence in these waters—the vessel's position might become a very perilous one, but Captain Briggs is a capable mariner, and it is safe to assume that he will not do anything reckless or careless, especially at such a time when the safety of his wife and child, in addition to that of his crew, is at stake. Can it be that he is ill or otherwise incapacitated, that some accident, or even something more serious, has befallen him, that other hands are directing the course of the *Mary Celeste?* Why is the vessel going into a more northerly latitude, when she should be going to the southward?

But now the ship's bell sounds eight times, indicating that it is eight o'clock, on this memorable Monday morning. By this time, the vessel, according to the track noted on her chart, has skirted the island's *north* shore, and now comes the final record when the log slate reads: "At 8,

South, within the limits of the trade winds (blowing from N.E.) which would put the vessel far from her route to Gibraltar. Do not forget that Columbus followed that course when he returned from his discovery, and every sailing-vessel coming from Africa or South America to Europe takes the same course."

Eastern point bore SSW. 6 miles distant." After this, silence! A silence which, after the passing of seventy years, still remains unbroken!

The "eastern point" observed by the forenoon watch on the *Mary Celeste* was, in all likelihood, Ponta Castello, a point on the southeastern shore of the island. This point is surmounted by a detached peak of considerable height and is higher than any other place along the island's eastern shore. In the morning light, it would stand out even more prominently than Ponta Matos, the island's northeastern extremity, lying about five miles to the northwest and probably somewhat nearer to the *Mary Celeste*.

Possible Time of Abandonment

It seems probable, therefore, that on this Monday, 25 November, at some time after 8 A.M., something of disturbing character happened. Whatever it may have been, it must have been sufficiently serious to cause an experienced master-mariner with his wife, child and crew, to abandon ship, and to do so in haste. As previously mentioned, Deveau testified that "the men's clothing was left behind; their oilskins, boots, and even their pipes as if they had left in a great hurry or haste." It is impossible to fix the hour when abandonment took place, but from the condition of the cabin-table on which there was no food; from the appearance of the galley where the stove was knocked out of place and no cooked food was found; from the Captain's bed which was as it had been left, after being slept in, not made — in the ménage of Mrs. Briggs, beds were not likely to go unmade until afternoon; with no sign of an interrupted or finished meal; no evidence of preparations for serving a meal; no log or log-slate record after

8 A.M. on a vessel where both the log and working chart had been systematically kept up to noon, 24 November; from all of these considerations, it seems reasonable to suppose, and it is our belief, that abandonment took place between 8 A.M. and the noon hour on Monday, 25 November.[2]

Possible Cause of Abandonment

It will be recalled that the seventeen hundred barrels of alcohol had been loaded in late October, loading having been completed on 2 November. The *Dei Gratia,* following eight days behind the *Mary Celeste,* had experienced stormy weather from the date of sailing, 15 November, up to 24 November. During that time, her crew never took off their fore hatch, and the main hatch was off for one hour. It is, therefore, probable that the *Mary Celeste* also had encountered stormy weather and that in all likelihood her hatches had remained closed during most, if not all, of the voyage up to the day of abandonment. Under such circumstances, the hold had been getting little or no ventilation. The vessel having left the comparatively cool temperatures prevailing in New York at that season, and having passed through the Gulf Stream into the milder climatic areas of the Azores, it would not be surprising if the atmospheric changes had been producing some effect

2. Mr. Lincoln Colcord points out in correspondence: "It can be stated conclusively that this abandonment took place in pleasant weather, since the cabin skylight was open. The battened cabin windows show that they had been through heavy weather, but the open skylight means only one thing, a pleasant and moderate morning. It stands to reason that the gale of the night before, which had been dead aft, since the brig's yards were found squared, had moderated sufficiently for them to start making sail before leaving the ship. And the fact that a boat apparently was launched without bringing the vessel to or stopping her headway gives further proof that the wind must have fallen away to a light breeze."

upon a non-ventilated hold containing seventeen hundred barrels of alcohol, some of which may have leaked.[3] According to a letter from the Servico Meteorologico dos Açores, "calm or light wind prevailed on the forenoon of the 25th." It is possible that Captain Briggs, mindful of the character of the cargo and the necessity for ventilating the vessel's hold, took advantage of the comparatively calm weather and, sometime during the forenoon, ordered the removal of the bar of the forward hatch.

It will be noted from the testimony, that the salvors found the fore hatch lying on deck, on the port side of the hatchway, about three feet away from it. Although there have been newspaper and other reports to the effect that this hatch was found upside down (which, to a sailor, would indeed have seemed an ominous circumstance—something likely to be remembered and worthy of mention) there is nothing in the testimony to confirm the report. Not a few writers have advanced the theory that an explosion of some kind occurred in the vessel's hold and that the hatch was blown off, but the *Dei Gratia's* men, as well as John Austin, the Surveyor of Shipping at Gibraltar, testified that there were no signs of an explosion. With seventeen hundred barrels, stowed in three or four tiers in the vessel's hold, it would have been difficult if not impossible to make a thorough examination at this time. It is, however, a matter of official record that, while the *Mary Celeste* was at Gibraltar, the Marshal of the Vice-Admiralty Court had

3. United States Consul O. M. Spencer, writing from Genoa, 26 April 1873, to United States Consul H. J. Sprague at Gibraltar, regarding the out-turn of the *Mary Celeste's* cargo, said: "There were landed 1701 bbls. of Alcohol agreeing with the bills of lading — 9 of which were empty — (a not unusually large number) proof 93 35 — and specific gravity 0.815. The cargo came out in excellent condition, so much so that the consignee who wished to relinquish in favor of the underwriters, could find no excuse for doing so."

fifty casks taken on deck from the hold of the vessel. "The cargo and the stowage," it is reported, "were found in excellent order, and the casks showed no signs of having been handled in any way, also the contents, the casks being full and in good shipping order." In the circumstances, the possibility of the occurrence of an explosion of major proportions seems considerably diminished, although it is still a question whether even the removal of fifty casks would have enabled the investigators to see more than a comparatively small part of the remainder of the cargo.

Opinions differ widely as to whether or not leakage from the alcohol would have produced gases, and whether, even if gases were produced, it would have been possible to cause a minor explosion or rumbling sounds in the hold. It is conceivable that the cargo gave forth a noticeable odor. Even apart from the possibility of an explosion, if, on removing the hatch, any vapor accompanied by a strong odor had issued from the hold, there can be no question as to the alarming effect it would have had upon the ship's company.

In this connection, it may be of interest to mention the fact that Oliver W. Cobb, who assisted the mate of the brigantine *Julia A. Hallock* in checking sixteen hundred barrels of petroleum unloaded from that vessel at Naples, noticed that some of the metal hoops around the barrels were bright, the paint having been worn off in places as a result of constant chafing in the hold. It was customary to load such barrels with their heads and bottoms facing fore and aft, and with their bungs up. Wooden billets were stuck in, here and there, between the barrels, in order to keep them steady, but that expedient, apparently, did not prevent some of the barrels from rubbing against each other. If, then, there was sufficient friction in the hold of the *Julia A. Hallock* to wear off the paint on the metal barrel hoops, is it beyond the bound of possibility to suppose that friction in the *Mary Celeste's* hold containing seventeen hundred barrels of alcohol could have produced a spark and a resulting explosion?

Precisely what happened will probably remain for all time in the category of conjecture. According to the theory of Dr. Cobb, as we understand it, Captain Briggs, confronted by a sudden and imminent peril, and fearing for the safety of his wife and child, and the members of his crew, gave orders to launch the ship's boat which was lying across the main hatch. As the wind was, presumably, from the west at the time, and the vessel's course was approximately east by south, it is probable that the boat was launched from the leeward side, which, under the circumstances, would then have been the port side of the vessel. As an additional precautionary measure, Captain Briggs may have directed one of his men to break out a coil of rope for a tow-line, so that if the threatened danger should pass, they could return to their vessel. The place where such ropes were customarily stowed was the lazarette, a low, headroom space below the deck in the after part of the vessel. According to Dr. Cobb's theory, they had already removed the lazarette hatch (reported as found "off" by the salvors) when it may have suddenly occurred to one of the company that it would take less time to utilize the main peak halyard, conveniently at hand, than to bother with breaking out a new, and perhaps stiff, coil of rope from the lazarette. This halyard, a stout rope of about three inches in circumference, and approximately three hundred feet long, stood ready for almost instant use. According to the Court testimony, the mainsail was furled. The gaff of this sail would, therefore, have been resting on it, presumably with a stop around the gaff, the sail and the boom, encircling all three. Assuming that on this vessel the halyard was secured at one end to the gaff (although on some vessels it began at a ring-bolt on the mast-head) and that it ran thence upward and downward, through a treble block on the mast-head and two single blocks on the gaff, it would finally descend to the deck where it would be secured to a belaying pin in the pin-rack or to the pin-rail at the foot of the mast. According to Dr. Cobb's theory, it would have taken but a few moments to release this end of the halyard and then pull it through the gaff and mast-head blocks until its entire length, with one end still secured to the gaff, would have been available for towing purposes. The free end of the halyard could then have been passed between the wooden stanchions supporting the topgallant rail (the vessel having no bulwarks) and then connected with the painter (rope) of the small boat which, by this time, no doubt, would have been alongside, with most of the ship's company already aboard. The tenseness of the situation can easily be imagined as they anxiously awaited the moment when all hands would be in the boat and they could cast off from the *Mary Celeste* and put as much distance as possible between themselves and the danger threatening them. At the end of such a long tow-line, they would doubtless have felt comparatively safe while awaiting further developments. As reported by the Servico Meteorologico dos Açores, "calm or light winds" prevailed on the forenoon of that day, and it seems probable that the abandonment of the vessel occurred during this period of calm, as the launching of a small boat on a wild sea would have meant little more than the substitution of a new peril for the one immediately impending.

The picture thus presented is that of a small boat—probably 16 to 20 feet long with perhaps not more than 9 to 12 inches free-board, carrying ten persons—and a few hastily gathered necessaries, including, no doubt, a small supply of food and drinking water. They are trailing astern of the *Mary Celeste,* somewhat off to port. The vessel's speed which at 8 A.M. that morning was recorded as eight knots, must now be considerably reduced, as her mainsail, gaff-topsail, middle staysail, topmast-staysail, topgallant-sail, royal and flying-jib are all furled. Her main-staysail is probably lying loose on top of the forward-house as if it had been hurriedly let down, and the only sails set are her foresail, upper and lower topsails, jib and fore-topmast staysail.

If this brief portrayal of the situation conforms at all closely to the actuality, it is reasonable to suppose that the occupants of the boat continued to hope for the eventual return to their vessel. They could not foresee that such hopes were not destined to be fulfilled and that the morning calm was not to continue. Sudden and violent squalls are of frequent occurrence in the Azores, and according to the meteorological report, something of this character must soon have happened, for it states that in the afternoon of that date, a wind of gale force prevailed over this area of the Azores. Under the impact of a wind of such violence, the vessel may have lunged forward with such suddenness as to break the improvised tow-line, leaving the occupants of the boat striving with frantic but futile effort to overtake the on-sweeping *Mary Celeste.* A heavy rain accompanying such a gale would have materially increased the difficulties of the people in the small boat, and it is possible that rain was present as, according to the report previously mentioned, at Ponta Delgada, only fifty miles distant, there was a rainfall of 29 mm. between noon on 24 November and noon on 25 November. This, according to the Hydrographic Office at Washington, D.C., meant a precipitation of 1.14 inches, representing a departure from normal, as during the rainiest season, December, the monthly average total is 4.42 inches.

It is barely possible that the boat, while being towed through rough waters, with her nose held down by a taut tow-line, was swamped by the heavy seas, resulting in the drowning of all hands. Had this occurred, however, it seems probable that some remnant either of the boat or

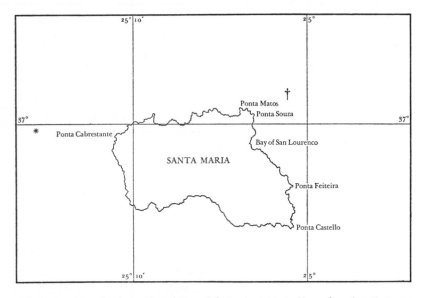

* *Indicates approximate position of* Mary Celeste *at 5 A.M., 25 November 1872. Entry on her Log Slate reads as follows, viz.: "At 5 o'clock, made the Island of S. Mary's bearing ESE."*

† *Indicates approximate position of* Mary Celeste *on the morning of 25 November 1872, when, according to her Log Slate, "At 8, Eastern point bore S.S.W. 6 miles distant."*

her painter would have been noticed by the men of the *Dei Gratia* when they discovered the *Mary Celeste*. According to Dr. Cobb's most recent theory, the tow-line parted at the point where it came over the side of the vessel around the corner of a stanchion.

Presumably, the nearest land was Santa Maria, the eastern point of which, at eight o'clock that morning, bore six miles SSW. This island, the easternmost of the Azores group, with its abrupt and precipitous coast, would have offered little accommodation even for a small boat of this character, had wind and wave borne them in that direction, but as it appears from the meteorological report that, after the passing of a "cold front" between 3 and 8 P.M. on 25 November, the wind veered from SW to NW, it seems more probable that the boat, with its little company, was blown to the southeastward, away from the island and out into the broad reaches of the Atlantic— with about eight hundred miles between them and the coast of Portugal, the nearest land to the eastward, and that they were soon overwhelmed in a gale-swept sea.

The *Mary Celeste,* undirected by human hands, apparently kept on her eastward course, however unsteadily, for several days, constituting a menace to every vessel which may have crossed her path, and becoming the plaything of the winds which tore two of her sails and made havoc with some of her rigging. It is not known how far she travelled eastward, but when found by the *Dei Gratia,* her head was pointed westward. Fanciful indeed it would be to suppose that the *Mary Celeste,* having been led by the vagabond winds into a betrayal of those who had confidently trusted her, was returning to the scene of the tragedy as if troubled by the realization of her participation in it. Although she was destined to end her career as a vessel thirteen years later on the Reef of the Rochelais, off Haiti, the memory of her has continued for threescore years and ten to haunt the imagination of people in every walk and clime. Moreover, it seems probable that, for generations to come, wherever men may foregather in forecastle or by fireside, and their thoughts turn to the unfathomed mysteries of the deep, the name that will inevitably come to their lips will be that of *Mary Celeste.*

To the families and friends of her company, her tragic experience brought full measure of sorrow. Once more, amid the tranquil surroundings of the old home "Rose Cottage" at Marion, Mrs. Nathan Briggs is to learn of the loss of more loved ones at sea. Already, her eldest son Nathan Henry, victim of yellow fever, sleeps beneath the waters of the Gulf of Mexico; Maria, her only daughter,

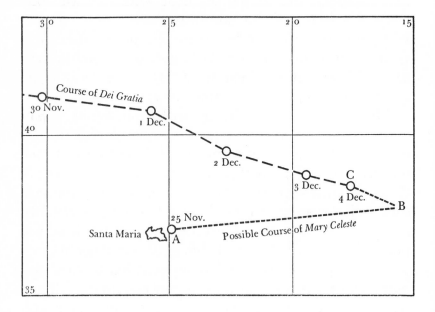

Possible course of Mary Celeste *after abandonment — A–B–C*

(A) *indicates last position recorded on vessel's log slate. Abandonment is presumed to have occurred not far from this point.*

(B) *indicates a point somewhere to the eastward where the abandoned vessel, with five sails set, may have encountered a squall, lost two sails and had her head turned about so that she headed westward.*

Under reduced speed, she may then have continued westward to the place of meeting (C) *with the* Dei Gratia *on* 4 December, *at about* 1:30–2:00 P.M. *approximately* 378 *miles east of Santa Maria (Saint Mary's).*

drowned in shipwreck, near Cape Fear; and now Death takes triple toll, when Benjamin, Sarah and their child Sophia perish off the Azores. Soon thereafter she will also learn of the loss of her son Oliver, drowned in the Bay of Biscay. To her, in the long afternoon of her life along the Massachusetts shore, the voices of the sea, the burial place of so many of her dead, must have spoken in tones which other ears could not have heard, and in a language which only a spirit sensitized through sorrow such as hers could have understood.

To Frances Richardson in her Brooklyn home, came word of the loss of her beloved sailor husband—a loss which overshadowed the remainder of her days. Sixty-five years of widowhood were terminated by her death, in 1937, at the age of ninety-one. She never remarried, and until the close of her long life, her husband's picture, kept on her dresser, was one of her most cherished possessions.

In January 1873, the parents of the Lorenzen brothers, and also the wife and daughter of Volkert, the elder brother, all living at Utersum, a village on the Island of Föhr, Prussia, received the sorrowful intelligence that their two seafarers were lost. There also, the betrothed of Boz Lorenzen learned that her sailor-lover would never return. Presumably at the same time, the parents of Arian Martens, and his wife and children, all living in the neighboring island of Amrum, received the melancholy news. The loss of these three respected seamen was not without its effect upon the material circumstances of their families who, according to the record, continued to mourn the loss of their loved ones, and heard with sorrow and indignation the evil reports circulated about them.

For almost seventy years, the facts of the case of the *Mary Celeste* (including the almost universal misspelling of her name) have been so largely obscured by the mass of legendary literature which has grown up around it, that much uncertainty exists in the public mind as to what actually occurred. For the sake of historical accuracy, and in the interest of justice, however belated, to persons who have been grossly maligned, but who, being dead, cannot speak in their own behalf, the author has deemed the present a propitious time to rectify the record and present the facts so far as they are known to him. Such a presentation requires no theatrical showmanship or flights of fancy in order to invest the story with dramatic interest. The simple story of the vessel's experience, involving the complete disappearance of an honorable and capable shipmaster, his wife and child, along with seven respectable seamen, is in itself a tragedy which has become a classic of maritime literature. The fate of the vessel's small company is still an unsolved mystery, and seems destined to remain forever unrevealed until the coming of that Day when all whom the sea hath sundered shall be re-united, and all that now lies hidden shall be made plain.

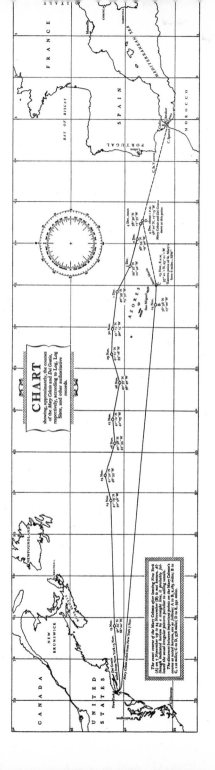

CHART

showing, approximately, the courses of the *Mary Celeste* and *Dei Gratia*, respectively, according to Log, Log Slate, and other authoritative records.

The exact course of the Mary Celeste after leaving New York (A) on 7 November up to 24 November (B) is not known, although indicated hereon by a straight line; it probably followed the usual irregular pattern peculiar to sailing vessels.

The distances between important points on the Mary Celeste's course as noted hereon, are as follows: A to B, 2,285 miles; B to C, 1.0 miles; C to D, 378 miles; D to E, 592 miles.

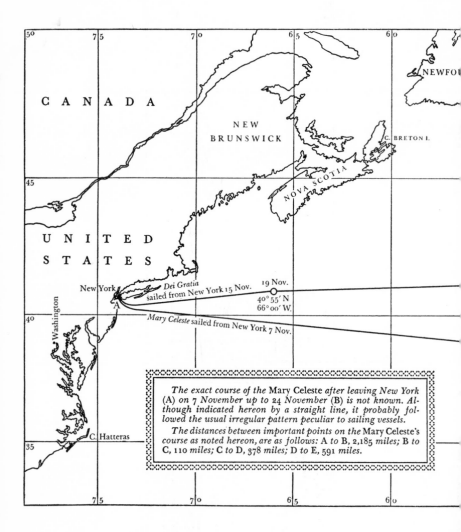

C A N A D A

NEW
BRUNSWICK

C. BRETON I.

NOVA SCOTIA

NEWFOU

U N I T E D

S T A T E S

New York

Dei Gratia
sailed from New York 15 Nov.

19 Nov.
40°55′ N
66°00′ W.

Mary Celeste sailed from New York 7 Nov.

Washington

C. Hatteras

The exact course of the Mary Celeste *after leaving New York (A) on 7 November up to 24 November (B) is not known. Although indicated hereon by a straight line, it probably followed the usual irregular pattern peculiar to sailing vessels.*

The distances between important points on the Mary Celeste's *course as noted hereon, are as follows: A to B, 2,185 miles; B to C, 110 miles; C to D, 378 miles; D to E, 591 miles.*

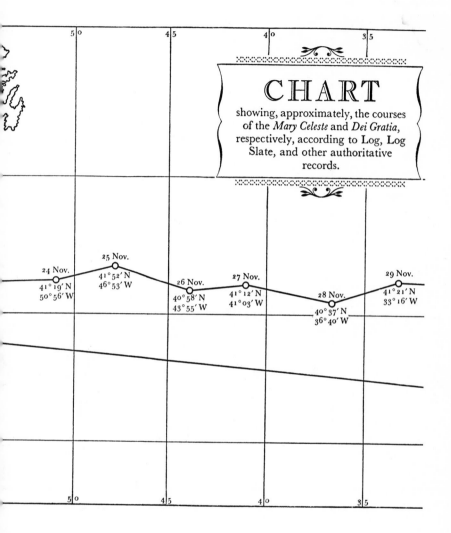

CHART

showing, approximately, the courses
of the *Mary Celeste* and *Dei Gratia*,
respectively, according to Log, Log
Slate, and other authoritative
records.

24 Nov.
41° 19′ N
50° 56′ W

25 Nov.
41° 52′ N
46° 53′ W

26 Nov.
40° 58′ N
43° 55′ W

27 Nov.
41° 12′ N
41° 03′ W

28 Nov.
40° 37′ N
36° 40′ W

29 Nov.
41° 21′ N
33° 16′ W

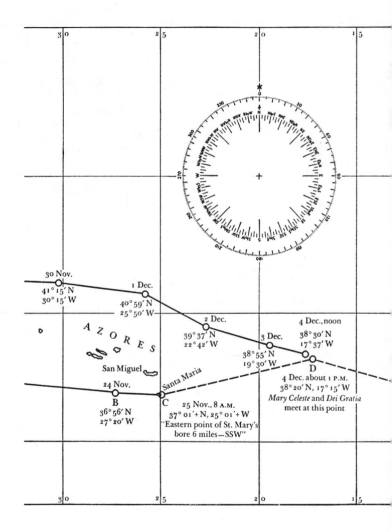

30 Nov.
41° 15′ N
30° 15′ W

1 Dec.
40° 59′ N
25° 50′ W

2 Dec.
39° 37′ N
22° 42′ W

4 Dec., noon
38° 30′ N
17° 37′ W

3 Dec.
38° 55′ N
19° 30′ W

D

A Z O R E S

San Miguel

Santa Maria

24 Nov.
B
36° 56′ N
27° 20′ W

C

25 Nov., 8 A.M.
37° 01′+ N, 25° 01′+ W
"Eastern point of St. Mary's
bore 6 miles—SSW"

4 Dec. about 1 P.M.
38° 20′ N, 17° 15′ W
Mary Celeste and *Dei Gratia*
meet at this point

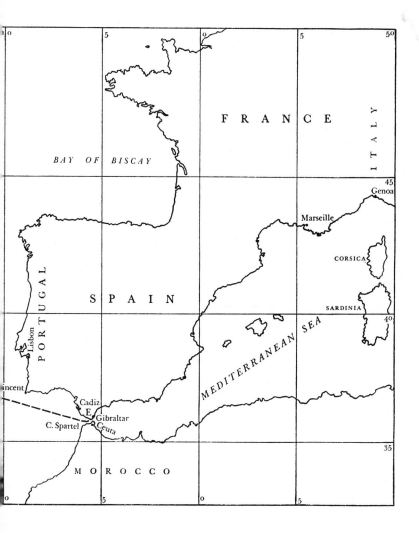

Mary Celeste

PART II

CHAPTER XII

Salvage Award and Insurance

a. *Salvage Award*

THE Atlantic Mutual Disaster Book[1] under date of 9 April 1873 contains the following undated newspaper clipping: "In the Vice Admiralty Court yesterday,[2] the Honorable the Chief Justice gave judgment in the *Mary Celeste* salvage case and awarded the sum of £1,700. to the master and crew of the Nova Scotian Brigantine *Dei Gratia* for the salvage services rendered by them; the costs of the suit to be paid out of the property salved. The *Mary Celeste* was valued at $5,700.00, and her cargo at $36,943.00, total $42,673.00, so that the award may be set down as one-fifth of the total value. The Judge further thought it right to express the disapprobation of the Court as to the conduct of the master of the *Dei Gratia* in allowing the first mate, Oliver Deveau, to do[3] away with the vessel which had rendered necessary the analysis of the supposed spots or stains of blood found on the deck of the *Mary Celeste* and on the sword, and his Lordship also decided that the costs of the analysis should be charged against the amount awarded to the salvors."

The late Anton Adolph Raven, former President of the Atlantic Mutual Insurance Company, in the course of an

1. Disaster Book No. 96, page 267.

2. Verdict rendered 14 March 1873, *Gibraltar Chronicle & Commercial Intelligencer,* 15 March 1873.

3. This reference is not clear. The suggestion has been made that, through typographical error in copying, the word "go" may have become "do." Deveau did "go" away with his own "vessel," the *Dei Gratia,* leaving Morehouse at Gibraltar, but this does not clarify the matter.

address on Marine Insurance at Yale University,[4] commented on the case of the *Mary Celeste,* and spoke of the salvage award. "The Admiralty Court awarded a Salvage of £1700, the equivalent of about $8300. This was a moderate compensation, being only about 18% on an aggregate value of $47,000. for vessel, freight and cargo." He added "that it is not unusual when derelicts i.e. abandoned vessels, are picked up at sea, for a salvage award of more than twice that percentage to be made to the Salvors."

In the opinion of Dr. Cobb,[5] formerly Treasurer and General Manager of the Davis Coast Wrecking Co. of New Bedford, Massachusetts, the award was inadequate in view of the service rendered. According to his view, the award should have been nearer $23,000.

There can be no doubt that the hazards of the six hundred mile trip to Gibraltar were considerably increased for the *Dei Gratia* which, by putting three of her men, including the first mate, aboard the *Mary Celeste,* had reduced her own working force from eight to five. The *Dei Gratia* (built in 1871 and slightly larger than the derelict) with her cargo of petroleum must have been worth more than $40,000, and it was no negligible feat of seamanship for three men to bring in the *Mary Celeste.*

b. *Insurance*

According to Atlantic Mutual Records,[6] the cargo of alcohol was insured in Europe. The hull of the vessel was

4. 22 February 1904, published in *Yale Alumni Weekly* (supplement), 2 March 1904.

5. Letter of 16 May 1940 to the author.

6. Atlantic Mutual Insurance Company, Disaster Book No. 93, page 192, 14 December 1872.

insured in the following American companies:[7]

	Sum insured
Maine Lloyds	$6,000.00
Orient Mutual Insurance Company	4,000.00
Mercantile Mutual Insurance Company	2,500.00
New England Mutual Insurance Company	1,500.00
Total sum insured on hull	$14,000.00
Not insured on hull	$ 600.00

In addition thereto, the following insurance was effected on freight on charter by the Atlantic Mutual Insurance Company — $3,400. The total insured value of all interests insured in the United States was therefore $17,400.

For salvage purposes the valuations of the respective interests were appraised as follows:

Cargo	$36,943.00 [8]
Hull	5,700.00 [8]
Freight on charter	3,400.00
	$46,043.00

The amount awarded to the salvors by the Vice-Admiralty Court was £1,700, equivalent in United States currency to about $8,300.

The proportionate share of the cargo owners, about eighty per cent of the total, was therefore about $6,640, leaving a balance of about $1,660 to be contributed, pro rata, by the American underwriters insuring the respective interests of hull and freight.

7. Atlantic Mutual Insurance Company, General Average Book, 1873, page 79.

8. Letter of 9 January 1885 from Frederick Solly Flood to Consul Sprague; *Journal of Commerce,* 9 April 1873; Atlantic Mutual Insurance Company Disaster Book No. 96, page 267.

As finally adjusted on 26 June 1873[9] by Jones & Whitlock, Average Adjusters, New York, the amounts paid by the American underwriters were as follows, viz.:

Maine Lloyds (hull)	$568.30
Orient Mutual Insurance Company (hull)	378.87
Mercantile Mutual Insurance Company (hull)	236.79
New England Mutual Insurance Company (hull)	142.07
Atlantic Mutual Insurance Company (freight on charter)	322.04
	$1,648.07
Amount uninsured[10]	56.83
	$1,704.90

It is not known how the salvage money was distributed, but evidence is not wanting that there was some dissatisfaction on the part of the owners of the *Dei Gratia* and of Oliver Deveau, first mate, in connection with their respective shares of the award.

Of the five American companies named above, the Atlantic Mutual Insurance Company is the sole survivor.

9. Atlantic Mutual Insurance Company, General Average Book No. 10, page 79.

10. Loss borne by vessel owners.

CHAPTER XIII

Oliver Deveau, First Mate of *Dei Gratia*

A CAREFUL reading of the testimony given in the Vice-Admiralty Court by the *Dei Gratia's* first mate, Oliver Deveau, cannot fail to make clear the fact that he was a mariner of more than usual intelligence, well versed in the ritual of the sea. In the circumstances, a brief review of his career may not be unrewarding, as it will better enable the reader to form his own conclusions as to the value of Deveau's testimony.

According to the parish records of Plympton, Digby County, Nova Scotia,[1] Oliver Deveau, son of Cyril Deveau and Madeleine Comeau, was born on 9 September 1837, and baptized 1 July 1838.

The following comment is quoted from the *Digby Courier* of 20 September 1912:

Death of Captain Oliver E. Deveau

The last survivor of the Brigt. *Mary Celeste* mystery has passed away.

Captain Oliver E. Deveau died at his home in Brighton on Tuesday, the 10th. instant, aged 76 years. The deceased was born at Cape St. Mary's, moving to Brighton when he was a young man. He was an old-time sailor, a thorough officer, and a man capable of sailing a ship to any part of the world. His last voyage was to Cuba some four or five years ago when he was obliged to leave his ship, owing to illness, and return home. He is survived by a widow, one son, James Deveau, who holds a responsible position with the telephone company in Springfield, Mass. and two daughters, Mrs. Jessie Melanson, of Plymouth, Mass., and Miss Addie A., at home.

1. Copied by Rev. L. Gaudet, P. P. from the parish records for Mr. J. Franklin Briggs, to whom the author is indebted for the information.

The funeral was held from his late home on Friday with interment in the St. Croix Cemetery at Plympton. The *Courier* extends its deepest sympathy to the bereaved ones.

Captain Deveau has been interviewed by hundreds of newspaper men during the past forty years. He related the entire story to the editor of the *Courier* in the cabin of the old tern schooner *Xebec* of Bear River more than thirty years ago, when Captain Deveau was chief officer of that vessel, and the editor "a small cabin boy."

It was thought that Capt. Deveau and his men would be well paid for his heroic work in saving the *Mary Celeste* and her valuable cargo, but the whole affair got involved in litigation, and the captain's share became a small one. . . . The vessel's boat and papers were gone. The entire crew appeared to have left in great haste, taking practically nothing with them. Marine men from all parts of the world put forth different ideas as to why the vessel was abandoned, but Capt. Deveau could always explain by referring to some circumstance in connection with the way the vessel was found, that they were wrong. Capt. Deveau himself could not account for their strange disappearance, nor could any one else from that day until the present time, and we very much doubt if the mystery will ever be solved.[2]

2. Excerpt from the same issue of the *Digby Courier*.

CHAPTER XIV

Theories and Attempted Solutions

LIMITATIONS of space preclude the recounting of the wide variety of theories and attempted solutions which, over a period of almost seventy years, have appeared in books, magazines and newspapers in various parts of the world. A few of them are given herewith.

1. *Theory of the Late Captain Marcus H. Tracy*

In the course of a conversation at the writer's office, on 31 July 1930, with Captain Marcus H. Tracy of New York (at one time Chairman of the Board of Governors, New York State Schoolship)—he stated that he was at Gibraltar when the *Mary Celeste* was brought in. According to his theory, when the sailors removed the bars of the forward hatch, the gases which had accumulated from the cargo of alcohol, blew the hatch covers off so that they fell upside down on the deck.[1] He thought that, owing to the superstitious fears entertained by the sailors when hatches were found upside down, and the additional fear that explosions were likely to follow, Captain Briggs, as a precautionary measure, having in mind the safety of his wife and child, as well as that of the crew, ordered all hands to take to the vessel's boat.

Captain Tracy thought that the vessel had, at first, more than one boat, and that Captain Winchester, observing the age of one of the boats on board, and knowing that the captain's wife and child were to accompany him, decided

1. Record of the court testimony does not show that any hatch covers were found upside down.

as an extra measure of precaution, to put an additional boat on board. This boat, according to Captain Tracy, was placed in a cradle over the hatch, and was not part of the vessel's regular equipment. He recalled, however, having heard that, prior to the vessel's departure from New York, one of her boats had been smashed during the process of loading.

2. *Oliver Deveau's Theory*

Oliver Deveau, first mate of the *Dei Gratia,* was of the opinion that "there was a panic from the belief that the vessel had more water than had afterwards proved."[2]

3. *"Drunken Crew" Theory*

The commentators who have entertained the theory of violence on the part of the crew may be divided into two groups: those who believe that Captain Briggs and his wife were the victims of a carefully premeditated mutiny on the part of the crew; and those who think the crew gained access to the cargo of alcohol, and, while intoxicated, made an attack. Among the proponents of the latter theory was the Queen's Advocate, Mr. Frederick Solly Flood.

In the course of his letters of 22 and 23 January 1873 to the London Board of Trade, he says: "My own theory or guess is, that the crew got at the alcohol, and in the fury of drunkenness murdered the master, whose name was Briggs, his wife and child, and the chief mate; that they then damaged the bows of the vessel with the view of giving it the appearance of having struck on rocks, or suffered a collision, so as to induce the Master of any vessel which might pick them up, if they saw her at some distance, to

2. See court testimony.

think her not worth attempting to save; and that they did, sometime between 25 November and 5 December, escape on board some vessel bound for some North or South American port or the West Indies."

In view of Captain Shufeldt's comment to the effect that "the damage about the bows of the brig appears to me to amount to nothing more than splinters made in the bending of the planks which were afterwards forced off by the action of the sea, neither hurting the ship nor by any possible chance the result of an intention to do so. . . ." Mr. Flood's theory on this point seems rather tenuous.

Whether or not the crew broached one of the barrels, cannot be proved. It will be noted that the following statement made on the subject by Mr. Flood, in the above mentioned communication to the Board of Trade, contains qualifications which tend to weaken the force of it. "On descending through the fore-hatch, a barrel, *ostensibly* of alcohol, *appeared* to have been tampered with." It is, however, noticeable that neither John Austin, who spent five hours in examining the vessel, nor Oliver Deveau who sailed her to Gibraltar, made any mention of such a finding. If the crew had been crazy for liquor, it seems probable that the alcohol would have been the only immediate source of supply, as Captain Briggs would not have allowed any liquor on board, and Deveau testified that he "found no wine, beer or spirits whatever on the ship."

4. *Theory of Captain Henry O. Appleby*

Some time during the summer of 1930, Captain Henry O. Appleby called at the New York office of the writer and made the following statement, notes of which were made at that time. According to Captain Appleby, escaping gas in the *Mary Celeste's* cargo of alcohol may have caused an explosion, frightening all hands, and causing them to take to the boat. He said that while in command of the *Daisy Boynton,* on a voyage to Bilbao, Spain, with a cargo of petroleum, gases blew the hatches off, and steam or vapor, accompanied by a crackling sound, began to come from the vessel's hold. The crew came running aft, and urged Captain Appleby to lower the boats, believing the ship to be on fire. The captain reassured them by explaining that the dunnage, consisting of pine wood—several cords of it —from the south, loaded during cold weather with frost in it, would sometimes crackle that way and make a noise, like that of fire, when the vessel encountered warmer temperatures. He told them that they were in no greater danger than he was, and thereby succeeded in calming them. If a similar situation existed on the *Mary Celeste,* it must be remembered that Captain Briggs had with him his wife and child, and it may have seemed necessary that extraordinary precautionary measures should be taken. A letter[3] from Mrs. Thomas J. Port, daughter of Captain Appleby, states: "My father's theory was that the dunnage wood was covered with ice when it was put aboard, and that as the ice melted, it made vapor with the fumes of the alcohol with which she was loaded, and then blew off the fore-hatch which was found on the deck beside the opening. The people, fearing a general explosion, took to one of the boats. He said that Captain Winchester told him he had put aboard a new boat which was missing when the brig was brought in. The fore-brace was trailing over the side when they found her, and my father believed they were fast to it, intending to go back aboard if nothing more happened, when a sudden squall struck the brig and they had to let go to avoid being towed under. They lost the ship— couldn't keep near her, and eventually perished."

3. 22 March 1941 to the author.

5. *Theory of Mutiny*

The theory of deliberate and premeditated mutiny has been advanced perhaps more frequently than any other, but the motive for such action is difficult to find. Captain Briggs was not a hard master. He was known to have had experience in handling men and vessels. His vessel was well supplied with everything needful for the voyage. According to the letter written by Captain Briggs to his mother a few days before he sailed, the *Mary Celeste* was "in beautiful trim." Had there been any discontent or trouble on board, it is reasonable to assume that some mention would have been made of it, in the ship's log, which had entries up to 24 November and was produced in court. Moreover, it seems apparent from what is known of Captain Briggs, that he would have been extremely careful in the selection of a crew for a voyage on which his wife and child were to accompany him. For the theory of mutiny, therefore, there seems to be no foundation.

6. *Theory of Piratical Attack*

Not a few commentators have attributed the abandonment of the *Mary Celeste,* and the disappearance of her company of ten, to a piratical attack, no doubt recalling the days when the Barbary Coast pirates attacked American and other merchantmen off the coast of Africa. Such an attack, it would seem, could hardly have been made without leaving some traces of the struggle which would have ensued, either bloodstains on the decks or other woodwork of the vessel, or at least some evidence of disorder. According to the testimony, however, such signs were lacking. There was definite testimony to the effect that, with a few minor exceptions, everything in the cabin was found in orderly shape.

In reply to an inquiry addressed, by the writer, to the Department of State, the following communication was received, from the National Archives, Washington, D. C. The letter, dated 15 January 1941, reads as follows:

> The Department of State has referred to this office your letter of January 2nd, 1941 concerning the possibility of pirates seizing the Captain, his family, and the crew of the brig *Mary Celeste*.
>
> An examination of the records does not reveal that any piratical operations took place as late as 1872 between the Azores and the coast of Portugal. Captain Shufeldt of the United States Navy who investigated the case of the *Mary Celeste* stated that there was no evidence of violence about the decks or cabins of the brig.

Had a piratical attack taken place, it seems likely that some attempt would have been made to loot the vessel, but there was no indication of such an attempt, and Consul Sprague's voluminous inventory of the effects found on board included clothing and other articles of considerable value.

7. *Iceberg Theory*

The theory has been advanced by some, that an iceberg, bearing down on the vessel and threatening to sink or damage her, frightened the captain and crew, causing them to take to the boat and resulting in its being smashed by the iceberg or overturned in a heavy sea, with consequent death to all hands.

The Hydrographic Office, Navy Department, at Washington, D. C., replying to an inquiry on the subject, writes under date of 7 December 1940 as follows:

> Replying to your inquiry as to possibility of icebergs being found in the locality in which the *Mary Celeste* was abandoned,

you are advised that this is highly improbable, due to the long drift through comparatively warm water necessary for any ice to reach this vicinity. However, small pieces of ice have been sighted exceptionally far south as follows: Sept. 2, 1883 Lat. 35° 40′ North, Long. 30° 00′ West, a lump of ice *Olivette* (Bark); Oct. 15, 1883 Lat. 37° 00′ N. Long. 18° 00′ W. a piece of ice, *Elenora* (S. S.); Oct. 3, 1934 Lat. 36° 53′ N. Lon. 29° 13′ W. Growler, approximately 20 x 4 feet, *Rhexenor* (S. S.); Oct. 4, 1934 Lat. 36° 16′ N. Lon. 29° 26′ W. Growler, approximately 15 x 3 ft., *Imperial Valley* (S. S.).

Inasmuch as such comparatively small pieces of ice found floating in the areas indicated were noted and officially reported to Washington, it seems reasonable to assume that an iceberg of sufficiently formidable proportions to frighten Captain Briggs and his men into abandoning their vessel would almost inevitably have been sighted by other vessels plying those waters and reported to the Hydrographic Office.

8. *Theory of Dr. Oliver W. Cobb*

Of all the vast body of literature which has been inspired by the abandonment of the *Mary Celeste* and the disappearance of her company, nothing conforms more closely to the ascertained facts than a recent article[4] by Dr. Oliver W. Cobb of Easthampton, Massachusetts. Dr. Cobb was a cousin of Captain Benjamin Briggs and also of the Captain's wife, who was Sarah Elizabeth Cobb prior to her marriage.

To quote Dr. Cobb: "I think that the cargo of alcohol, having been loaded in cold weather at New York, early in November, and the vessel having crossed the Gulf Stream and being now in comparatively warm weather, there may

4. *Yachting*, February 1940.

have been some leakage, and gas may have accumulated in the hold. The Captain having care for his wife and daughter, was probably unjustifiably alarmed and, fearing a fire or an explosion, determined to take his people in the boat away from the vessel until the immediate danger should pass.

"Knowing what the duty of each man would be, it is comparatively easy to reconstruct the scene with the evidence which we have. The boat was launched on the port side. The Captain got his wife and daughter into the boat and left them in charge of Mr. Richardson[5] with one sailor in the boat, while the Captain went for their Chronometer, sextant, Nautical Almanac and the ship's papers.

"Mr. Gilling[6] with one sailor would be getting the peak halliard ready to use as a tow rope. Another sailor would tend the painter[7] of the boat and a fourth would be at the wheel. The cook gathered up what cooked food he had on hand and some canned goods.

"There is some evidence of haste in the act of leaving the vessel. The sailors left their pipes. The main staysail was not furled. The wheel was left loose. The binnacle was displaced and the compass broken, probably in a clumsy attempt to get the compass quickly.

"It may well have been that just at that time came an explosion which might have accounted for the fore hatch being upside down on deck as found.[8]

"Whatever happened, it is evident that the boat, with ten people in her, left the vessel and that the peak halliard was taken as a tow-line, and as a means of bringing the boat

5. Albert G. Richardson, first mate.

6. Andrew Gilling, second mate.

7. Painter: "A length of rope made fast to the inner side of the stem of boats, and used for making fast to anything in order to hold the boat." *Patterson's Nautical Encyclopedia.*

8. See footnote 1, Chapter XIV.

back to the *Mary Celeste* in case no explosion or fire had destroyed the vessel. Probably a fresh northerly wind sprang up, filled the square sails, and the vessel gathered way quickly. The peak halliard made fast at the usual place on the gaff, would be brought at an acute angle across the bulwarks[9] at the gangway. With the heavy boat standing still at the end, I do not wonder that the halliard parted. This would tally exactly with the evidence given in court, —that the peak 'halliard was broken.'—This fact was impressed upon the sailors as they had to get up a coil of rope from the lazarette and reeve off a new peak halliard before they could set the mainsail.

"When the tow-rope parted, these people were left in an open boat on the ocean as the brig sailed away from them. The wind that took the vessel away may have caused sea enough to wreck them. Nothing has appeared in all these sixty-seven years to tell us of their end."

9. *Main Peak Halyard Theory*

The theory of the main peak halyard mentioned elsewhere in this narrative depends primarily upon the statements of the four men of the *Dei Gratia* who appeared before the Vice-Admiralty Court and, under oath, testified as to the conditions noted by them while they were on board the *Mary Celeste*. Their statements, while differing in some particulars, present no serious conflict of opinion. Second Mate Wright, who spent only a half-hour on board and therefore had limited opportunities for observation, said: "The running gear I did not notice," and added later: "I observed no remains of any tow-line." Mate De-

9. In a letter to the author, written by Dr. Cobb since the publication of his article in *Yachting*, he has changed "across the bulwarks" to "around a stanchion," to conform to information recently received.

veau, who went on the first boat trip to the derelict and later took her into Gibraltar said: "I saw no remains or pieces of a painter or boat's rope *fastened to the rail*." (The italics are the author's.) However, Seaman Anderson, one of the two who helped Deveau sail her to Gibraltar, testified that "there were ropes hanging over the side" and that "there was all kind of running gear hanging overside—sheets and braces hanging over both sides." "Running gear" would include halyards and Deveau testified that "the main peak halyards were broken," while Seaman Lund (one of the two who accompanied him to Gibraltar) said: "The peak halyards were broke and gone." (If the halyard was gone, how could it be said to be broken?) At what point the break occurred is not indicated by either Deveau or Lund, and Anderson's testimony does not give us any idea as to the length of the running gear hanging over the side. Nobody knows what actually happened, and every reader is at liberty to form his own conclusions in the light of the evidence as given.

During the seventy years which have passed since the event occurred, numerous theories and attempted solutions have appeared in newspapers, magazines and books in various parts of the world. Dr. Cobb appears to have been the first to suggest the possible use of the main peak halyard as a tow-line. His theory is based on his own sea experiences with sailing vessels, both as a hand "before the mast" in his earlier years, and later as Treasurer and General Manager of the Davis Coast Wrecking Co. of New Bedford, Massachusetts. His activities in connection with that organization, which he served for five years, extended to South American and West Indian waters as well as to the coastal waters of the United States. To the author, whose file of bibliographical material contains the principal magazine and other articles written on the subject since the inception of the case, Dr. Cobb's theory seems by far the most deserving of consideration.

10. *Comment on Mr. Flood's Theory Regarding Time of Abandonment*

It is apparent from the record that, at the very inception of the incident, the Queen's Proctor entertained the idea that foul play had been committed by the crew of the *Mary Celeste,* and from that time forward, every circumstance was made to fit into the preconceived pattern of his thought about it. Even Captain Winchester, according to his letter[10] to Consul Sprague, was not immune from suspicion on the part of the Queen's Proctor. As Consul Sprague observed, in his letter to the Department of State,[11] Mr. Flood had "a vivid imagination," and evidence is not wanting that in the case of the *Mary Celeste,* it somewhat impaired his judgment.

In his supplementary letter of 23 January 1873, the Queen's Proctor raises a point which, whether one agrees with it or not, deserves consideration. In his opinion, abandonment of the *Mary Celeste* took place several days *after* the eight o'clock log slate entry on the morning of Monday, 25 November, and probably "much further to the eastward." According to his idea, as more fully expressed in his letter[12] written twelve years later to Consul Sprague: "The evidence proved [?] the crew to have been in possession of the vessel for sometime longer than the Master, the chief mate, and as I expect, the second mate, they had had an ample opportunity to remove appearances of violence had there been any."

10. 10 March 1873, Chapter x.
11. 4 March 1885, Letter No. 488.
12. 9 January 1885.

This view appears to have been based largely upon the assumption that the *Mary Celeste,* without direction, could not have traversed the distance from the location indicated by the last log-slate entry (six miles NNE. off the eastern point of St. Mary's) to the location (latitude 38° 20', longitude 17° 15') where she was sighted by the *Dei Gratia.* According to the computation made by the Branch Hydrographic Office, New York,[13] the distance between the two points was 378½ nautical miles.

When the *Mary Celeste,* headed *westward,*[14] was sighted by the *Dei Gratia,* she was making 1½ to 2 knots.[15] This would mean a possible accomplishment of 36 to 48 nautical miles per day. About 9¼ days intervened between her probable time of abandonment (forenoon of 25 November) and the time when she was sighted—1.30 to 2 P.M., 4 December, civil time (5 December, sea-time).[16] Had the same rate of speed been maintained throughout the 9¼ day period, it seems probable that she could have travelled at least 333 (1½ knots x 24 hours x 9¼ days) and even 444 (2 knots x 24 hours x 9¼ days) nautical miles.

Inasmuch as a sailing vessel's course is often a series of tacks, determined by changing wind and other conditions, it does not always run in a straight line. In the circumstances the actual mileage covered by the *Mary Celeste* was probably even greater than 444 miles. When she was picked up, the only sails set were her jib, fore-topmast staysail and lower topsail; her fore-sail and upper topsail were gone; the main-staysail was found lying loose on top of the forward house; all the other seven sails were furled. It is probable that when the *Mary Celeste,* abandoned,

13. Letter of 18 June 1941 to the author.
14. On starboard tack, with wind from the north.
15. Court testimony.
16. The date is advanced one day, at noon, and sea-time begins.

started on her undirected course, she was then carrying the two sails later found gone. This would have given her five sails during the first part of the 9¼ day period; just how long cannot be determined. Therefore, it seems reasonable to assume that, during the first part of the 9¼ day period when she had five sails set, she was making better speed than the 1½ to 2 knots she was making when discovered with only three sails set, and could therefore have covered a greater distance than 444 nautical miles.

From Dr. O. W. Cobb, who in his early years sailed before the mast, comes the following interesting theory of the vessel's probable behavior after she had been abandoned. He writes:[17] "As the vessel sailed away after the change of wind which is reported to have come about this time (and being headed easterly with a northerly wind), there were three sails drawing: foresail, lower topsail and upper topsail. The foretopmast staysail and jib, being set on the port side, would not be of much use except as they would tend to prevent the vessel from coming into the wind and so keep her more steadily on her course. From 25 November to 5 December, northerly winds prevailed. The speed would be 3 to 4 miles per hour with ordinary winds, but the course sailed would be far from straight. She probably went easterly at about 2½ miles per hour, or, say 60 miles per 24 hours, for nearly eight days—or 480 miles. Then came a sudden change of wind—a squall perhaps. She came into the wind—shipped a sea (which accounted for the water in the galley and most of that in the hold, as the fore hatch was off)—lost her foresail and upper topsail, and then filled away on the starboard tack. . . . The jib and foretopmast staysail were now set to draw, and the yards had worked around so that the lower topsail would draw on the starboard tack. She was now headed westerly.

17. Letter of 10 May 1941 to the author.

If she went westerly for two days at 2 miles per hour, a total of 96 miles," Dr. Cobb reasons, "the net distance covered would be 384 (480 less 96) miles, approximately the distance of 378½[18] between the probable point of abandonment and the point of actual discovery.

In this connection, the *New York Journal of Commerce*[19] mentions that the schooner *William L. White,* abandoned off Delaware Bay, 13 March 1888, during the great blizzard, affords an interesting illustration of what a derelict vessel may do, and the speed at which, with few sails or none at all, she may drift. In the course of ten months and ten days, she traversed a distance of more than five thousand miles. From the record of her track, compiled from forty-five different vessel reports, it appears that, previous to May, she followed a course about ENE at an average of about thirty-two miles a day, which would indicate a speed of one and one-third knots.

The foregoing observations would therefore appear to negative the theory of the Queen's Proctor, with its implications of foul play on the part of the crew, that an undirected vessel could not have compassed the distance within the time period indicated.

18. As computed by the Branch Hydrographic Office, New York, letter of 18 June 1941.

19. 25 January 1889.

CHAPTER XV

Subsequent History—*Mary Celeste* Ends Her Career on Haitian Reef

A<small>T</small> some time after the arrival of the *Mary Celeste* at Genoa on 21 March and prior to 24 April, "she was hove down in Genoa in order to have her bottom surveyed, and it was found in perfect order. This vessel was laying [*sic*] there awaiting the settlement of damages, the charterers having cancelled her charter-party."[1] She left Genoa on 26 June[2] for Boston, with Blatchford, captain, arriving at Boston on 1 September.[3] On 13 September she sailed from Boston for New York, arriving at the latter port on 19 September.[4]

She was destined to continue in service for twelve years longer, during which period the ownership changed several times. Her last register, No. 28, issued 4 August 1884, was the last of seventeen registers after the one issued 29 October 1872, just prior to her eventful passage.

In December 1884, the *Mary Celeste,* under the command of Captain Gilman C. Parker, sailed from Boston for a port in Haiti. This passage was destined to be her last. The *Maritime Register* of 28 January 1885, contains the following item:

Mary Celeste (bg) Parker, from Boston for Hayti, went ashore on Rochelais Bank, Lon. 73°; lat. 18° 38′, Jan. 3, and would probably be a total loss. She had the following cargo: 475 bbls. alewives, 135 pkgs. ale, 64 cases boots and shoes, 10 bbls. bread, 4000 lbs.

1. *Maritime Register,* 14 May 1873.
2. Ibid., 27 August 1873.
3. Ibid., 10 September 1873.
4. Ibid., 24 September 1873.

butter, 10 bbls. beef, 87 boxes codfish, 66 drums do., 30 coils cordage, 34 cases canned fish, 30 pkgs, domestic[s], 50 pkgs. furniture, 10 hlf. drums fish, 150 bbls. flour, 75 kegs herrings, 472 boxes do., 500 bbls. do., 15 cases hardware, 460 bbls. mackerel, 209 tubs do., 37 kegs paint, 500 gals. petroleum, 3 bales twine, 5 nests trunks, 2 bbls. varnish, 20 kegs white lead, 21 pkgs. yeast powder, 25 bbls. pork. The master was at Miragoane.

The back of the register contains the following brief obituary: "Date of Surrender, January 3, 1885; Where Surrendered: Miragoane, Hayti: Cause of Surrender: Vessel lost by stranding Jan. 3, 1885 on the Reefs of the Rochelais, near Miragoane, Haiti; 7 on board, none lost." Elsewhere on the back of the register is the following notation: "Surrendered Port-au-Prince and Miragoane, Hayti. Total loss by stranding, Jan. 3 1885. T. B. S." According to this last register, her ownership was divided up as follows: Wesley A. Gove, six-sixteenths; Andrew W. Martin, two-sixteenths; Charles A. Grant, three-sixteenths; John S. Weeks, three-sixteenths; Sidney F. Waterhouse, two-sixteenths. All of the above were described as "of Boston."

On 29 March 1885 it was reported in the daily press that Captain Parker of Winthrop, Massachusetts, had been arrested the day before by the United States Marshal, "on a charge of having purposely wrecked his brig, the *Mary Celeste* on a coral reef off Hayti." The willful wrecking of a vessel, defined as barratry, was an offense "which was punishable with death under the United States laws."

It was testified in court that "it was a clear day and the sea was smooth: that the reef on which the vessel struck was plainly marked on the chart and clearly visible"; that "the wheelman saw the reef, changed his course, and, on the Captain's orders, immediately set it back, with the result that the vessel went on the centre of the reef."

It was also testified that "what was practically, a dummy cargo of fish, rubber shoes etc., was put on board and heavily insured." The vessel, according to report, was insured for $25,000 and "the arrest was made at the instance of the insurance companies on the testimony of the mate."

Captain Parker appears to have been arraigned in court at Boston on 20 April 1885. Bail having previously been taken, "the Commissioner ordered the defendant to appear before the Circuit Court to answer the charge on May 15th."

In the *Nautical Gazette*[5] may be found an interesting account of the experiences of Mr. Kingman N. Putnam, a New York surveyor, who, while in Haiti on other matters, was engaged by some of the underwriters interested in the *Mary Celeste* to make certain investigations in their behalf. His activities in the case appear to have been partly, if not largely, responsible for the arrest of Captain Parker.

According to Mr. Putnam, "Captain Parker was indicted for barratry and conspiracy, and the shippers of the cargo were indicted for conspiracy." Mr. Putnam is further quoted as saying that "the result of the trial in Boston was that the jury disagreed. They stood nine to three in our favor. The three men declined to convict Captain Parker on the charge of conspiracy for fear it might influence the jury who were going to try him for barratry. . . . A notice for a new trial was immediately given. All the shippers came forward and acknowledged their guilt. One firm which had collected a loss of $5,000 on some rotten fish, paid it back with interest. It also paid $1,000 to the Government toward the cost of the suit. . . . Captain Parker died in three months, and the mate in six months."

The companies interested in the insurance were report-

5. *Nautical Gazette* (New York), 31 December 1913.

ed in the press notices of the time as the New York Mutual, Commercial Mutual, Phoenix Insurance Company, Boston Marine and Switzerland Marine.

CHAPTER XVI

Conan Doyle, Pioneer of the Romanticists

PROBABLY the first, and apparently the best known of all stories written about the vessel was that written in 1884 by Conan Doyle, but without the use of his name. It appeared in the January issue of the *Cornhill Magazine,* a British publication, and was entitled "J. Habakuk Jephson's Statement." Altering the vessel's name to *Marie Celeste,* he unfolded a fantastic tale which bore only a remote resemblance to the known facts. He correctly stated the name of the vessel performing the salvage operation as the *Dei Gratia* and was approximately correct in giving latitude and longitude. Other than these items, his story was wholly inaccurate, but richly meriting a high place in the category of literary entertainment.

This article, with its ingenious and quite successful attempt at verisimilitude, was noticed not only by Queen's Advocate Flood at Gibraltar, but also by Consul Sprague who promptly sent a copy of it to the Department of State at Washington, along with the following letter (No. 451):

UNITED STATES CONSULATE
Gibraltar, January 12, 1884

HONORABLE JOHN DAVIS,
Assistant Secretary of State, Washington.
SIR:

My attention has been called to an article which appears in the *Cornhill Magazine* for this month, entitled "J. Habakuk Jephson's Statement" in which is referred the American brigantine *Mary Celeste* of New York, which was met at sea on the 4th December 1872 in latitude 38° 20′ longitude 17° 15′ W. by the British brigantine *Dei Gratia,* and brought into this port as a derelict, the full particulars of which were at the time duly transmitted to the Department.

It having ever since remained a mystery, regarding the fate of the master and crew of the *Mary Celeste,* or even the cause that induced or forced them to abandon their vessel which, with her cargo, were found when met by the *Dei Gratia* to be in perfect order, I ask [*sic*] to myself, what motives can have prompted the writer of the article in question to refer to this mysterious affair, after the lapse of eleven years; especially as the statement given, is not only replete with inaccuracies as regards the date, voyage and destination of the vessel, names of the parties constituting her crew, and the fact of her having no passengers on board beyond the master's wife and child, but seems to me to be replete with romance of a very unlikely or exaggerated nature.

As the Department cannot fail to feel a certain interest to ascertain whether there be the least suspicion of truth in any portion of what is stated in the article referred to in the *Cornhill Magazine,* I have taken the liberty to call its attention to it, especially as it may have the opportunity of examining the author of this extraordinary composition.

With reference to the crew of the *Mary Celeste,* I beg to enclose herewith a list of their names, according to her clearance for Genoa at the New York Custom house; also copy of a communication I received in 1873 from Prussia, referring to two of the crew, represented as being brothers, and evidently of German extraction.

I am, Sir,   Your obedient Servant,
                   [Signed] HORATIO J. SPRAGUE, U. S. Consul.

Enclosures:

1. List of crew of the *Mary Celeste.*
2. Copy of a letter from T. A. Nickelsen.

From the Department of State, Consul Sprague received the following reply (No. 289):

DEPARTMENT OF STATE
Washington, April 2, 1884

HORATIO J. SPRAGUE ESQ.
   Consul of the United States, Gibraltar
SIR:
   I have to acknowledge the receipt of your despatch numbered 451 of the 12th of January last, relating to the statement of J. Ha-

bakuk Jephon [*sic*] which appears in the *Cornhill Magazine* for January 1884 in regard to the brigantine *Mary Celeste* of New York, which vessel was met at sea by the British brigantine *Dei Gratia* and brought into the port of Gibraltar on the 4th. of December 1872, as a derelict.

The article to which you refer has been read with attention and much interest. The mystery which surrounds the fate of the master and crew and the passengers, or even the cause that induced or forced them to abandon their vessel, is in no wise satisfactorily explained in that statement, and it is conceived that, from the information we now possess, no solution of the mystery has yet been presented.

Under the circumstances, the Department has not deemed it essential to pursue any particular enquiries into the antecedents of the writer of the article in question, leaving the matter to a further development of the facts which time alone may or will develop.

Agreeing with the interest you have expressed in the matter, the Department will be gratified to receive any further information upon the subject that may reach you in the future.

I am, Sir, Your obedient servant,

[Signed] JOHN DAVIS, Assistant Secretary.

The real authorship of the story was not known until several years later, when it appeared in a volume of short stories written by Conan Doyle. To him belongs, beyond doubt, the responsibility for altering the vessel's name from Anglo-Saxon "Mary" to French "Marie," which latter, while admittedly more homogeneous with French "Celeste," does not accord with the official records of the vessel's name. Innumerable writers since have followed in his wake in the use of the wrong name, and with the tenacity of the familiar barnacle, it persists to this day in the majority of the articles on the subject.

CHAPTER XVII

The Surprising Claim of Frederick Solly Flood

1. *Consul Sprague Informs Department of State*

TWELVE years after the award of the Vice-Admiralty Court to the salvors of the *Mary Celeste*, Consul Sprague, still at the Consulate at Gibraltar, received a surprising communication from Frederick Solly Flood. Mr. Sprague in his official communication (No. 488), dated 4 March 1885, to the Department of State, disclosed the nature of it.

Honorable Assistant Secretary of State,
   Washington.
SIR:

   I regret being under the necessity of transmitting for the information of the Department, copies of a correspondence which has lately taken place with Mr. Frederick Solly Flood, lately Her Majesty's Attorney General in Gibraltar and this Consulate, regarding a claim he has advanced for services, as he states, to have rendered in the case of the American brigantine *Mary Celeste,* which vessel was brought into this port in December 1872 as a derelict by the British brigantine *Dei Gratia.*

   The Department will notice that I have from the commencement thought proper to decline holding any correspondence with Mr. Flood on the subject, or even to forward to the Department his claim for remuneration for services alleged to have been rendered by him in this case in the Vice Admiralty Court of Gibraltar.

   This action on my part is prompted by the belief that Mr. Flood has no right whatever to make any such claim in his capacity then of chief law officer of the Crown, he then being a salaried official of Her Majesty's Government appointed at Gibraltar for the purpose of discharging such duties, and in this opinion I am fully borne out by the leading professional men in Gibraltar who were engaged in the case in the Vice Admiralty Court, and who, therefore, are familiar with its details. I beg to inclose herewith their written opinion on the subject, which declares Mr. Flood's claim as utterly inadmissible.

Regarding the effects of the missing Captain, Mates and crew of the *Mary Celeste* to which Mr. Flood alludes, I must remark that his observations are inaccurate, inasmuch as these effects were delivered to me by the Vice Admiralty Court unconditionally, and this is clearly shown by my despatches to the Department of the 10th, and 21st. March 1873, No. 135 and No. 138, respectively.

Being the effects of an American master and crew, I do not see what right Mr. Flood could have, to expect me to store them here for an indefinite period, twelve years having already elapsed without even a vestige of the missing parties being traced.

I will not dwell upon the rather severe and gratuitous imputations which Mr. Flood has thought proper to cast upon some of the missing crew of the *Mary Celeste* whose fate, up to the present moment, is involved in the deepest mystery. Such groundless imputations have been advanced in spite of favorable reports regarding the characters of the missing men, supposed to be Danes and Germans, whose relatives and friends (some of them of an official character) have on several occasions corresponded with the German and Danish Consuls in this City asking for any information regarding these missing seamen, and offering, at the same time all the particulars they possessed respecting some of the missing men, relative to whom, the inclosed press-copies, kindly handed over to me by my German colleague, will afford additional interest.

In conclusion, I would beg to state confidentially, that Mr. Flood is an Irish gentleman. Although reported as being over eighty years of age, has always been considered an individual of very vivid imagination, and to have survived, to some extent at least, the judicious application of his mental faculties; such is, I believe, the general opinion of the community at large, even among his most intimate and personal friends.

I am, Sir, Your obedient servant,

[Signed] HORATIO J. SPRAGUE, U. S. Consul.

Enclosures.

1. Copy of Mr. Flood's letter to Mr. Sprague 9th. January — P. S. 20th. February, 1885.
2. Copy of Mr. Flood's letters to Advocates for *Mary Celeste* and her cargo, 18th. April 1873.
3. Copy of Mr. Sprague's reply to Mr. Flood, 23rd. Feb'y. 1885.
4. Copy of Mr. Flood's further letter to Mr. Sprague, 25th. Feb'y. 1885.
5. Copy of Mr. Sprague's reply, 26th. February 1885.
6. Press copy of a translated German communication to German Consul, 7th. Feb'y. 1885.
7. Legal opinion declaring Mr. Flood's claims inadmissible.

Mr. Flood's remarkable letter, with its belated post-script written forty-two days later, is given herewith:

2. *Mr. Flood's Letter to Consul Sprague*

Gibraltar, 9th. January 1885

P. S. 20th, February 1885

MY DEAR MR. SPRAGUE:

I have the honor to recall to your attention an event in which you have felt no inconsiderable interest. In December 1872 it became my duty as H. M.'s Advocate General and Proctor for the Queen in Her Office of Admiralty to institute and conduct in the Vice Admiralty Court of Gibraltar against a vessel and cargo and effects on board, which had been found derelict and brought into the port of Gibraltar by the British Brigantine *Dei Gratia*. It was alleged and afterwards proved that the derelict vessel was, when found, perfectly seaworthy and to have sustained no damage whatever from the perils of the sea or any accident, or to have been in any danger whatever, and that her cargo was such that under no circumstances could she have foundered, but that she had been wantonly disfigured and damaged for the obvious but ill disguised purpose of making her appear to have been abandoned as unseaworthy. She was well found and well provisioned. The whole, or at least apparently the whole of the personal effects of the Master, even including his watch, purse, hat and *trowsers with braces attached,* were found in his cabin. Effects of his two mates and crew, of which some were new and of very good quality, were also found on board. The after hatchway through which access was obtained to the provisions, and the fore-hatch through which access was obtained to stores and barrels of alcohol, one of which had been tampered with, were both found open and uncovered, the provisions immediately under the open after hatchway, and the stores immediately under the open forehatchway, were found perfectly dry; the deck house and after cabins were found artificially deluged with water. A few and inconsiderable marks of violence were found on deck, but as the evidence proved the crew to have been in possession of the vessel for sometime longer than the master, the chief mate, and, as I expect, the second mate, they had an ample opportunity to remove appearances of violence had there been any. The vessel turned out to be the American Brigantine *Marie [sic] Celeste* valued in her damaged state at Gibraltar at $5,700 for salvage purposes, and her cargo to have been alcohol only which was valued at Gibraltar at $36,943 for salvage purposes, shipped by Messrs. Ackermann & Co., American citizens in New York, for Genoa. The vessel was owned by Mr. J. H. Winchester and other American Citizens. She had been commanded by Benjamin S. Briggs, a brave and experienced American Citizen, and also had on board when she sailed, his wife, the accomplished daughter of an American clergyman and their little girl aged two years. Albert G. Richardson, also a brave and experienced American Citizen, had been her first mate. Her compliment [sic] had consisted of a second mate and five seamen, of whose nationality and antecedents nothing was then known, but the name of the second mate and the names of four of the five seamen indicated them to have been either Germans or Danes. She had no passengers except the Master's wife and child, and had no accommodation for any.

Under these circumstances, I felt it necessary to cause repeated and minute surveys to be held on the vessel and on her cargo and to be present during all of them, and to spare no exertions no pains and no trouble to discover the fate of all the ten persons who had left New York in the vessel and also, whether any, and if any, what, and by whom, any outrage or other serious crime beside that of disfiguring and casting away the vessel, had been committed on board her or after her abandonment. After a prolonged enquiry the vessel was delivered to Mr. Winchester who had the largest interest in her, and had claimed her and made good his claim upon giving security for salvage and the expenses of the Queen, and the cargo was delivered to the representatives of Messrs. Ackermann & Co. who had claimed and made good their claim, upon giving security for salvage and the expenses of the Queen, but the effects of the Master, Officers and crew not having been claimed, remained in the custody of the Marshal subject to the costs and expenses of the Queen and to abide such claims as might be preferred thereto and be established to the satisfaction of the Court, and in default as forefeited to the Queen. The Court having learnt from an affidavit of the Marshal sworn in the cause that you were willing to become custodian of the effects supposed to have belonged to the Master, Officers and crew for which neither he nor the Court had convenient accommodation, and to have the care of them on his behalf as Marshal without prejudice to the warrant under which he held them and subject to the jurisdiction of the Court, made an order permitting him to deliver, and you to have the care of them in the manner stated. The retention of these effects within the jurisdiction of the Court was a necessity, inasmuch as it was the duty of the Court to investigate and decide upon all claims which might be made thereto and condemn them as forfeited to the Queen, and to insure their delivery to the proper officer of Her Majesty's Revenue if unclaimed within a certain period. There was a further reason why it behooved the Court to be especially cautious to retain these effects within its own jurisdiction, namely, that in the event of any claim being made to them, an opportunity would be afforded to the Court of making a further and more rigid judicial inquiry into the fate of all persons known to have been in the vessel, and especially whether any, and if any, what violence had, as there was too much reason to fear, being committed against any of them, and thus advance the administration of justice which could not possibly be effected elsewhere. The effects were accordingly delivered into your care and a receipt taken for them which was filed in the Registry. Shortly afterwards but before final judgement was given, namely on the

4th April 1873 you favored me with the perusal of a letter which you had just received from a gentleman at Uetersum in the island of Fohr under date of the 24th. of the previous month making inquiries respecting the condition and appearance of the vessel when found, which impressed me very strongly — I may almost say, convinced me, that it was dictated by or on behalf of some of the crew who had left the vessel conscious of having been guilty of a great crime and desirous to learn whether they could safely emerge from concealment. Feeling assured that if they were kept in total ignorance of the evidence given in the cause, the retention of their effects, within the jurisdiction of the Court, aided by silence would probably reveal the mystery on which the fate of all who had sailed in the vessel and the cause of her abandonment were involved, I immediately requested you to inform the parties that you were not at liberty to give any information whatever respecting the condition or appearance of the vessel, and that all inquiries relating thereto should be addressed to me. I added that so great was the necessity of caution, that the Judge refused to permit a certain paper to be opened for the present, even for the purpose of furnishing a copy to the Governor who had officially requested a copy.

Under these circumstances, I decided to postpone making a demand for remuneration for my services. There is no salary attached to the office of H. M's Advocate General and Proctor or other emolument in suit[s] relating to derelict vessels except such as is customarily paid by the owners of the vessel, and of the cargo and other property found on board, for the recovery of which he has a lien which he may detain upon the vessel and upon cargo and upon all other property found in her if he has any fear that the owners or their bail are untrustworthy, but having had personal experience of the high honor, liberality and trustworthiness of the Citizens of the United States, I had no such fears either of the owners who had appeared or of their bail and having in view that the suit so far as it related to the effects of the Master, Officers and crew had not yet terminated and that the retention of those effects within our jurisdiction might lead to and assist further inquiry by the Court into their fate, and being desirous to expedite the payment of the fees then due to the Judge and the Registrar and of the Marshal's disbursements, I wrote to the Counsel who represented the owners of the vessel and their bail, and the counsel who represented the owners [ ]¹ and their bail, the letters of which I inclose a copy. Neither of those letters has ever been yet answered or even acknowledged by either of the gentlemen to whom they were addressed, or by their clients or otherwise; it cannot therefore be denied that those letters were, and ever have been understood by them, not as an abandonment or offer of an abandonment of my right to remuneration by them, but merely as an offer of an intention on my part to waive my lien upon the vessel and cargo and place my right to remuneration by them on the footing of a debt of honor, for it is inconceivable that if my letters were understood as conveying an abandonment of my right to remuneration, any Gentleman should condescend to accept even an offer of that nature or, above all, to treat it as unworthy of acknowledgment.

I refrained for some years from making any representation with reference to my remuneration, under the firm conviction that a proper time to make it would be when the retention of the effects and silence had elicited claims to those effects and renewed enquiry by the Court into the fate of the Master, Officers and crew, or when all hope that the effects would be claimed had imposed upon Her Majesty's Advocate General and Proctor the duty of applying to the Court to condemn the effects subject to my lien, to the use of her Majesty. The necessity for performing that duty had not arisen when in January last year, a Statement appeared in the *Cornhill Magazine* professing to have been written by an eyewitness, and to describe the master² of the Captain of the *Marie* [*sic*] *Celeste,* his wife and child, and the death of all the crew. This was followed up by the insertion in a newspaper published at Kropp, a small village in Holstein, of false statement[s], the obvious object of which was to stifle inquiry into the fate of the Master, Officers and crew of the *Marie* [*sic*] *Celeste.* I, and the German and

1. It is apparent from the context that the words "of the cargo" after the word "owners" were inadvertently omitted. Author's Note.

2. The word "murder" appears to have been inserted here by Consul Sprague, in the belief, no doubt, that murder was what Mr. Flood intended to say but wrote "master" instead.

Danish Consuls at my request, entered into a correspondence with various persons, which is not yet completed, but which, as far as it has proceeded, has tended to confirm my belief that the letter which, in April 1873 you sent to me for my perusal was dictated by survivors of the crew of the *Marie [sic] Celeste*. In the meantime, I have learnt from you that the effects upon the retention of which, in Gibraltar, I had for so many years been relying, for a solution of the mystery, had unfortunately been removed from the Jurisdiction of the Courts of Gibraltar, in January 1874, and consequently that the prosecution of a Judicial Inquiry into the fate of the missing persons, in which I might have assisted, had become impossible, and I should then have felt it no longer necessary to forbear from making a representation of my claim to remuneration, but that an inquiry by means of correspondence was then in progress. That correspondence has been protracted and is still being continued, but as it may last for some time longer, I think further postponement of my claim unnecessary. While abstaining from considering from a legal point of view the non-acceptance of the proposal contained in my letters of the 18th. April 1873, I desire to express my unabated confidence in the honor, liberality and trustworthiness of all the American people, and that in response to this communication, means will not be found wanting to requite my arduous labors and zeal not merely for the protection of the rights of individuals, but for the advance of public justice in which the whole American people are interested.

I further transmit for your perusal a fair copy of my minutes of such of the proceedings in the cause as I took part in, down to the 18th. April 1873, but these dry minutes exhibit to a very limited extent my efforts for the attainment of justice, and my special sympathy with the families of the Captain and his wife, and the Chief Mate and his wife.

I have the honor to be, my dear Mr. Sprague,
Yours most truly,
[Signed] FRED'K. SOLLY FLOOD,

Her Majesty's Counsel and lately Her Attorney General and also Her Advocate and Proctor.

Horatio Jones Sprague Esq.
  U. S. Consul at Gibraltar, &c. &c.

P. S. 20th February 1885.

I delayed transmitting this letter as I had no sooner written it than I was led to expect further information respecting the missing persons who had been in the *Marie* [*sic*] *Celeste*. I have now received some information, but it is so imperfect as to render further inquiries.[3] However, I now transmit this letter as I think it contains all that is necessary for the present purpose.

[Signed] FRED'K. SOLLY FLOOD

3. *Consul Sprague Declines to Transmit Claim to Washington*

Mr. Sprague's letter in reply speaks for itself.

CONSULATE OF THE UNITED STATES
Gibraltar 23rd, February 1885

FREDERICK SOLLY FLOOD ESQRE.
  &c &c Gibraltar
DEAR MR. FLOOD.

I beg to return herewith the enclosures contained in your communication of the 9th. ultimo, with an appending postscript of the 20th instant, and to state in reply, that I feel wholly unauthorized to enter into the subject matter to which it refers.

Any claims of the character or nature you may think proper to advance in the *Mary Celeste* case, can only be entertained or considered by the highest authority in the United States: therefore, it is obvious that I cannot enter into the case in any form whatsoever, and must respectfully decline any further communication on the subject.

Believe me, Yours most truly,

[Signed] HORATIO J. SPRAGUE, U. S. Consul

3. Word missing.

4. *Mr. Flood Renews Request*

Mr. Flood, apparently not discouraged by Mr. Sprague's refusal, renews the matter in the following communication:

Gibraltar 25th. February 1885

SIR:

I have the honor to request that you will be good enough to transmit through your Consulate to the United States Minister the enclosed documents together with the letter from myself dated 9th. January ultimo, and a copy of your reply thereto having reference to a claim which I am desirous of submitting to the favorable consideration of the Government of the United States in connection with services rendered by me in the case of the *Marie* [*sic*] *Celeste*.

You are aware that I am only availing myself of the customary channel of official communication, and I shall feel obliged if you will make any recommendation or explanation you may think fit in transmitting the papers in question.

I have the honor to be Sir, Your most obedient servant,

[Signed] FREDK. SOLLY FLOOD

Her Majesty's Counsel, and lately Her Attorney General and also Her Advocate General and Proctor.

Soon after receiving Mr. Flood's first communication, Consul Sprague consulted with Mr. Martin W. Stokes and Mr. George F. Cornwell, the attorneys who, twelve years before, had, respectively, represented the cargo and vessel interests when the *Dei Gratia's* salvage claim was presented before the Vice-Admiralty Court. These attorneys were still practising at Gibraltar, and, no doubt, because of their familiarity with the case, Consul Sprague asked them for a legal opinion on the subject of Mr. Flood's claim. Fortified by their opinion contained in a prepared statement (a copy of which is published below) Consul Sprague continued his policy of refusing to have anything to do with Mr. Flood's claim, as evidenced by the letter which follows:

5. *Consul Sprague Again Declines to Transmit Claim*

CONSULATE OF THE UNITED STATES
Gibraltar 26th. February 1885

FREDERICK SOLLY FLOOD ESQRE.
&c &c. Gibraltar
SIR:

In returning the inclosed papers relating to your proposed claim in reference to the *Mary Celeste* I beg to confirm my letter to you of the 23rd. instant, and to repeat that I feel unauthorized as Consul of the United States to enter into any correspondence with you as to any claim you may think yourself justified in submitting on this subject to the Government of the United States, and therefore I must respectfully decline forwarding the papers as requested by you.

I have the honor to be, Sir, Your obedient servant,

[Signed] HORATIO J. SPRAGUE, U. S. Consul

6. *Opinion of Proctors Martin W. Stokes and George F. Cornwell on Validity of Mr. Flood's Claim*

We the undersigned Proctors and Advocates in the Vice Admiralty Court of Gibraltar say, That we were retained in the action — *Mary Celeste* — on behalf of the owners of that Vessel and of the Cargo laden on board her. The Circumstances of the case were as follows. The *Mary Celeste* left the Port of New York in or about the Month of October 1872[4] laden with a cargo of Alcohol bound for an Italian Port — The Wife of the Master was on board her and an infant child. The Vessel was found derelict, and abandoned to the Westward[5] of the Azores in the Month of November 1872[6] by the British Vessel *Dei Gratia* which was bound to the

4. Error, sailed 7 November 1872.
5. Eastward, not westward, of the Azores.
6. Error, found 4 December 1872.

Mediterranean. The Mate of the *Dei Gratia* and two seamen were put on board the *Mary Celeste* and both Vessels proceeded to the Strait of Gibraltar. The *Mary Celeste* had evidently met with very bad weather and appeared to have been left by the crew in a moment of sudden panic. There was not the slightest appearance of anything criminal having occurred. The Boat in which the crew had left her had not been hoisted up by Tackles but forced over the side of the Vessel. The Boat and crew had never been heard of since and there can be no doubt that in attempting to reach land, probably the Azores, the boat was swamped.

The two Vessels arrived safely in the Port of Gibraltar, and the *Mary Celeste* and her cargo were forthwith arrested as derelict by Mr. Solly Flood the Proctor and Advocate of the Queen in Her Office of Admiralty as perquisites of Her Majesty — property thus arrested if no claimants appear within one year is then sold and the proceeds paid over to the Consolidated fund: — if the property is claimed, and the Queen's Proctor is satisfied with the title of the claimants, it is handed over to the claimants on their paying the expenses (not the costs) of the Crown — and giving Bail to pay the amount awarded to the Salvors for their Services. The owner of the *Mary Celeste* appeared, claimed his Vessel and the claim was allowed — and the owners of the cargo appeared and their claim was allowed, they undertaking to pay the expenses of the Crown — and giving Bail to answer the claims of the Salvors — the property being restored to the owners. The action became one of Salvage and the Queen's Proctor ought not to have interfered any further in the action — but Mr. Flood persisted in doing so, not on behalf of the American Government but as the Proctor and Advocate of the Queen in Her Office of Admiralty. The action was in the instance side of the Court — a Civil Action — Vice Admiralty Courts have no criminal Jurisdiction. Mr. Flood has no right to make any professional charges after the claims of the owners were allowed. When the suit finished, and the Salvors were paid the sum awarded them for their Service, Mr. Flood desired the owners of the Vessel and Cargo by their Counsel to pay the expenses of the Crown Viz. the Judge's, Registrar's, and Marshal's fees which were paid, but no claim was then made by him for his professional charges — in fact no such claim could be made — he should have obtained his fees from the Crown — as the Crown in Admiralty Courts neither receives nor pays costs. From that time to the present no steps have been taken in the Vice Admiralty Court of Gibraltar in respect of Mr. Flood's claims. The Court indeed could not entertain any question in the case which has been concluded since the date of the Judgement and the payment of the salvage and the Queen's Expenses. Mr. Sprague has informed us that Mr. Flood is now claiming compensation for services rendered by him professionally in the Matter of the *Mary Celeste* from the American Government and he has shewn to us a letter addressed by Mr. Flood to him as consul of the United States of North America and a proforma Bill of Costs — and requested Mr. Sprague to transmit the same to the American Government.

Mr. Sprague having consulted us professionally in the subject, our opinion is that Mr. Flood has no claim on the American Government — that he never was authorized in the *Mary Celeste* suit to act for the American Government and he never intimated that he was, he acted solely as the Proctor, and Advocate of the Queen. Under these circumstances we recommended Mr. Sprague to decline having any correspondence with Mr. Flood on the claims now set up by him for compensation from the U. S. Government and not to consent on any account to transmit officially, as consul of the United States of North America, the papers, which Mr. Flood is desirous of sending through the medium of the United States Consul at Gibraltar — as we are of opinion that Mr. Sprague by so doing would to some extent be countenancing and supporting the claims of Mr. Flood, now first made after the lapse of 12 years: the action — *Mary Celeste* — having been adjudicated on and settled in the years 1872 and 1873 — We beg to add that if any crime had been committed on board the *Mary Celeste,* the only court which could have adjudicated — would be an American Court of Criminal Jurisdiction.

Gibraltar 3 March 1885   MARTIN W. STOKES, *Advocate.*

GEORGE F. CORNWELL, *Advocate,*
Lincoln's Inn, London, practising in Gibraltar.

CHAPTER XVIII

Correspondence in 1887 between Department of State and Consul Sprague Regarding Chemist's Report on "Blood Stains"

O N 9 July 1887 some fourteen years after the Vice-Admiralty Court had rendered its decision on the salvage claim against the *Mary Celeste*, the Department of State at Washington wrote to Consul Sprague inquiring for information regarding the result of the analysis of the stains on the sword found on the *Mary Celeste* and on her woodwork. In reply, Consul Sprague wrote the Department as follows:

CONSULATE OF THE UNITED STATES OF AMERICA

Gibraltar, 26th, July 1887

WORTHINGTON C. FORD, ESQRE.
    Dep't. of State, Washington
DEAR SIR:

I beg to acknowledge the receipt of your note of the 9th instant, asking for any information I might possess regarding the result of the analysis made on the stains which appeared on a sword and woodwork on board the derelict *Mary Celeste* in 1873.

I have to say in reply, that although the result was never publicly disclosed by the Vice Admiralty Court, it was, however, well-known at the time, that the result of such analysis negatived anything like blood existing, and I, on the 7th, February, 1873, informed the Department of State to that effect in my despatch No. 132.

Nevertheless, anxious to obtain the fullest and most reliable information for you, I yesterday called upon the Registrar of the Vice Admiralty Court, who did me the great favor to look for the sealed evelope containing the report of the analysis, which he, in my presence opened and handed over to me the said report for perusal, which proved to be a confirmation of the information I had forwarded to the Department of State on the 7th Feb'y. 1873.

This case of the *Mary Celeste* as you justly remark, is startling, since it appears to be one of those mysteries which no human ingenuity can penetrate sufficiently to account for the abandonment of this vessel, and the disappearance of her Master, family and crew about whom nothing has ever transpired.

Believe me, Very truly yours,

HORATIO J. SPRAGUE.

P. S. It is possible that I may yet be favored with a copy of the report itself of the analysis made, which is pretty lengthy,— in that event, I shall not fail to transmit it to you.

A few days later, 29 July 1887, Consul Sprague again addressed the Department of State, enclosing copy of Dr. Patron's analysis and also the following letter received from the Registrar:

SUPREME COURT, GIBRALTAR, JUDGE'S CHAMBERS

28*th, July* 1887

DEAR MR. SPRAGUE:

I have much pleasure in transmitting a copy of the Analysis ordered to be made by the Vice Admiralty Court of Gibraltar, 14th March, 1873[1] in that very mysterious case of the *Marie* [*sic*] *Celeste*[2] which was brought before the Court as a derelict having been picked up abandoned totally on the high seas without any apparent reason for such abandonment.

This analysis which was made by Dr. Patron, M. D. at the instance of Mr. Solly-Flood, Advocate General, speaks for itself, it being rather remarkable, however, that the analysis or report so

1. The Registrar obviously erred in stating 14 March 1873 as the date when the analysis was ordered, inasmuch as Dr. Patron's report (see Appendix Q) was dated 30 January 1873 a month or more previous to the date above mentioned. Consul Sprague informed the Department of State about it on 7 February 1873.

2. This letter was written about three years after Conan Doyle had published (1884) his story about the *Marie* [*sic*] *Celeste*, indicating the influence already exerted by that publication in giving the vessel a wrong name.

brought in, was brought in under seal on the 14th, March 1873, and the seal remained unbroken until I opened it for the purpose of giving you the copy.

Believe me,   Yours very truly,

EDWARD J. BAUMGARTNER, *Registrar*.
Vice Adm. Court Gibraltar.

Mary Celeste

PART III

APPENDIX A
Bibliographical Notes

The writer has on file a number of books and copies of many newspaper and magazine articles written on this subject, dating from the time when the news of the disaster first reached this country, in December 1872, to the time of writing this narrative. This includes photostatic copies of the extensive collection of "Celesteana" over a long period, by the late Frederick J. Shepard, for many years Librarian of the Buffalo Public Library. Mr. Shepard had made a thorough study of the case and was a fearless critic of those who, in his opinion, had deliberately made false statements concerning it.

We have read, with interest, *A Great Sea Mystery*[1] the well-written work of J. G. Lockhart, an English author. Although we are not in accord with this writer in regard to certain statements in the realm of fact, his book is manifestly the sincere and earnest effort of an author intent only upon telling the truth.

For the source material of this book, the writer has gone to the records of the Atlantic Mutual Insurance Company of New York; the National Archives at Washington, D. C., and to other government departments in the United States and Canada.

The only publications on which requisition has been made for material found in this book, or which have proved useful as works of reference, were Dr. Oliver W. Cobb's excellent article "The Mystery of the *Mary Celeste*" (*Yachting*, February, 1940) and his more recent book *Rose Cottage* giving particulars of the Briggs family and their home-life in Marion, Massachusetts; the address by the late Anton A. Raven, former President of the Atlantic Mutual Insurance Company, *Yale Alumni Weekly*, 1904; *Patterson's Illustrated Encyclopedia*, published by The Marine Review Publishing Co., Cleveland, Ohio; *More About Nova Scotia* by Dr. Clara Dennis; *Nautical Gazette*, New York (31 December 1913); *Marine Journal*, New York (7 November 1891); H. O. No. 134—*East Atlantic Pilot*—1928.

Edmund Burke, the English statesman, is quoted as saying: "It is not only our duty to make the right known, but to make it prevalent." In the case of the *Mary Celeste*, where error has long been entrenched in the public mind, to "make prevalent" the right—the truth concerning her—becomes an ungracious and distasteful office whenever critical reference to the works of previous writers has to be made. Our preference would have been to omit all comment on *The Great* Mary Celeste *Hoax* by Laurence J. Keating, or on his previous magazine article, under the pseudonym of "Lee Kaye" on the same subject.

Mr. Keating declares in his book (p. 16): "The purpose of the present narrative is to put on record an exact and accurate account of what really

1. (London: Philip Alan & Co. Ltd., 1927.)

did happen on board the vessel during her famous and magical voyage etc. ... and to give the ruthless truth about the people who were connected with her." He further states (p. 18): "No evidence has been included which has not been investigated and corroborated; no document is quoted which has not been examined. The history is placed before the reader complete and accurate in all respects."

In view of these declarations, it becomes apparent that his book is not represented as a work of fiction, but as a record of fact, and must therefore, be dealt with on that basis.

We regret to say that Mr. Keating's book, because of the easily demonstrable inaccuracies with which it abounds, has proved valueless to the writer as a work of reference. Neither time nor space nor inclination permits any extended comment on its gross misstatements. In fact, no comment of any kind would have been made thereon had it not been for the utterly false and unjust reflections on Captain Briggs, on his honor as a man and his proved abilities as a master mariner. Charges involving irregularity of conduct, of conspiracy with Captain Morehouse, also unjustly accused of fraud, should not be permitted to pass without vigorous challenge and stern reproof. Furthermore, the coarse and vulgar references to Mrs. Briggs, who was described by Queen's Advocate Frederick Solly Flood in his letter to United States Consul Sprague as "the accomplished daughter of an American clergyman," cannot fail to arouse indignation where they do not cause disgust. The character of the book may be briefly epitomized as follows:

Here lies a book, of which it may be said:
It hoaxed the living and defamed the dead.

Excerpts from *New York Journal of Commerce*

From Atlantic Mutual Insurance Company, Record Book No. 7—"Amounts at Risk on Vessels Ashore, in Distress or Abandoned"

1872–1873

23 December 1872. Reports vessel "towed [*sic*] into Gibraltar 16th [*sic*] inst., and commanded by Capt. Benjamin Briggs of Marion, Mass. 'who had his wife and child with him.'"

11 January 1873. Reports vessel fallen in with derelict, Dec. 4, lat. 17° 37 [*sic*] long. 18° 20. The mate and two men were put on board. She proceeded to Gibraltar, arriving there 13th. . . . "There were no boats on board when she was found."

25 February 1873. Refers to cargo of alcohol, and reports fears that the crew might have been inflamed by liquor to commit murder.

3 March 1873. Suggests that vessel may not have been abandoned until "some days after" last entry on the log. Reports finding of sword with stains resembling blood and marks of blood on top-gallant rail.

14 March 1873. Reports Captain Winchester's views and refers to wife and child of Captain Briggs being lost with him—vessel worth more than her insurance. Mentions finding a $30 draft in a seaman's chest. Gives list of crew, ages and places of birth.

9 April 1873. Reports seventeen hundred pounds sterling awarded salvors by the Vice-Admiralty Court; the vessel being valued at $5,700 and the cargo at $36,943.

21 April 1873. Genoa (4 April). Reports *Mary Celeste* discharged all her cargo but [ ]² barrels. All the cargo came out in good condition and there appears to be no damage, as far as can be seen, in the quantity still on board.

13 May 1873. Reports vessel at Genoa, hove down, bottom surveyed and found in perfect order. Vessel lying in port "awaiting the settlement of her damages, the charterers having cancelled her charter-party."

Maritime Register

1872

Mary Celeste

11 September. At 17th St., North River. Wallace, master. Consignees J. H. Winchester & Co.

18, 25 September; 2, 9 October. At Pier 44, East River (master and consignees as above).

16 October. At Pier 44, East River (master and consignees as above). For Genoa.

23 October. At Hunter's Point (master and consignees as above). For Genoa.

30 October. At Pier 50 East River (master and consignees as above). For Genoa.

6 November. Briggs, master: N. Y. Nov. 4 [*sic*] Genoa (see corrected date below).

13, 20, 27 November; 4, 11 December. Briggs, master, Nov. 7, Genoa.

18 December. (Disaster column) "*Mary Celeste* — of and from N. Y., Nov. 7 with 1700 bbls. Alcohol for Genoa, was picked up derelict and towed [error] into Gibraltar—Dec. . . . . ."

25 December. Briggs, N. Y., Nov. 7., Genoa.

Dei Gratia

23 October. Bear River, N. S., Morehouse, master. Consignees Simpson and Shaw. For Curacao — at Erie Basin.

30 October. Bear River, N. S., Morehouse, master. Consignees as above. For Gibraltar. At Erie Basin.

2. Illegible.

30 October. Freight Report. Funch, Edye, & Co. Ship Brokers. Br. Brig *Dei Gratia*, 250, hence to Gibraltar, f. o. with petroleum at 6s. 9d.—7s. 9d.

6 November. Bear River, N. S., Morehouse, master. Consignees, Simpson and Shaw. For Gibraltar. At Venango Yard.

13 November. Bear River, N. S., Morehouse, master. Consignees, Simpson and Shaw. For Gibraltar (cleared) at Venango Yard.

20 November. Br. Morehouse, N. Y., Nov. 15 for Gibraltar.

27 November; 4, 11, 18 & 25 December. Br. Morehouse, N. Y., Nov. 15 for Gibraltar. Spoken 19 November—Lat. 40° 55′. Long. 66°.

1873

Mary Celeste

1 January. Briggs, N. Y. Nov. 7 for Genoa.

8 January. Briggs, N. Y. Nov. 7 for Genoa. Arr. Gibraltar, Dec. 13.

8 January. Reported as derelict, taken into Gibraltar, arr'd. December 13.

15 January. Reports vessel taken in charge by Vice-Admiralty Court. "There were no boats on board when she was found." This report errs in stating latitude and longitude and name of salvaging vessel.

22 January. Reports vessel at Gibraltar 25 December. Erroneously gives name of master as "Devon" (Deveau sailed her from lat. 38° 20′ N, long. 17° 15′ W to Gibraltar.)

29 January & 5 February. Reports vessel at Gibraltar, 6 January, and repeats error in name of master.

12 February. Reports vessel at Gibraltar 25 January. Repeats error of 22 January.

19 February. Reports vessel remained in hands of Court 28 January.

19 March. Reports vessel released by Court as of 28 February after bond had been given for ship and cargo.

9 April. Reports award of £1700 to salvors. Vessel valued at $5700, cargo $36,943.

14 May. Reports vessel hove down in Genoa. Bottom surveyed and found in perfect order. Vessel lying there awaiting settlement of damages, charterers having cancelled her charter-party.

4, 11 & 18 June. Reports vessel at Genoa 17 May, ready.

Dei Gratia

1, 8 January. "Br., Morehouse, N. Y. Nov. 15 for Gibraltar—Spoken 19 November—Lat. 40° 55′ Long. 66°.

15 January. Br., Morehouse, N. Y. Nov. 15 for Gibraltar.—Arr. 11 December [Error: arrived 12 December and sailed 23 December for Genoa].

22 January. Same as 15 January with additional: "In port 25 December for Genoa."

29 January & 5 February. Same as 22 January with additional, sailed 23 December for Genoa.

12 February. "Br. Morehouse, N. Y. 15 November Genoa—Arr. 16 January—

19 & 26 February. "Br. Morehouse, Genoa Jan. . . . Messina & N. Y.

5, 12, 19 & 26 March, 2 April. Br. Morehouse[3] Genoa—Jan.—Messina & N.Y.

9, 16 & 23 April. Br., Deveau, Genoa, 17 March Messina & N. Y.

30 April. Br., Deveau, Genoa, 17 March Messina & N. Y. Arr. 29 March Messina. In port 12 April—Palermo or Coast & N. Y.

7, 14 May. Br. Deveaux [sic] At Messina, 12 April for Europe.

21 & 28 May. Br. Deveaux [sic] Messina 27 April for N. Y.

4, 11 & 18 June. Br. Deveaux [sic] Messina 27 April for N. Y. Arr. Gib. 13 May and sld—

25 June. Br. Deveaux [sic] Messina, 27 April for N. Y. Arr. 19 June—

Bibliographical Review

1873

Gibraltar Chronicle (31 January). Report of survey of *Mary Celeste* by John Austin, Surveyor of Shipping, Ricardo Portunato, Diver, and T. J. Vecchio, Marshal of the Court at Gibraltar.

Gibraltar Guardian (14 February). Quotes letter from Frederick Solly Flood, Queen's Proctor and Attorney-General for Gibraltar, to the London Board of Trade, suggesting that action be taken to ascertain fate of *Mary Celeste's* company. (Reprint of article in *Shipping Gazette*, 5 February.)

Boston Post (24 February). Advancing theory of piratical attack or assault by vessel's crew inflamed with alcohol. (Reprinted 17 December 1913 in *Nautical Gazette.*)

Gibraltar Chronicle & Commercial Intelligencer (15 March). Announcement of salvage award by Vice-Admiralty Court.

Nautical Gazette (29 March). Quotes Captain Shufeldt's report, also Secretary of Treasury's notice to Collectors of Customs and mentions fears of the Department that murder had been committed by a drunken crew who either perished at sea or escaped on some other vessel. (Reprinted in issue of 17 December 1913.)

---

3. Although Morehouse was still master, the record shows that Deveau was in command of the vessel when she left Gibraltar for Genoa and also on the passage thence to Messina and thence to Gibraltar. It is not known at what point Morehouse again took charge of the vessel.

1884

Cornhill Magazine (London) (January). "J. Habakuk Jephson's Statement."
  In this fanciful story by Conan Doyle, anonymously published, the *Mary Celeste* makes her first public appearance as *Marie Celeste* except for one citation under that name in *Lloyd's List* of 25 March 1873. See Chapter XVI, "Conan Doyle, Pioneer of the Romanticists."

1886

New York World (Sunday, 24 January). "A Brig Fated to Ill Luck" by Captain Coffin.
  Highly interesting account but inaccurate in many particulars. Cites experience of another vessel carrying alcohol and advances theory of explosion.

1894

McClure's Magazine (November). "Real Conversations" by Robert Barr.
  Brief account which reports vessel loaded with clocks from Baltimore to Lisbon, and contains other inaccuracies.

1902

Brooklyn Daily Eagle (9 March). Interview with Mrs. A. G. Richardson widow of *Mary Celeste's* first mate.
  Quotes her as believing that murder had been committed by the crew, to whom the article, in many particulars inaccurate, makes unfavorable reference. Apparently first mention of alleged letter to "Fanny my dear wife." Mentions explosion theory.

1904

Yale Alumni Weekly (2 March). Address by Anton Adolph Raven, then president of Atlantic Mutual Insurance Company, at Yale University.
  Brief but interesting comment on salvage award.

Chambers's Journal (17 September). "The Case of the *Marie* [*sic*] *Celeste*" by J. L. Hornibrook.
  Suggests that an octopus rose from the deep and, after first encircling the helmsman, took the remainder of the crew, one by one. Article ten years "off" as to date of event, and inaccurate in other particulars.

New York Evening Post (Saturday Supplement) (15 October). "Strange Case of the *Mary Celeste*" by Allan Kelly.
  Advances theory of explosion due to escaping fumes from porous, red-oak barrels. One year "off" as to date, and inaccurate in other particulars.

1905

McClure's Magazine (May). "Terror of the Sea" by P. T. McGrath.

Writer gives sailing date as 1887, with total company of thirteen, boats at davits, rigging intact, sails set, and a half-eaten meal. No theory advanced.

Munsey's Magazine (September). "Mysteries of the Sea" by John R. Spears. Writer one year off in date. Reports vessel with most of her sails set, running before wind, rigging and sails in order, and other inaccuracies. Offers no theory.

1906

Overland Monthly (November). "Tales of the Sea" by Arthur H. Dutton.

Names Briggs as first mate, with a wife in Brooklyn who mysteriously disappears. Reports *Dei Gratia* on a voyage from Cape of Good Hope to England. Other factual errors too numerous to mention.

1909

Gibraltar Chronicle. A highly fantastic tale by one Ramon Alvarado, of Cincinnati, Ohio.

Purporting to be a solution of the mystery. All dates given by the writer are almost a year after the vessel's abandonment.

1912

The Digby Weekly Courier, Digby, Nova Scotia (20 September). Obituary of Oliver E. Deveau, first mate of *Dei Gratia*.

Refers to abandonment of *Mary Celeste* and Deveau's small share of salvage money. No theory advanced as to disappearance of the latter's company.

1913

New York World (Sunday, 9 February).

Erroneously states sailing date as 7 October and vessel found with "sails set" and fore hatch "upside down." Quotes Captain Winchester as believing alcohol fumes escaped through red-oak barrels, generated gas and forced off fore hatch.

Nautical Magazine (April). "An Unsolved Mystery" by J. S. C.

This long article contains numerous inaccuracies, gives name of captain as "Griggs" and that of *Dei Gratia's* master as "Boyce," mentions log entry dated 2 September, two months *before* vessel left New York.

Maritime Exchange Bulletin (August). Letter dated Red Bank, 9 August 1913 from Captain C. B. Parsons:

This writer recalls having had a conversation with Captain "Boyce" (?) of the *Dei Gratia*, a year or two after that vessel had found the *Mary Celeste* and speaks of Island of Corvo as the place where the vessel was apparently abandoned. According to the record, however, Morehouse was master, and the vessel had reached St. Mary's Island. The error of Captain Parsons in describing, from memory, a conversation which had occurred forty years before, is understandable.

New York Times (Magazine Section) (23 November). Quotes letter to *Strand Magazine* from A. Howard Linford, of Magdalen College, Oxford, headmaster of a preparatory school.

Tells of finding a story of the *Mary Celeste* among papers committed to him by an old servant, Abel Fosdyk, while the latter was on his deathbed. The story, while highly imaginative, is well told. Fosdyk claimed to have been one of *Mary Celeste's* company, but not one of the names of his companions, as stated in his account, appears on the official records. Tells of the captain and mate wearing each other's clothes while they engage in a swimming contest around vessel. Improvised quarterdeck for "Baby" collapses, precipitating all hands into the water. Sharks do their deadly work. Fosdyk survives and is picked up by a "boat" the name and nature of which are not stated. Mr. Linford cautiously states: "I do not vouch for the truth of anything narrated." (See Review by Frederick J. Shepard, in *Buffalo Express*, 14 December 1913.)

Buffalo Express (14 December). "The *Mary Celeste*" by Frederick J. Shepard.

Errs in stating Captain Briggs was owner of one-eighth interest (instead of one-third as indicated in vessel's register No. 122). Erroneously mentions Boyce and Devon as master and mate, respectively of the *Dei Gratia*, instead of Morehouse and Deveau. Repeats unconfirmed report of finding letter from Mate Richardson to his wife. In other respects, this well-written article conforms very closely to the known facts.

Nautical Gazette (17 December). "The *Mary Celeste* Mystery."

A very sensible review of article in *Strand Magazine*, professed to have been written by a man named Abel Fosdyk who claimed to have been a member of the crew. Points out various weaknesses and inaccuracies in Fosdyk's story.

Washington Post (19 December). Quoting article published by London *Daily Express*.

Refers to latest alleged solution furnished by R. E. Greenhough. Tells of finding document in a bottle, found off St. Paul's Rocks, describing forcible seizure of men aboard a becalmed brig, *Marie* [*sic*] *Celeste*, in order to make up for losses sustained among crew of another vessel. The woman and child presumably met with violent death. Fanciful and unconvincing narrative.

New York Times (21 December). Letter from Kingman N. Putnam.

Advances theory that a sailor went down into the forepeak with a lighted match. "Some gas from leaky packages of spirits exploded and blew off hatch cover." In 1885, after vessel went ashore off coast of Haiti, Mr. Putnam, representing certain insurance companies, made investigation with interesting results.

Nautical Gazette (24 December). "The *Mary Celeste* Mystery Explained."

Gives views of Mr. Winchester Noyes, grandson of Captain J. H. Winchester. Mr. Noyes erred in giving Bath, Maine, as place of construction and his account, in a number of other instances, does not fully accord with the record as it appears today. Quotes Captain Winchester as believing that gas in hold caused spontaneous combustion which blew off hatch cover.

Nautical Gazette (31 December). "Sequel to the *Mary Celeste* Mystery."

Quotes Kingman N. Putnam as favoring explosion theory. Refers to hatch being found upside down—a statement not confirmed by Court testimony. Refers to vessel's stranding on Haitian reef and Mr. Putnam's investigations.

Youth's Companion (date ?), by John Newton Swift. Contains one brief paragraph in which vessel's name is incorrectly stated and date of discovery is given as 4 December 1873, one year after actual happening.

1914

Nautical Magazine (March ?). An abbreviated account of Abel Fosdyk's Narrative.

(See comment under 23 November 1913, *New York Times* [Magazine Section].)

1922

Lloyds—Yesterday and To-day, by Henry M. Gray.

Incorrectly reports sailing date as November 1875, "a crew of 13," "all sails set" and "not a spar or rope out of place." It also erroneously states that "not one of the brig's boats was missing" and that "both in the cabin and forecastle a freshly-cooked and half-consumed meal was on the table." Repeats but questions the Abel Fosdyk story .

1924

New York Times (Magazine Section) (12 October). By Kathleen Woodward.

This fanciful narrative follows the usual pattern, with inaccuracies too numerous to mention. Gives vessel a crew of seventeen. Mentions story by Captain H. Lucy, R.N.R. telling of information received from a man named Triggs, who claimed to have been bos'n's mate of the *Mary Celeste*. According to the latter, Captain Briggs and his men boarded a derelict steamer; rifled a safe containing £3500 in gold; divided the loot; escaped in steamer's boats with name of a London schooner painted thereon; landed at Cadiz; made false report to authorities; Triggs, Briggs, wife and daughter went to Marseille. Triggs convinced Lucy by giving evidence of having signed on *Mary Celeste* at Boston [*sic*].

New York Times (Saturday Review) (26 October). "A Mystery of the Seas" by Dr. Oliver W. Cobb.

A cousin of Captain Briggs refutes the allegations made in the *Times* article of 12 October, previously quoted. Dr. Cobb errs in stating date of discovery of *Mary Celeste* as 13 December. His subsequent article in *Yachting* (February 1940) corrects this and a few other items not in complete accord with the record as it now appears. Believes rumbling noises due to gases generated in hold, frightened captain and crew, causing them to take to boat; that the vessel sailed away and all hands are believed to have been drowned.

1925

The Yachting Monthly, London (August). "The Mystery of the *Mary Celeste*" by Dr. Oliver W. Cobb.

See comment on article in the *New York Times* (Saturday Review), 26 October 1924.

1926

Chambers's Journal (12 June, July in monthly issue). "The Truth About *Marie* [*sic*] *Celeste*" by Lee Kaye (alias Laurence J. Keating).

Reports finding an aged survivor [?] John Pemberton, who claimed to have been cook on the *Mary Celeste*. Pemberton reveals an astonishing memory for things which never happened, but fails to recall the correct names of other members of the ship's company, except Captain and Mrs. Briggs. A mélange of inventions and easily demonstrable misstatements too numerous to mention.

New York Herald (24 July) Editorial. "The *Marie* [*sic*] *Celeste* Mystery."

Reviews article by Lee Kaye (alias Laurence J. Keating) and, like many others at the time, the writer seems disposed to accept the story at its face value. The writer incautiously accepts the Kaye-Keating discovery of the "port of Santa Marta" which geographers would have difficulty in locating in the Azores.

Boston Sunday Post (8 August). By John Lafitte (George Comstock).

Quotes Arthur S. Briggs[4] (son of Captain B. S. Briggs) and Frederick J. Shepard, Librarian of Buffalo Public Library, in refutation of Kaye-Pemberton story in *Chambers's Journal*. Mr. Shepard, usually very accurate, errs in reporting the *Dei Gratia* as loading at Liverpool while

4. Since deceased.

Mary Celeste was loading at New York. According to the record, both vessels were in New York harbor, in early November, but not alongside each other as often stated. Lafitte's article contains much information, but many regrettable inaccuracies, such as calling vessel *Mary Sellers*; naming "Boyce," instead of Morehouse, as master of *Dei Gratia*, repeatedly mentioned by him as *Dei Gracia*. Article contains other factual errors.

Boston Sunday Post (15 August). By John Lafitte (George Comstock).

Corrects previous error in naming "Boyce" instead of "Morehouse" as master of the *Dei Gratia* and quotes Captain D. R. Morehouse's widow as saying that her husband entertained the theory that gases in the hold of the *Mary Celeste* caused fear of explosion and the abandonment of the vessel.

Outlook Magazine (1 September). "The Mystery of the *Mary Celeste*" by Dr. Oliver W. Cobb.

The article points out the weaknesses of the story by one Triggs to Captain Lucy, R.N.R. and advances the theory of explosion from gases in the hold. The article contains a few misconceptions which are cleared up by Dr. Cobb in a subsequent narrative.

Literary Digest (18 September). Résumé of various articles on the subject, from Conan Doyle to date. Comments on error in naming Boyce as master of the *Dei Gratia* instead of Morehouse. Mentions various theories.

1927

A Great Sea Mystery by John Gilbert Lockhart (London: Philip Allan & Co., Ltd.).

A sincere, interesting and in many respects excellent presentation of the case. Mr. Lockhart refers to certain " 'solutions' which, for their author's purposes, light-heartedly convey the gravest charges against Captain Briggs or Captain Morehouse or other members of the ship's companies." He draws attention to the fact that their "unfortunate relatives have no remedy in law, for neither in Great Britain nor in the United States is there redress for a libel upon the dead." This author *repeats a number* of the familiar errors including the statement that the *Mary Celeste* previously bore the name of *Mary Sellers;* that the hatch lay wrong side up; that Captain Morehouse boarded the derelict; that all sails were set. We cannot agree with the statement (p. 13) that the *Mary Celeste* when found was only 300 miles from Gibraltar; or that (p. 15) she was "about 130 miles from the coast of Portugal"; or (p. 27) "some 750 miles E. of the Island of Santa Maria." Limitations of space preclude the mention of other inaccuracies, some of which, presumably, are typographical. Mr. Lockhart states that he "is inclined to accept Dr. Cobb's theory of an explosion in the vessel's hold, as the more likely."

1929

The Great Mary Celeste *Hoax* by Laurence J. Keating alias Lee Kaye (London: Heath Cranton Ltd.).

This unpleasant book has been thoroughly dissected and refuted by others. See subsequent comment in this list.

Evening Standard, London (6 May).

Reports an interview had by the paper's "Liverpool Correspondent" with John Pemberton, "aged 92." This nonagenarian asserts that he was cook of the *Mary Celeste,* and tells of his request to Keating to write a book vindicating him (Pemberton) of charge of poisoning everybody on board. Tells of a terrible storm in which the steersman is washed away— all hands thought the ship had gone. "A shriek from the cabin. The tinkling of the piano had stopped; Mrs. B. had been playing hymn tunes"—all of which shows remarkable dexterity on the part of Mrs. Briggs in a storm-tossed vessel, and supernatural hearing on the part of "Pemberton" in the midst of a gale. Names two companions apparently non-existent. "Pemberton's" tale is a product of a lively imagination and utter disregard for the facts.

New York Herald Tribune (29 July). "*Mary Celeste* Hoax Author Called Hoaxed" by Percy N. Stone.

Tells of interview with Mrs. Priscilla Richardson Shelton, sister of Mate Richardson of *Mary Celeste*. Quotes her as being exceedingly skeptical of Keating's story, and regarding Pemberton as an impostor. This article described *Dei Gratia* as a barkentine, names her master "Moorhouse," and repeats several familiar errors such as finding vessel with "all sails set . . . running before a brisk wind . . . with one of her life-boats on board . . . a breakfast still warm." Mentions "Fanny, my dear wife," message alleged to have been found on log slate and a "headless cask of alcohol," neither of which is mentioned in Court testimony. No solution offered.

New Bedford Standard (4 August). "Facts Refute *Mary Celeste* Solution" by Cooper Gaw.

Of all the commentaries which have come to our notice in connection with Keating's book, Mr. Gaw's article impresses us as most able and thorough. Its denunciation of the book seems well merited, and its factual content, in respect of accuracy, is almost unexceptionable. Presumably (albeit unwittingly) influenced by the Keating narrative, it refers to the *Dei Gratia's* master as "Moorhouse," instead of "Morehouse."

Buffalo News (8 August).

Frederick J. Shepard[5] of the Public Library, questions Keating's book, and is quoted as saying about John Pemberton: "I don't think there is

5. Since deceased.

such a person, and if there is, he is a colossal liar." He is further quoted as saying of the book: "There is scarcely a correctly stated fact in it." Mr. Shepard's reference to a hatch found upside down lacks confirmation. He advances theory of explosion.

New York Herald Tribune (11 August). Review by Walter Millis of Keating's book.

This careful reviewer cautiously states: "If one could be sure that Mr. Keating's book is entirely what it purports to be, one could hail a genuine service to maritime literature, but, unfortunately, one cannot be sure." He points out the absence of citation, by Author Keating, of "specific authority for specific statements." A temperate, well-written review, despite a few errors in the realm of fact.

New York Herald Tribune Book Review (11 August ?). "*Mary Celeste* Mystery Still Shrouds the Strange Ship."

The reviewer relies for his basic information, upon a book by Elliott O'Donnell; repeats the usual errors, including "boats on board," "under full sail," and the "freshly cooked breakfast." Calls the *Dei Gratia* a barkentine, her master "Moorhouse," and locates the place of finding the *Mary Celeste* as *west* of the Azores. The reviewer shrewdly points out lack of evidence in buttressing statements. Advances no theory and refrains from taking sides in the controversy.

New York Times Book Review (18 August). "A Forecastle Classic" by Captain David W. Bone.

A brief review of Keating's book previously mentioned. Considers the tale "ingenious and quite credible," and that "the author of it has apparently been at considerable pains to search for and examine all the evidence pertinent to the making of his book." The reviewer is very gentle in his comment.

New York Times Book Review (1 September).

Frederick J. Shepard expresses annoyance at Captain Bone's apparent acceptance of Keating's book, and points out various inaccuracies and weaknesses in the narrative.

Saturday Review of Literature (14 September). "The Bowling Green."

Christopher Morley quotes in full, with brief comment, a sales-appeal letter from the publishers of *The Great* Mary Celeste *Hoax*. This letter repeats the familiar errors, reporting that the vessel was found with "life-boats intact," with "all sails set," "apparently going normally along her course." [Actually, she was headed westward when found and had only three sails set.] It asserts that "Laurence Keating" has unravelled the story, step by step, "having made a thorough study of independent records," and "the Mystery of the *Mary Celeste* is a mystery no longer." [We are still without knowledge as to what became of the ten persons and what caused them to abandon their vessel.]

Sunday World (Magazine) (15 September). "William McFee Solves the Mystery of the *Marie* [*sic*] *Celeste*."

A well-written article which apparently shares Captain Winchester's reported belief that the vessel was abandoned through fear of explosion. The writer however errs in regard to the vessel's name, sailing date and the distance travelled after abandonment.

Saturday Review of Literature (21 September). "A Forecastle Classic."

Review of Keating's book by Captain David W. Bone. (See *New York Times Book Review*, 18 August, previously quoted herein.)

New York Times Book Review (13 October). "Objection and Reproof."

Here Mr. Keating makes reply to his critics. He points out "that the noise is all coming from one quarter — a corner of New England" [where else indeed could it more appropriately come from?]; makes a lame effort to explain that "the piano was not the melodeon," and counsels his readers to refer to certain pages of his book in order to discover the difference. [Such a quest, it is feared, will prove unrewarding to the average reader.] He denies the presence of a child on board the vessel and asserts that no boats were missing. [Mr. Keating's statements do not carry conviction.]

He questions the possibility of carrying 1,700 barrels alcohol, and could not "conscientiously accept" facts offered him regarding Sarah Elizabeth Cobb, preferring to rely upon his own investigations which resulted in his use of the name "Mary Sellars" of whom no one, up to the time of Laurence Keating, had apparently ever heard.

1930

Liverpool Post & Mercury (20 March). "Old Mystery of the Sea. The *Marie* [*sic*] *Celeste*."

Refers to advertisement in Liverpool *Echo* (19 March) reading: "If John Pemberton of the *Marie Celeste* mystery, said cook of that vessel in 1872 will communicate with J. C. Anakin, 181 Boaler Street, Liverpool, it will be to his advantage." Pemberton, said to be ninety-three, "believed to be the only living survivor" of the vessel. The article reports that the vessel, when found, was under "full spread of canvas," "the galley fire was still warm," and "three cups of tea were lukewarm," while "a cat was asleep on a locker" [manifestly a feline of unusual endurance and placidity of disposition after so long a period without water]. The article states that "Pemberton is known to have been seen in Liverpool as lately as a month ago" but "all attempts to trace him have so far come to nothing."

Mitropa—Zeitung, Frankfort, Germany (26 October). "The Mystery of the *Mary Celeste*" by Bernhard Freiherr von Friesen.

This narrative follows, with some variations, the usual pattern which shows a vessel "following her course, . . . fully equipped with life boats," and with evidence in the forecastle of "a meal eaten a short time before." In this account, the child is four, the crew numbers fourteen, the *Dei Gratia* is on her way from Europe, the hatches are not only in order, but "locked and sealed," and the log-book entry reads: "My good wife and my dear child. To-day is the . . . ." Here the derelict enjoys the distinction of having been towed into port by nothing less notable than "an English Cruiser." Even this unusual honor, however, does not serve to save the *Mary Celeste* from a catastrophe which, the writer states, soon overtook her, for we are told that on the first trip after this strange occurrence: "She went down with all on board." [The *Mary Celeste* survived until 1885, despite the author, and was wrecked on 3 January of that year off the Haitian Coast with no loss of life.]

"Last Thoughts on the *Mary Celeste*" in *Strange Tales of the Seven Seas* by John Gilbert Lockhart.

This relates chiefly to Keating's book, published in 1929, and disproves a number of that author's statements. Mr. Lockhart, himself the author of an interesting book on this subject and manifestly a sincere seeker after the truth, deals with the subject in his usual gentlemanly manner. However, in saying that Mr. Keating's book "covers most of the facts and is supported by a wealth of detail indicating exhaustive research," it is feared that Mr. Lockhart has not gone very deeply into the matter. For example, after referring to errors in Mr. Keating's previous magazine article (*Chambers*, 12 June 1926) under the pseudonym of Lee Kaye, Mr. Lockhart says: "In the book, the sailing dates are correctly given." Without multiplying instances, the reader is referred to page 203 (American edition) where Author Keating states: "This interesting voyage of the *Dei Gratia* started from New York for Gibraltar via Azores on 12th November 1872"; but even a casual reference to any one of the following six issues of the *Maritime Register* 20, 27 November; 4, 11, 18 and 25 December would have disclosed the fact that her sailing date was 15 November. After adopting, with a slight variation, Mr. Keating's erroneous statement (page 47) that "it seems to be the case that neither the ship nor the cargo was insured," Mr. Lockhart passes to surer ground when he concludes his article by inquiring: "Can it be that Mr. Keating christened his book more appropriately than he intended?"

1931

Quarterly Review. "Light on the Mystery of the *Mary Celeste*" by Harold T. Wilkins.

This well-written article is especially deserving of consideration. Writer errs however in stating that twelve (instead of nine) days elapsed between log-slate entry and the date of vessel's discovery by *Dei Gratia*. The distance covered by the abandoned vessel was nearer 378 than 507 miles (Hydrographic Office, Washington, D. C.). The author is apparently unaware that when found, she had turned about, and was headed westward. He suspects (in our opinion, unwarrantedly) the men of the *Dei Gratia* of foul play, and alleges that Morehouse sailed under an alias. There is abundant evidence to refute this charge. Captain Parsons' reference to "Boyce" as master was, manifestly, a slip of memory after the passing of many years. We find no record of Captain Winchester calling Morehouse by the name of Boyce. There is no evidence to prove Mrs. Priscilla Richardson Shelton's statement, which he quotes, that the vessels lay alongside each other at New York. There is, however, abundant proof that the *Dei Gratia* did not sail before the *Mary Celeste*, as alleged, but eight days later, on 15 November. (See *Maritime Register*, 20, 27 November, 4, 11, 18 & 25 December.) We cannot agree with the implications of Mr. Wilkins's question as to "why the authorities at Gibraltar in 1872-1873 did not set in motion legal machinery in London which would have led to the arrest of the Captain, mate and crew of the British Brig *Dei Gratia*."

1933

Chambers's Journal (March). New Light on the *Marie* [*sic*] *Celeste* Case" by J. L. Hornibrook.

In this article, the vessel is erroneously described as hailing from Boston, and as being "under a full spread of canvas . . . off Gibraltar when sighted," by the *Bark* [*sic*] *Dei Gratia* under Captain "Moorehouse" (à la Keating), "Not a boat was missing," and "breakfast was on the table in the after-cabin . . . Some of the food had already been consumed . . . Three cups of tea were lukewarm . . . The galley range, though raked out, was still hot . . . Lying on the deck was a rusty cutlass." This author, after citing and quite successfully exploding several theories previously advanced, acquits Captain Morehouse and his men of guilt and attributes the disappearance of the vessel's company to Riff Pirates. "That," maintains the writer, "is the true story of the *Marie* [*sic*] *Celeste*." (Government records at Washington with respect to pirate activities do not support such a theory.)

About 1936 (date uncertain)

Shipping Wonders of the World. "Mystery of the *Mary Celeste*" by Lt.-Commander. R. T. Gould, R. N.

This thoughtful, well-written article is marred by the repetition of oft-repeated errors published during the preceding half-century. Had Commander Gould consulted the record of Court proceedings, it would have been discovered that as the *Dei Gratia* was headed eastward, she could hardly be said to be "overhauling" a vessel proceeding toward her. He incorrectly reports both vessels as sailing on the port tack. The *Mary Celeste* was on the starboard tack, the wind being out of the north. The record does not confirm statement that Captain Morehouse boarded the derelict at any time before reaching Gibraltar. According to the testimony, there were no remains of a meal; the captain's watch was not found, nor was there any unfinished letter written by the mate. It would be interesting to ascertain Commander Gould's authority for asserting that the log contained only seven entries, and that it was negligently kept and that one of the "hatchway covers" lay upside down. He disposes of the mutiny theory and shrewdly observes that no one but the Queen's Proctor Flood raised the question about a barrel of alcohol having been "broached."

1936

Canadian Magazine (May). "Question Mark of the Sea" by Burton Robinson.

This writer launches the *Amazon* (later re-named *Mary Celeste*) in 1865 — or four years too late — and asserts that "half-way down the ways, she stuck fast," a statement which lacks confirmation. He states that one boat was missing; that her hatch cover was overturned; that she was not in the most seaworthy condition. (Her sea voyage must have overcome that defect as she was pronounced fit on arrival at Gibraltar.) He asserts that her log was written up to a few days before she was found. The article then follows the course of the "Keating-Pemberton" story and concludes by saying: "No explanation that has ever been given, however, seems quite as satisfying as the statement of John Pemberton and it is obviously untrue."

Boston Globe (26 September 1936). "Why Was the *Marie* [*sic*] *Celeste* Abandoned?"

Here the vessel becomes a "bark," sailing a year late — 7 November 1873 — and is picked up by the *Dei Gratia*, now also a "bark," with the phantom Captain "Boyce" invented by a previous chronicler. The "Fanny — my dear wife" message, which constantly re-appears in the legendary literature, is to be found here also, written this time by the Captain; this, notwithstanding the fact that his wife was named Sarah and was his companion on the voyage. No solution of the mystery is offered.

1937

New York Sun (8 March). By Robert Wilder.

Here, the *Marie* [*sic*] *Celeste* is found on the port instead of the starboard tack. The writer incorrectly reports that she was built at Parrsboro and repeats the Keating invention about her being named *Mary Sellars*. There is no dependable evidence that the two vessels lay at adjacent wharves before departure from New York and none that Captain Morehouse did the unseamanlike thing of leaving his own vessel at any time before reaching Gibraltar. The story is well told and leaves the mystery still unsolved.

Bangor Daily News (2 July). By Henry Buxton.

Reports death of widow of Mate Albert G. Richardson of *Marie* [*sic*] *Celeste*. This writer places thirteen persons on board, and names "Moorhouse" (à la Keating) as master of *Dei Gratia*. Quotes Gilson Willett's description of the Captain's table from which "four persons had risen from a half-eaten meal to leave the cabin forever." We are informed that the meal consisted of oatmeal, coffee, bacon and eggs. (Mate Deveau's Court testimony that there was no food on the cabin table is out of harmony with this description.) Breakfast was also being served in the fo'c'sle, according to the same narrator, but here again Deveau's testimony is quite clear that there was none. The story also errs in giving date of last log entry as 2 December, and saying that "every life-boat was in place." Quotes a friend of Richardson family as saying that the log book had been sent to Mate Richardson's widow, and that part of the cargo was glycerine. Quotes various theories but does not profess to have penetrated the mystery.

New York Times (1 August).

A brief statement, with only a few factual inaccuracies. Quotes some of the interesting theories including that of the octopus, the swimming contest and the "Keating-Pemberton" stories as well as the late F. J. Shepard's theory of explosion in the hold.

Oregonian (8 August). "Yawl Held Clue to Phantom Ship Mystery," by Rollin Palmer.

For the most part a re-print of *Times* article of 1 August.

Bangor Daily News (19 October).

This further article by Henry Buxton, with the exception of a few apparent misquotations, gives a more accurate portrayal of the case than most of its predecessors. Mr. Buxton again erroneously places a crew of thirteen on board, continues to call the *Dei Gratia's* master "Moorhouse" and makes the interesting assertion, which we find it difficult to credit, that the *Mary Celeste's* log book was sent to the widow of First Mate Richardson. This would hardly have accorded with sea-practice. The vessel was built at Spencer's Island (not Shelter Island as stated). Mrs. Briggs before her marriage, was Sarah Elizabeth Cobb, and not as stated.

1938

Reader's Digest (September). Excerpt from *The Log of Bob Bartlett* (Putnam).

This brief article repeats the legend about "four half-eaten breakfasts on the table," and that "a life-boat hung on its davits." This statement however possesses the unique distinction of attributing to the little brigantine a far greater capacity than that acknowledged by previous chroniclers. It states that, "there was not a clue that might lead to the solution of the riddle of where those *two score* people had gone," an increase of 300% over the number of persons actually on board.

1939

Log of the Sea (28 January). "The *Marie* [*sic*] *Celeste*" by Felix Riesenberg.

This account erroneously reports the vessel as leaving a Brooklyn pier, and follows Conan Doyle's misspelling of her name. Captain Briggs was not forty-five, but thirty-seven, and his wife was thirty instead of thirty-two. The crew list makes no mention of a boy to which this article refers. The *Dei Gratia* was not a bark, her captain was not Boyce, and she was nearer 600 than 300 miles west of Gibraltar when she found the *Mary Celeste*. The latter did not have "all sails set," and it was Mate Deveau — not Devon — who first boarded her. There was no "food in galley-pots cooked to a crisp," and it was not the main hatch that was off, but the fore-hatch, and it was not reported upside down in the Court testimony. Quotes the late Captain Marcus H. Tracy as favoring the theory of explosion. Moreover (according to Court testimony) the ship's one boat did not hang "on the stern davits."

Marine Journal (date of issue ?). "New Light on an Old Sea Mystery" by Marjorie Dent Candee.

This well-written article errs in respect of a few factual matters. The *Mary Celeste*, when found, was about 600 miles west of Gibraltar and was not headed eastward, as she should have been, but westward. The Court testimony does not confirm the statement that "the remnants of a meal were found," nor that there was a "blood-stained axe." The derelict was not towed to Gibraltar. After mentioning and successfully refuting several theories, the writer introduces the theory of "yellow fever" propounded by Captain Robert Huntington, principal of the Merchant Marine School at the Seamen's Church Institute of New York. The writer in controverting the theory of Captain R. W. Shufeldt, U. S. N. that the vessel was abandoned during "a gale" asserts that "there was no sign of a storm — no injury to ship's rigging." This however, does not accord with testimony given at Gibraltar.

1940

Yachting (February). "The Mystery of the *Mary Celeste*" by Dr. Oliver W. Cobb.

This excellent article by Dr. Cobb, dean of *Mary Celeste's* chroniclers, bears the imprint of authority, especially as to the facts regarding the family of Captain and Mrs. Briggs to both of whom he was related, and whom he personally knew. Notwithstanding Author Keating's assertions that Mrs. Briggs, before her marriage, was "Mary Sellars," we prefer Dr. Cobb's statement and the evidence of the town records of Marion. Dr. Cobb also makes it clear that Sophia Briggs, aged two, accompanied her parents on the voyage, despite Author Keating's positive statement that "there was no child aboard." Dr. Cobb believes that an explosion occurred, that all hands took to the ship's only boat, and that as a precautionary measure, Captain Briggs used the main peak halyard as a tow-line. When the sails filled, the rope parted and the ten persons in the boat were unable to overtake the *Mary Celeste* and probably perished soon thereafter. Dr. Cobb discovered (but too late for correction) that a few errors had crept into his manuscript. The middle name of Sarah Cobb was "Elizabeth" and Glace Bay is in Cape Breton Island. The sword found on board was listed in Consul Sprague's inventory of Captain Briggs's effects which were sent to his relatives. What is believed to be the identical sword is now in the possession of his nephew, J. Franklin Briggs of New Bedford. Captain Briggs owned a one-third interest in the vessel.

New York Herald Tribune (8 February). "The Truth About an Old Friend."

It will suffice to quote from the concluding paragraph of this excellent editorial, which reviews Dr. Cobb's recent article in *Yachting*: "More mysterious than the mystery of the ship herself, is the enduring hold which ier abandoned and drifting form has established over the romantic imagination of three generations. Dr. Cobb's theory carries conviction and may suffice to bring her long voyage through the Sunday supplements to an end. But somehow, one doubts it. The *Mary Celeste*, like the *Flying Dutchman*, seems forever proof against mere verisimilitude."

National Geographic Magazine (May). "Salty Nova Scotia" by Andrew H. Brown.

This contains a brief reference to the *Mary Celeste*: correctly locates her place of construction at Spencer's Island and her course when found as westerly. It errs, however, in reporting that "ashes in the galley stove were still warm," a statement which contradicts the testimony given at Gibraltar.

Maritime Register (17 July).

This brief account rightly states the place of construction as Spencer's Island, whereas most of the previous chronicles mention Parrsboro which was the place of registry. It errs, however, in stating the number of persons on board as thirteen and in asserting that "meals had been left half eaten." Moreover, when found, only three of her sails were set, and not a little of her running rigging was out of order.

"The Progressive Salesman" (October). Reprinted from *Everybody's Digest*.

A clear, well-written account conforming closely to known facts. It errs, however, in describing the vessel as "under full sail" when found and incorrectly states the distance the vessel had travelled between the time of the last log-slate entry (25 November) and the date when she was found (4 December P.M.) which, according to the Hydrographic Office, Washington, was about 378 miles.

APPENDIX B

Calendar of Significant Events Chronologically Arranged

1860

Keel of *Amazon* laid at Spencer's Island, Nova Scotia.

1861

May. *Amazon* launched at Spencer's Island.

10 June. Registered at Parrsboro, Nova Scotia.

19 June. Robert McLellan, first master, dies at Spencer's Island.

November. Vessel at Marseille, France.

1867

November. Ashore at Cow (Glace) Bay.

1868

31 December. First Register in name of *Mary Celeste* issued by United States Government to Richard W. Haines.

1872

11 January. *Mary Celeste,* Fowler, master, Jamaica for New York, spoken lat. 30° 59', long. 79° 48'.

16 March. *Mary Celeste,* J. W. Spates, master, arrived St. Thomas, Virgin Islands, from Martinique.

31 March. *Mary Celeste* at St. Thomas.

5 April. *Mary Celeste,* J. W. Spates, master, sailed from St. Thomas for Porto Rico in ballast.

18 July. *Mary Celeste* Crew List issued at Boston.

5 September. *Mary Celeste* arrived at New York from Cow Bay, Cape Breton.

3 October. Date of receipt for $1500 from J. H. Winchester and Co. (found in Captain Briggs' desk).

16 October. Date of receipt for $500 from J. H. Winchester and Co. (found in Captain Briggs' desk).

22 October. Date of receipt for $1600 from J. H. Winchester and Co. (found in Captain Briggs' desk).

27 October. His wife, daughter Sophia, age two, arrive New York and go on board *Mary Celeste.* Mrs. Briggs writes letter to son Arthur.

29 October. Register No. 122 shows purchase of eight twenty-fourths interest in *Mary Celeste* by Benjamin S. Briggs.

30 October. *Mary Celeste* reported at Pier 50 East River. *Dei Gratia* reported at Erie Basin.

2 November, Saturday (P.M.). *Mary Celeste* completes loading.

3 November, Sunday. Captain Briggs writes to his mother.

4 November, Monday. Signs crew list and articles of agreement.

5 November, Tuesday (A.M.). Vessel leaves East River Pier, anchors off Staten Island.

6 November, Wednesday. *Dei Gratia* at Venango Yard.

7 November, Thursday. Mrs. Briggs writes from *Mary Celeste* off Staten Island. Vessel weighs anchor and proceeds on voyage.

13 November. *Dei Gratia* loaded with a cargo of 81,126 gallons of refined petroleum.

15 November. Brigantine *Dei Gratia* (Br.), Morehouse, sails from New York.

19 November. *Dei Gratia* spoken lat. 40° 55′ N: long. 66° 00′ W.

24 November (noon). Last entry on *Mary Celeste's* log.

25 November (8:00 A.M.). Last entry on log slate.

4 December (1:30-2:00 P.M.). *Mary Celeste,* headed westward, first observed by *Dei Gratia* on her port or windward bow (lat. 38° 20′ N, long. 17° 15′ W).

4 December. First Mate Deveau, Second Mate Wright, Seaman Johnson row over to *Mary Celeste*. Deveau and Wright go aboard. (5 December sea-time).

4 December (about 4 P.M.). Deveau, Seamen Anderson and Lund sent by Captain Morehouse to sail derelict to Gibraltar (5 December sea-time).

4 December (8-9 P.M.). Vessel pumped out and got under way.

12 December (Evening). *Dei Gratia* arrives at Gibraltar.

13 December (Early A.M.). *Mary Celeste* arrives at Gibraltar.

13 December. *Mary Celeste* arrested by Marshal of Vice-Admiralty Court.

13 December. Consul Sprague cables Board of Underwriters, New York.

14 December. Cable message received in New York from Captain Morehouse at Gibraltar reporting finding of *Mary Celeste* abandoned and brought into that port.

14 December. Cable message from insurance companies to United States Consul Sprague, Gibraltar.

18 December. First session of Vice-Admiralty Court to hear salvage claim of *Dei Gratia*. Deveau testifies.

20 December. Vice-Admiralty Court orders survey of *Mary Celeste*.

20 December.   Deveau concludes testimony. Wright and Lund testify.

21 December.   Seamen Anderson and Johnson testify.

23 December.   Vessel surveyed.

23 December.   *Dei Gratia* sails for Genoa with Deveau in command.

28 December.   Further survey of vessel.

1873

7 January.   Further survey of vessel.

15 January.   Captain J. H. Winchester arrives at Gibraltar.

16 January.   *Dei Gratia* arrives at Genoa.

22, 23 January.   Queen's Proctor informs London Board of Trade of incident.

30 January.   Date of report of analysis of supposed blood-stains.

February.   Captain Winchester leaves Gibraltar. Meets Captain Appleby at Cadiz.

5 February.   Captain R. W. Shufeldt, U. S. N. in command of U. S. S. *Plymouth* arrives. Surveys *Mary Celeste* 6 February.

6 February.   Winchester writes from Lisbon to Consul Sprague.

25 February.   *Mary Celeste* restored to her original owners.

26 February.   Captain J. H. Winchester arrives at New York by steamship *Caledonia.*

4 March.   Deveau recalled to testify.

6 March.   Receipt for chests, bags, etc., of missing seamen signed by new master, Captain G. W. Blatchford.

10 March.   *Mary Celeste* clears for Genoa with original cargo under Captain Blatchford.

10 March.   Captain J. H. Winchester writes from New York to Consul Sprague at Gibraltar.

14 March.   Salvage award £1700 to *Dei Gratia.*

17 March.   *Dei Gratia,* Deveau, master, sails from Genoa for Messina.

21 March.   *Mary Celeste* arrives at Genoa.

29 March.   *Dei Gratia,* Deveau, master, arrives at Messina. Painting of vessel made here.

13 May.   *Dei Gratia* arrives at Gibraltar.

19 June.   *Dei Gratia* arrives at New York.

26 June.   *Mary Celeste,* Blatchford, master, sails from Genoa for Boston.

1 September.   *Mary Celeste* arrives at Boston.

13 September.   Sails for New York.

19 September.   Arrives at New York.

19 November.   Consul Sprague notifies Department of State effects of Captain and Mrs. Briggs forwarded to United States.

11 December.   Collector of Customs, New York, reports receiving effects of Captain and Mrs. Briggs.

1885

3 January.   *Mary Celeste* wrecked on reef of the Rochelais, near Miragoane, Haiti, seven on board, all saved.

APPENDIX C

Common Errors and Misconceptions

1. *Name of Vessel*

Since the anonymous publication in 1884, of "J. Habakuk Jephson's Statement" by Conan Doyle, the name of the vessel has been repeatedly stated as *Marie Celeste*.

Correction: The correct name of the vessel was Mary Celeste.

Authorities: Records of the American Bureau of Shipping, New York. All registers issued by the United States Government from the time when the vessel came under the American flag, 31 December 1868 (register No. 485) up to the final register (No. 28) issued 4 August 1884, give, in every instance, the name of the vessel as *Mary Celeste* stating, in every instance, that previously she was the "British Bg. *Amazon*." Records of the Atlantic Mutual Insurance Company, and correspondence (1872 to 1885) between Consul Sprague and Department of State, Washington, D. C.

2. *Ship's Boat*

Erroneously reported as found on board.

Correction: It has been authoritatively established that no boat was found on board.

Authorities: Testimony before Vice-Admiralty Court, Gibraltar, 1872. Consul Sprague's letter (No. 123) 13 December 1872 to Department of State; Atlantic Mutual Insurance Company, Disaster Book No. 93, page 192, 14 December 1872. Sprague's Cable 13 December 1872 to Board of Underwriters, New York, as recorded in Atlantic Mutual Insurance Company, Disaster Book No. 94, page 178.

3. *Food on Cabin Table*

Erroneously reported that the salvors found hot food, and cups of tea or coffee still warm on cabin table.

Correction: There was nothing to eat or drink on the cabin table and no evidence of preparations being made for eating. The rack was on the table.

Authority: Testimony before Vice-Admiralty Court, Gibraltar, 1872.

4. *Galley Stove*

Erroneously reported that the stove was warm and that there was cooked food on it.

Correction: There was no cooked food on the galley stove, or elsewhere in the galley. The galley stove was knocked out of place. Pots and kettles were all washed up. The water in the galley was a foot or two deep.

Authority: Testimony before Vice-Admiralty Court, Gibraltar, 1872.

5. *Sails*

Erroneously reported that, when found, all sails were set.

Correction: The only sails set were the lower topsail, jib and fore-topmast staysail. The fore-sail and upper topsail were gone — apparently blown away. The main staysail was lying loose on top of the forward-house. All other sails were furled.

Authority: Testimony before Vice-Admiralty Court, Gibraltar, 1872.

6. *Date when Found*

Erroneously reported found on 5 December.

Correction: The vessel was found on 4 December between 1:00 and 2:00 P.M. Inasmuch as in those days the date, at sea, changed daily at the noon hour, the entry on the Dei Gratia's *log was therefore dated 5 December, sea-time, which fact has caused some confusion as to the exact date.*

Authority: Cable received by the Atlantic Mutual Insurance Company, 14 December 1872, Disaster Book No. 93, page 92. Testimony before Vice-Admiralty Court at Gibraltar, 1872. Letter from Consul Sprague (No. 123) on 13 December 1872 to Department of State.

7. *Rig of Vessel*

Erroneously reported as brig.

Correction: The Mary Celeste *was a half-brig. Vessels of this type were also called hermaphrodite brigs and brigantines.*[1] *For the sake of convenience, all such vessels, have customarily been grouped with brigs in the Port List of the New York Maritime Register under the caption of "Brigs." For the same reason, barkentines were grouped with barks under the single caption "Barks."*

Authority: Records of American Bureau of Shipping, New York, and the Atlantic Mutual Insurance Company.

8. *Method of bringing Derelict into Gibraltar*

Erroneously reported as "towed" by the *Dei Gratia*.

Correction: The Mary Celeste *was sailed all the way from the place where she was picked up latitude 38° 20′ N, longitude 17° 15′ W to Gibraltar by Mate Deveau and Seamen Lund and Anderson.*

Authorities: Testimony before Vice-Admiralty Court, Gibraltar, 1872. Correspondence between Consul Sprague and Department of State.

9. *"Mary Sellars"*

Erroneously reported as one of the names previously borne by the *Mary Celeste*. This name appears to have first been mentioned by "Lee Kaye" (the pseudonym used by Laurence J. Keating) in article published by *Chambers's Journal* in 1926.[2]

Correction: It seems clear from available records that the vessel bore only two names — Amazon and Mary Celeste — during her entire career.

1. See explanatory note, Chapter VII, page 55.
2. See Appendix A.

Authorities: Records of American Bureau of Shipping, *Maritime Register,* and Atlantic Mutual Insurance Company.

10. *Character of Cargo*

Erroneously reported that the vessel's cargo consisted principally of sperm oil and spirit.

Correction: The cargo consisted of 1,700 barrels alcohol shipped by Meissner, Ackerman & Co. of New York and insured in Europe.

Authorities: Records of the Atlantic Mutual Insurance Company Disaster Book No. 193, page 192. Consul Sprague's letter (No. 123) 13 December 1872 and No. 134, 25 February 1873 to Department of State. Letter of Frederick Solly Flood, Advocate-General, to British Board of Trade, published in *Shipping Gazette* (London), 5 February 1873 and *Gibraltar Guardian,* 14 February 1873. Statement,[3] 3 March 1885, published by Martin W. Stokes, Proctor for claimants of cargo and George F. Cornwell, Proctor for Claimants of vessel, accompanying Sprague's letter No. 488, dated 4 March 1885 to Department of State.

11. *Names of Crew*

The names of Pemberton, Dossell, Hullock and Venholdt constitute part of the ghostly crew invented by Laurence J. Keating, author of *The Great Mary Celeste Hoax.*

Correction: These names are not found in any of the official records. The correct names are as follows: Albert G. Richardson, first mate; Andrew Gilling, second mate; Ed. William Head, steward and cook; Volkert Lorenzen (also spelled "Lorensen" in the same record), Arian Martens[4] (also called Adrian Martens, Arian Mardens and Andrew Marten in the same record); Boz Lorenzen (also spelled "Lorensen" in the same record), Gottlieb Goodschaal (also spelled Goudschaad in the same records).

Authorities: "Engagement Book" in United States Shipping Commissioner's Office, New York City, and "List of Persons Composing the Crew" in The National Archives, Washington, D. C.

12. *Place of Construction and Name of Builder*

Erroneously reported as having been built at Parrsboro in the shipyard of "Henry Matthew Colfax"—a name apparently invented.

Correction: The vessel was built at Spencer's Island about twenty-five miles south of Parrsboro, in the shipyard of Joshua Dewis, shipwright and boss-builder. The vessel was first named Amazon.

Authorities: Correspondence on file from R. Lester Dewis and Captain William M. Collins, present residents of West Advocate, Nova Scotia. Let-

3. See pp. 154-156.

4. A translation of a letter from Kunot Martens, father of Arian Martens, to the German Consul at Gibraltar and sent by him to Consul Sprague who transmitted it to the Department of State, indicates the correct name of this seaman.

ter of 13 May 1941[5] from Rev. C. R. Harris, Rector, St. George's Church, Parrsboro, Nova Scotia. Dr. Clara Dennis, author of *More About Nova Scotia.* Professor H. E. Bigelow, Mount Allison University, Sackville, New Brunswick.

13. *Name of Master of* Dei Gratia

Erroneously reported as "Boyce."
Correction: The name of the master was David Reed Morehouse.
Authority: New York *Maritime Registers* (23, 30 October; 6, 13, 20, 27 November; 4, 11, 18, 25 December and others—1872 to 1873). Atlantic Mutual Insurance Company Disaster Book No. 93, page 192, showing cable received from Morehouse. Testimony before Vice-Admiralty Court, Gibraltar, including Justice Cochrane's comment about Morehouse remaining at Gibraltar and Deveau departing.

14. *Locations of* Mary Celeste *and* Dei Gratia

Erroneously reported that they were anchored alongside each other at New York before departure in November 1872.
Correction: Available evidence from Maritime Register *records indicate vessels' positions as follows: Issue of 23 October 1872, Port List—Mary Celeste at Hunter's Point;* Dei Gratia *at Erie Basin. Issue of 30 October 1872, Port List—Mary Celeste at Pier 50, East River;* Dei Gratia *at Erie Basin. Issue of 6 November 1872, Port List does not mention* Mary Celeste, *but under the caption "Weekly Compendium," she is reported as having sailed 4 November for Genoa. The Port List of this issue reports* Dei Gratia *at Venango Yard, believed to be part of the premises of the Venango Oil Works on the Weehawken river front, where there were various slips of different depth for vessels to load.*

15. *Latitude and Longitude*

There have been many erroneous reports of latitude and longitude. Last entry on log of the *Mary Celeste* was dated 24 November and indicates lat. 36° 56′ N, long. 27° 20′ W. Last entry on vessel's log slate was dated 8 A.M., 25 November, reading "eastern point of St. Mary's bore 6 miles SSW." The correct latitude and longitude of this position, although not given in the testimony would appear to be 37° 01′ N, and 25° 01′ W, respectively. The position where the *Dei Gratia* found the *Mary Celeste* was latitude 38° 20′ N, longitude 17° 15′ W.

16. *The Testimony given before the Vice-Admiralty Court at Gibraltar,* 1872-1873, *affords no Evidence*

That the fore-hatch was found upside down, or that a cat was found on board. It is however known that, after the arrival of Mrs. Briggs and her child, there was a cat on board. It is not known whether or not it left the ship before sailing.

5. To the author.

APPENDIX D

First Register issued to Brigantine *Amazon* by the
Government of Nova Scotia, 10 June 1861

[*See reproductions on following two pages.*]

OFFICIAL NUMBER OF SHIP 37671

| Port Number... Five | Port of Registry ... Parrsboro | British or Foreign built } ... British |

| Number of Decks - One |
| Number of Masts - Two |
| Rigged - Brigantine |
| Stern - Square |

| Build - - - - Carvel |
| Galleries - - - none |
| Head - - - none |
| Framework - - - Wood |

Tonnage.

	No. of Tons
Tonnage under Tonnage Deck	
Closed-in Spaces above the Tonnage Deck, if any, viz.:	177 . 34
Space or Spaces between Decks	
Houses forward and aft 29.94 less to of tonnage	21 . 08
Under Deck - 8.36 excess added	
Other enclosed Spaces (if any), naming them	198 . 42
Gross Tonnage, being Register Tonnage, if a Sailing Ship -	
If a Steamer, Deduct Allowance for propelling Power, as per other side	
Register Tonnage, if a Steamer	

Names, Residence, and Description of the Owners, and Number of Sixty-fourth Shares held by each Owner

George Reed of Parrsboro in the Province of Nova Scotia Farmer
Josiah Spicer of Parrsboro in the Province of Nova Scotia Shipwright
Jacob Spicer of Parrsboro in the Province of Nova Scotia Farmer
Morton McKellan York of Economy in the Province of Nova Scotia Mariner
William Morrison ...
William Huyes Bigelow of Parrsboro ... in the Province of Nova Scotia Merchants and
Lewis ...
William Hores Barnard of Cornwallis

Dated at Parrsboro 10th June 1861.

Col. 1.	Col. 2.	Col. 3.	Col. 4.	Col. 5.	Col. 6.	Col. 7.
Number of Transaction.	Letter denoting Mortgages, and Certificates of Mortgages.	Name of Person from whom Title is derived.	Number of Shares affected.	Date of Registry	Nature and Date of Transaction.	Name, Residence, and Occupation of Transferee, Mortgagee, or other Person acquiring Title or Power.
1		Robert McLellan	4	Sepr 11 June 1864. 10 A.M. on the 19th day of June 1861.	dies at Spencers Island in the County of Cumberland Intestate, Letters of Administration of this Estate Granted by the Probate Court of County of Colchester on 29th October 1862 to Mary Ann McLellan Widow of deceased.	Mary Ann McLellan Widow and Hannah ... Parish Lest of Canning ... County ... McKerystonof Parrsboro County of Nova Scotia
2	—	Mary Ann McLellan	4	Sepr 12. 1864 10 A.M.	Bill of Sale dated 13th September 1863	W. H. Spicer and Daniel Cox of Canning and William Bigelow of Parrsboro N Scotia

NAME OF SHIP *Amazon* *Lady*

| Whether a Sailing or Steam Ship; if Steam, how propelled | *by Sails* | Where built... *Parrsboro: in the Province of Nova Scotia* | When built... *in the Year* 1860 |

Measurements
Length from the foreport of the Stem under the Bowsprit to the aft side of the Head of the Stern-post *99* Feet *3* Tenths.
Main Breadth to outside of Plank *25* Feet *5* Tenths.
Depth in Hold from Tonnage Deck to Ceiling at Midships *11* Feet *7* Tenths.

Additional Particulars for Steamers.

Tons.

Deduction for Space required for Propelling Power (as measured).

Length of Engine Room (if measured). Feet Tenths.

Number of Engines

Combined Power (estimated Horse Power)

Joint owners

(Signed) *T. Ratchford* Registrar.

Col. 8. Number and Amount of subsequent Transaction, showing how Interest disposed of.	Col. 9. Number of Shares in which Title is separated	Col. 10. Names of Owners	Col. 11. Mortgages and Certificate of Mortgages	Col. 12. Names of Mortgagees or Attorneys under Certificate of Mortgage.	Col. 13. Number of Shares	Col. 14. REMARKS.
	1	Mary Ann McLellan George Reed Joshua Dewis Isaac Spicer Jacob Spicer William Thompson Willm H. Bigelow {Daniel Cox Willm H. Payzant} *Joint owners* Total 11th Jany. 1864.			4 8 16 8 8 8 12 64	Return Made & forward 27 August 1861 Return Made & forwd 5th August 1864
2		George Reed Joshua Dewis Isaac Spicer Jacob Spicer William Thompson Willm H. Bigelow {Daniel Cox Wm H. Payzant} *Joint Owners* Total 12 Jany. 1864			8 16 8 8 8 8 16 104	Return Made & forward 5 August 1864

The above named Ship was wreck at Big Glace Bay C.B. and Registered at the Port of Sydney on 9th November 1867. Old Certificate Cancelled, and returned to this office. Registry Closed 18th Novr. 1867. See letter from D.B. Leonard, dated Sydney 11 Novr. 1867.

Certificate Sent to London 6 Dec. 1867
1867

APPENDIX E

Last Register issued to Brigantine *Amazon* by the Government of Nova Scotia, 9 November 1867

[*See reproductions on following two pages.*]

OFFICIAL NUMBER OF SHIP _37671_

Port Number ... _eight_   Port of Registry.. _Sydney, C.B._ .   British or Foreign built } .... _British_

Number of Decks - - _one_
Number of Masts - - _two_
Rigged - - _brigantine_
Stern - - _square_

Build - - - - _carvel_
Galleries - - - - _none_
Head - - - - _none_
Framework - - - - _wood_

Tonnage.

Tonnage under Tonnage Deck - - - - - - - - - -   177 . 34

Closed-in Spaces above the Tonnage Deck, if any, viz.:
Space or Spaces between Decks
~~Poop~~ Houses _forward and aft_ - _29: 94 less to of tonnage_
~~Round-house~~ _under deck_   _21: 08 - Even added_
Other enclosed Spaces (if any), naming them -   }   21 : 08

Gross Tonnage, being Register Tonnage, if a Sailing Ship - -
If a Steamer, Deduct Allowance for propelling Power, as per other side -   198 : 42
Register Tonnage, if a Steamer - - - - -

Names, Residence, and Description of the Owners, and Number of Sixty-fourth Shares held by each Owner } _Alexander Mac Bean, of Big Glace Bay, in the Island of Cape Breton, Gentleman_ { _Sixty four 64 Shares_

Dated _9th November 1867_   _Registered by order of the_

Col. 1.	Col. 2.	Col. 3.	Col. 4.	Col. 5.	Col. 6.	Col. 7.
Number of Transaction.	Letter denoting Mortgages, and Certificates of Mortgages.	Name of Person from whom Title is derived.	Number of Shares affected.	Date of Registry.	Nature and Date of Transaction.	Name, Residence, and Occupation of Transferee, Mortgagee, or other Person acquiring Title or Power.
1		_Alexr. Mc Bean_	64	_9 Novr 1867 at 12¾ A.M._	_Bill of Sale dated 9th Novr 1867_	_John Howard Beatty at present of Big Glace Bay aforesaid, formerly of Newton, Westmorland County, New Brunswick, Gentleman_

NAME OF SHIP _Amazon_

Whether a Sailing or Steam Ship ; if Steam, how propelled	_Sailing._	Where built.. _Pershore, in the Province of Nova Scotia_		When built... _in the year_ 18_67_

Measurements
{ Length from the forepart of the Stem under the Bowsprit to the aft side of the Head of the Stern-post _ninety seven_ Feet — _three_ — Tenths.
Main Breadth to outside of Plank _twenty five_ Feet — _five_ — Tenths.
Depth in Hold from Tonnage Deck to Ceiling at Midships _eleven_ Feet _eleven_ Tenths.

Additional Particulars for Steamers.

	Tons.
Deduction for Space required for Propelling Power (as measured)	
Length of Engine Room (if measured), Feet Tenths.	
Number of Engines	
Combined Power (estimated Horse Power)	

Lieutenant Governor of Nova Scotia (Signed) _H. W. Hardy_ Registrar.

Col. 8.	Col. 9.	Col. 10.	Col. 11.	Col. 12.	Col. 13.	Col. 14.
Number and Account of subsequent Transaction, showing how Interest disposed of.	Number of Transaction under which Title acquired.	Names of Owners.	Mortgages and Certificates of Mortgages.	Names of Mortgagees or Attornies under Certificates of Mortgage.	Number of Shares.	REMARKS.
						Copy of Register sent to C.R. 30 March /68
						Copy of Transaction sent 30 March /68

APPENDIX F

First Register, No. 485, issued to *Mary Celeste* by the
United States Government, 31 December 1868

[*See reproduction on following page.*]

In Pursuance of an Act of the Congress of the United States of America, entitled "An Act concerning the registering and recording of Ships or Vessels," approved December 31, 1792, and of "An Act to regulate the admeasurement of Tonnage of Ships and Vessels of the United States." approved May 6, 1864.

Richard W Haven of the City County & State of New York

having taken or subscribed the *Oath* required by the said Act, and having *Sworn* that

He is the

485

only owner of the Ship or Vessel called the *Mary C Haven* of *New York* whereof

is at present Master, and a citizen of the United States,

and that the said Ship or Vessel was *formerly the Bt. Brig Amazon & Rigrin &c in Pursuance of the Act of Congress of 23 Dec 1852*

And *Ly Surveyor* of this Port having certified that the said Ship or Vessel has *one* Deck and *two* Masts, and that

	FEET.	TENTHS		TONS.	TENTHS.
her length is	98	3	Under Tonnage deck	177	02
her breadth	23		Between decks above ditto		
her depth	11	6	Enclosures on upper deck	28	84
her height					

and that she measures *Two Hundred & six* $^{2}/_{100}$ Tons ; that she is *a Brig* has *a square stern* and *a Billet* head. And the said *Richard W Haven*

having agreed to the description and admeasurement above specified, and sufficient security having been given, according to the said Acts, the said *Brig* has been duly registered at the Port of *New York*

Given under *our* hands, and seals at the Port of *New York*, this *31* day of *Dec* , in the year one thousand eight hundred and sixty *eight*

APPENDIX G

Register, No. 122, issued to *Mary Celeste*, 29 October 1872

No. 122

IN PURSUANCE of an Act of the Congress of the United States of America, entitled "An Act concerning the Registering or Recording of Ships or Vessels," approved December 31, 1792, and of "An Act to regulate the admeasurement of Tonnage of Ships and Vessels of the United States," approved May 6 1864.

JAMES H. WINCHESTER of New York State of New York having taken or subscribed the Oath, required by the said Act, and having sworn that He 12/24 SYLVESTER GOODWIN 2/24 DANIEL T SAMSON 2/24 & BENJAMIN S BRIGGS 8/24 of Marion State of Maine [*sic*] are the

(ss.)

only owner of the Ship or Vessel, called the MARY CELESTE of NEW YORK whereof BENJAMIN S. BRIGGS is at present Master, and a CITIZEN of the UNITED STATES: and that the said Ship or Vessel was formerly the Br Brig Amazon Registered in pursuance of act of Congress Dec 23rd 1852 as per Register No. 16 issued at this Port 11 January 1870 now cancelled Property changed in part vessel Readmeasured

REGISTER

(ss.)

and J. LAX BENEDICT Deputy Surveyor of this Port having certified that the said Ship or Vessel has Two Decks and Two Masts, and that her length is One hundred three feet, her breadth Twenty five seven-tenth feet, her depth Sixteen two-tenth feet, her height [   ] one-tenth feet, and that she measures Two hundred eighty two Tons, Twenty eight hundredths, viz.:

DEPUTY COLLECTOR

	Tons	100ths
Capacity under tonnage deck,	271	79
Head Room	3	69
Deck House	6	80
Total tonnage,	282	28

(ss.)

that she is a Brig has a Square Stern and a Billet head: and the said JAMES H. WINCHESTER having agreed to the description and admeasurement above specified, and sufficient security having been given according to the said Act, the said Brig has been duly registered at the Port of New York.

DEP'Y NAVAL OFFICER

GIVEN under our Hands and Seals, at the Port of New York, this 29 day of October in the year one thousand eight hundred and Seventy-two 1872

APPENDIX H

Digest of Certificates of Registry and Enrollment issued by U. S. Government to *Mar*

No. of Register	Date of Issue	Issued at	Owners	Address of Owners	Number of Shares	Hailing Port
485	31 December 1868	New York	Richard W. Haines	New York	Only owner	New Yo
486	31 December 1868	New York	Richard W. Haines	New York	7/8	New Yo
			Sylvester Goodwin	New York	1/8	
339	31 October 1869	New York	James H. Winchester	New York	6/8	New Yo
			Sylvester Goodwin	New York	1/8	
			Daniel T. Samson	New York	1/8	
16	11 January 1870	New York	James H. Winchester	New York	4/8	New Yo
			Sylvester Goodman (*sic*)	New York	1/8	
			Daniel T. Samson	New York	1/8	
			Rufus W. Fowler	Searsport, Me.	2/8	
122	29 October 1872	New York	James H. Winchester	New York	12/24	New Yo
			Sylvester Goodwin	New York	2/24	
			Daniel T. Samson	New York	2/24	
			Benjamin S. Briggs	Marion, State of Maine[1]	8/24	
108	10 October 1873	New York	James H. Winchester	Brooklyn, N. Y.	16/24	New Yo
			Simpson Hart	New Bedford, Mass.	8/24	
109	10 October 1873	New York	James H. Winchester	Brooklyn, N. Y.	3/4	New Yo
			John Q. Pratt	West Hanover, County of Plymouth, Mass.	1/4	
326	3 February 1874	New York	James H. Winchester	Brooklyn, N.Y.	Only owner	New Yo
327	3 February 1874	New York	Frederick H. Harrison	Brooklyn, N.Y. } Co-partners	4/8	New Yo
			David O. Cartwright	Brooklyn, N.Y. }		
			John Bukbeck	Brooklyn, N.Y.	1/8	
			Edward Crabb	Great Neck, N. Y.	1/8	
			John B. Wilson	Philadelphia	2/8	
278	2 June 1876	Boston	(Same ownership as No. 327)	(As above)	(As above)	New Yo
107	16 December 1876	Boston	Frederick H. Harrison	Brooklyn, N.Y. } Co-partners		New Yo
			David G. Cartwright	Brooklyn, N.Y. }		
			John Burbeck (Birkbeck)	Brooklyn, N.Y.	(As above)	
			Edward Crabb	Great Neck, N. Y.		
			John B. Wilson	Philadelphia		
95	11 September 1877	New York	(Same ownership as No. 107)	(As above)	(As above)	New Yo
305	25 February 1880	New York	Wesley A. Gove	East Boston	Only owner	Boston

[1] Error. Should read "Massachusetts."

Name of Master	Former Name	Decks	Masts	Length	Breadth	Depth	Capacity under Tonnage Deck	Enclosures on Upper Deck	Head Room	Deck House	Total Tonnage
ot stated)	Br. Bg. *Amazon*	1	2	98 5/10	25	11 6/10	177.42	28.86			206.28
chard W. Haines	Br. Bg. *Amazon*	1	2	98 5/10	25	11 6/10	177.42	28.86			206.28
alter S. Johnson	Br. Bg. *Amazon*	1	2	98 5/10	25	11 6/10	177.43	28.86			206.29
fus W. Fowler	Br. Bg. *Amazon*	1	2	98 5/10	25	11 6/10	177.43	28.86			206.29
njamin S. Briggs	Br. Bg. *Amazon*	2	2	103	25 7/10	16 2/10	271.79		3.69	6.80	282.28
ot stated)	Br. Bg. *Amazon*	2	2	103	25 7/10	16 2/10	271.79		3.69	6.80	282.28
an Q. Pratt	Br. Bg. *Amazon*	2	2	103	25 7/10	16 2/10	271.29 (*sic*)		3.69	6.80	282.28 (*sic*)
ot stated)	Br. Bg. *Amazon*	2	2	103	25 7/10	16 2/10	271.29 (*sic*)		3.69	6.80	282.28 (*sic*)
M. Tuthill	Br. Bg. *Amazon*	2	2	103	25 7/10	16 2/10	271.29 (*sic*)		3.69	6.80	282.28 (*sic*)
gar M. Tuthill	Br. Bg. *Amazon*	2	2	103	25 7/10	16 2/10	271.29 (*sic*)		3.69	6.80	282.28 (*sic*)
gar M. Tuthill	Br. Bg. *Amazon*	2	2	103	25 7/10	16 2/10	271.79		3.69	6.80	282.28
gar M. Tuthill	Br. Bg. *Amazon*	2	2	103	25 7/10	16 2/10	271.79		3.69	6.80	282.28
os. L. Fleming	Br. Bg. *Amazon*	2	2	103	25 7/10	16 2/10	271.79		3.69	6.80	282.28

No. of Register	Date of Issue	Issued at	Owners	Address of Owners	Number of Shares	Hailing Port
334	8 March 1880	New York	Wesley A. Gove	East Boston	Sole owner	Boston
218	27 April 1880	Boston	Wesley A. Gove	Boston	Only owner	Boston
28	10 August 1880	Boston	Wesley A. Gove	Boston	6/16	Boston
			Andrew M. Martin	Boston	2/16	
			Charles A. Grant	Boston	3/16	
			John S. Weeks	Boston	3/16	
			Sidney F. Whitehouse	Boston	2/16	
44	8 December 1882	Providence	Wesley A. Gove	Boston	6/16	Boston
			Andrew M. Martin	Boston	2/16	
			Charles A. Grant	Boston	3/16	
			John S. Weeks	Boston	3/16	
			Sidney F. Whitehouse	Boston	2/16	
201	28 December 1882	New York	Wesley Gove	Boston	6/16	Boston
			Andrew M. Martin	Boston	2/16	
			Charles A. Grant	Boston	3/16	
			John S. Weeks	Boston	3/16	
			Sidney F. Whitehouse	Boston	2/16	
273	1 May 1883	New York	Wesley Gove	Boston	6/16	Boston
			Andrew M. Martin	Boston	2/16	
			Charles A. Grant	Boston	3/16	
			John S. Weeks	Boston	3/16	
			Sidney F. Whitehouse	Boston	2/16	
18	21 May 1883	Brunswick, Ga.	Wesley Gove	Boston	6/16	Boston
			Andrew M. Martin	Boston	2/16	
			Charles A. Grant	Boston	3/16	
			John S. Weeks	Boston	3/16	
			Sidney F. Whitehouse	Boston	2/16	
410	25 June 1884	New York	Wesley Gove	Boston	6/16	Boston
			Andrew M. Martin	Boston	2/16	
			Charles A. Grant	Boston	3/16	
			John S. Weeks	Boston	3/16	
			Sidney F. Whitehouse	Boston	2/16	
28	4 August 1884	Boston	Wesley A. Gove	Boston	6/16	Boston
			Andrew M. Martin	Boston	2/16	
			Charles A. Grant	Boston	3/16	
			John S. Weeks	Boston	3/16	
			Sidney F. Waterhouse (sic)	Boston	2/16	

(ENDORSEMENT ON BACK)

Date of surrender: Jan'y 3, 1885.

Where surrendered: Miragoane, Haiti.

Cause of surrender: Vessel lost by stranding, Jan'y 3, 1885, on the Reefs of the Rochelais, near Miragoane, Haiti. 7 on board — none l
Surrendered — Port au Prince and Miragoane, Haiti. Total loss by stranding — Jan. 3, 1885. T. B. S.

Name of Master	Former Name	Decks	Masts	Length	Breadth	Depth	Capacity under Tonnage Deck	Capacity between decks above Tonnage Deck	Capacity of Enclosures on Upper Deck	Total Tonnage
os. L. Fleming	Br. Bg. *Amazon*	2	2	103	25 7/10	16 2/10	271.79	3.69	6.80	282.28
os. L. Fleming	Br. Bg. *Amazon*	2	2	103	25 7/10	16 2/10	271.79	3.69	6.80	282.28
os. L. Fleming	Br. Bg. *Amazon*	2	2	103	25 7/10	16 2/10	271.79	3.69	6.80	282.28
							Deduct by Act Aug. 5, 1882			14.11
									Nett	268.17
omas L. Fleming	Br. Bg. *Amazon*	2	2	103	25 7/10	16 2/10	271.79	3.69	6.80	282.28
							Deduct by Act Aug. 5, 1882			14.11
									Nett	268.17
omas L. Fleming	Br. Bg. *Amazon*	2	2	103	25 7/10	16 2/10	271.79	3.69	6.80	282.28
							Deduct by Act Aug. 5, 1882			14.11
									Nett	268.17
os. L. Fleming	Br. Bg. *Amazon*	2	2	103	25 7/10	16 2/10	271.79	3.69	6.80	282.28
							Deduct by Act Aug. 5, 1882			14.11
									Nett	268.17
omas L. Fleming	Br. Bg. *Amazon*	2	2	103	25 7/10	16 2/10	271.79	3.69	6.80	282.28
							Deduct by Act Aug. 5, 1882			14.11
									Nett	268.17
omas L. Fleming	Br. Bg. *Amazon*	2	2	103	25 7/10	16 2/10	271.79	3.69	6.80	282.28
							Deduct by Act Aug. 5, 1882			14.11
									Nett	268.17
man C. Parker	Br. Bg. *Amazon*	2	2	103	25 7/10	16 2/10	271.79			
				Capacity of enclosures on upper deck			10.49			282.28
				Deductions under Act of Aug. 5, 1882						14.11
									Nett	268.17

APPENDIX I

Articles of Agreement—Crew of *Mary Celeste*

Reproduced from the original in The National Archives (Records of the Department of the Treasury, Bureau of Customs), Washington, D. C.

[See reproductions on following two pages.]

United States  of America.

Articles of Agreement Between Master and Seamen in the Merchant Service of the United States.

REQUIRED BY ACT OF CONGRESS, APPROVED JUNE 7th, 1872.

U. S. SHIPPING COMMISSIONER'S OFFICE, PORT OF *New York Nov ᵗ 4ᵗʰ* 1872

It is Agreed *between the Master and seamen, or mariners, of the* Brig

Mary Celeste of New York *of which*

Benj. S. Briggs *is at present master, or whoever*

shall go for master, now bound from the port of New York

to¹ Genoa. and such other ports and places in the Mediterranean and Europe

as the Master may direct, and back to her final port of discharge in the United States

	Bread	Beef	Pork	Flour	Peas	Rice	Tea	Coffee	Sugar	Water
Sunday......	1	1½		¼			¼	¼	2	3
Monday.....	1		1½		¼		¼	¼	2	3
Tuesday....	1	1½		¼			¼	¼	2	3
Wednesday.	1		1½		¼		¼	¼	2	3
Thursday...	1	1½		¼			¼	¼	2	3
Friday......	1		1½		¼		¼	¼	2	3
Saturday....	1	1½				¼	¼	¼	2	3

Scale of Provisions to be allowed and served out to the Crew during the Voyage, in addition to the daily issue of Lime and Lemon Juice and Sugar, or other anti scorbutics in any case required by Law.

SUBSTITUTES.

One Ounce of Coffee or Cocoa or Chocolate may be substituted for one quarter ounce of Tea, Molasses for Sugar, the quantity to be one half more ; one pound of potatoes or yams ; one half pound of Flour or Rice ; one third pint of Peas or one-quarter pint of Barley, may be substituted for each other. When Fresh Meat is issued, the proportion to be two pounds per man, per day, in lieu of Salt Meat. Flour, Rice and Peas, Beef and Pork, may be substituted for each other, and for Potatoes, Onions may be substituted.

And the said crew agree to conduct themselves in an orderly, faithful, honest and sober manner, and to be at all times diligent in their respective Duties, and to be obedient to the lawful Commands of the said Master, or of any Person who shall lawfully succeed him, and of their Superior Officers, in everything relating to the said Ship and the Stores and Cargo thereof, whether on board, in boats, or on shore ; and in consideration of which service to be duly performed, the said Master hereby agrees to pay to the said Crew, as Wages, the sums against their Names respectively expressed, and to supply them with Provisions according to the annexed or above Scale : And it is hereby agreed, That any Embezzlement or wilful or negligent Destruction of any part of the Ship's Cargo or Stores shall be made good to the Owner out of the Wages of the Person guilty of the same : And if any Person enters himself as qualified for a duty which he proves himself incompetent to perform, his wages shall be reduced in proportion to his incompetency : And it is also agreed, That if any Member of the Crew considers himself to be aggrieved by any breach of the Agreement or otherwise, he shall represent the same to the Master or Officer in charge of the Ship in a quiet and orderly manner, who shall thereupon take such steps as the case may require : And it is also agreed, That (2)

⁴The authority of the Owner or Agent for the allotments mentioned within is in my possession.

{ Shipping Commissioner or Consular Officer.

This is to be signed if such an authority has been produced, and to be scored across in ink if it has not.

In witness whereof, the said parties have subscribed their Names on the other Side or Sides hereof on the days against their respective Signatures mentioned.

Signed by *Benj. S. Briggs* Master, on the *4ᵗʰ* day of *November* 1872

Date of Commencement of Voyage.	Port at which Voyage Commenced.	Date of Termination of Voyage.	Port at which Voyage Terminated.	Date of Delivery of Lists to Shipping Commissioner	I hereby declare to the truth of the Entries in this Agreement and account of Crew, &c.
					Master.

These Columns to be filled up at the end of the Voyage.

¹ Here the Voyage is to be described, and the places named at which the Ship is to touch, or, if that cannot be done, the general nature and probable length of the Voyage is to be stated, and the port or country at which the voyage is to terminate.
² Here any other stipulations may be inserted to which the parties agree, and which are not contrary to Law.

N. B.—This Form must not be unstitched. No leaves may be taken out of it, and none may be added or substituted. Care should be taken at the Time of Engagement that a sufficiently large Form is used. If more men are engaged during the Voyage than the number for whom signatures are provided in this Form, an additional Form should be obtained and used.

Eight Pages.

Any Erasure, Interlineation or Alteration in this Agreement will be void, unless attested by a Shipping Commissioner, Consul or Vice-Consul, to be made with the consent of the persons interested.

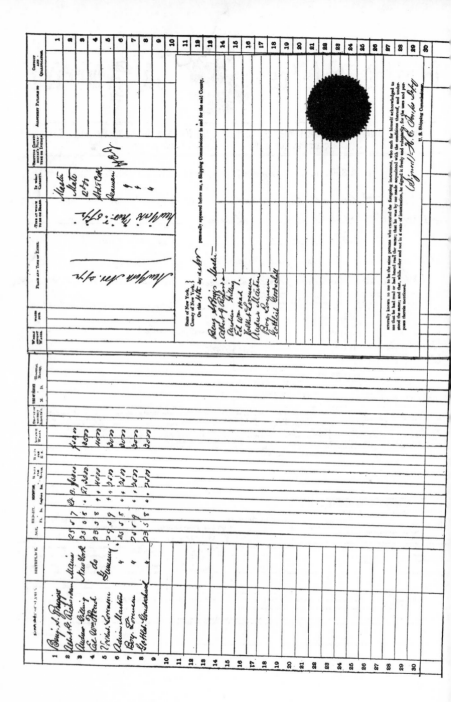

APPENDIX J

List of Persons composing the Crew of the *Mary Celeste*

Reproduced from the original in The National Archives (Records of the Department of the Treasury, Bureau of Customs), Washington, D.C.

[See reproductions on following two pages.]

CREW LIST.

T. W. Son & Co., Stationers and Printers, 45 Wall St., N. Y.

LIST OF PERSONS

COMPOSING THE CREW of the *Brig Mary Celeste* of *New York* _____ whereof
Benj. S. Briggs _____ is Master, bound for *Genoa*

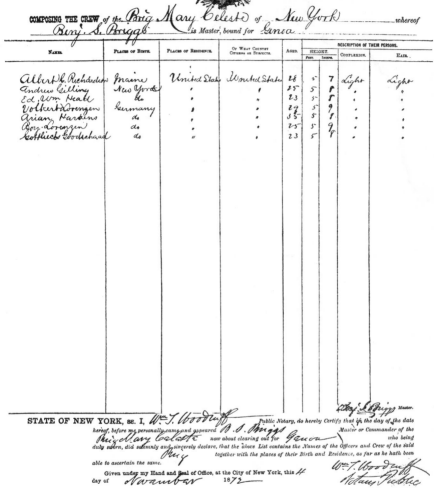

NAMES	PLACES OF BIRTH	PLACES OF RESIDENCE	OF WHAT COUNTRY CITIZENS OR SUBJECTS.	AGED.	HEIGHT.		COMPLEXION.	HAIR.
					Feet.	Inches.		
Albert G. Richardson	Maine	United States	United States	28	5	7	Light	Light
Andrew Gilling	New York	"	"	25	5	8	"	"
Ed. Wm Head	do	"	"	23	5	8	"	"
Volkert Lorenzen	Germany	"	"	29	5	9	"	"
Arian Martens	do	"	"	35	5	8	"	"
Boy Lorenzen	do	"	"	25	5	9	"	"
Gottlieb Goodschaad	do	"	"	23	5	8	"	"

Benj. S. Briggs Master.

STATE OF NEW YORK, ss. I, *Wm. T. Woodruff* _____ Public Notary, do hereby Certify that on the day of the date hereof, before me personally came and appeared *B. S. Briggs* _____ Master or Commander of the *Brig Mary Celeste* now about clearing out for *Genoa* _____ who being duly sworn, did solemnly and sincerely declare, that the above List contains the Names of the Officers and Crew of the said *Brig* together with the places of their Birth and Residence, as far as he hath been able to ascertain the same.

Given under my Hand and Seal of Office, at the City of New York, this *4* day of *November* 18*72*

Wm. T. Woodruff
Notary Public

Mary Colvin
Nov. 1/72

APPENDIX K

Copy of Log Slate of *Mary Celeste*, 25 November 1872, according to Letter of Frederick Solly Flood, Queen's Advocate, Gibraltar, to London Board of Trade, 22 January 1873

(*Copy M.* 1802)

Entries on Slate

H.	K.	Course	Wind	Monday 25th.
1	8			Comes in fresh.
2	8			
3	8			
4	8			
5	8			
6	8			
7	9			
8	9			At 8 P.M. fresh.
9	8			Got in Royals & top G sail.
10	8			
11	8			
12	8	E. by S.	West	M. P. rainy.[1]
1	8			
2	8			
3	8			
4	8			
5	8			At 5 made the island of S. Mary's bearing E. S. E.
6	8			At 5 o'clock made the Island of S. Mary's bearing E. S. E.
7	8			
8	8			At 8 Eastern point bore S. S. W. 6 miles distant.
9				
10				
11				
12				

1. M. P. probably means "Middle Part."

211

APPENDIX L

Extracts from Log of Brigantine *Dei Gratia* as reported 23 January 1873 by Frederick Solly Flood, Queen's Advocate, Gibraltar, to the London Board of Trade, Marine Department

[From photostatic copies (in author's possession) of copies sent to Department of State, Washington, D. C., by British Minister to the United States.]

(*Copy M.* 1802)

H.	K.	Course	Wind	24 November
2	9	E. S. E.	W. N. W.	
4	8	"	"	
6	8	"	"	
8	8	"	"	
10	8	"	"	
12	8	"	"	
2	8	"	"	
4	8	"	"	
6	8	"	"	
8	8	"	"	
10	8	"	"	Dist. per Log Lat. 41 19.
12	8	"	"	Long. 50 56 by chron.

H.	K.	Course	Wind	25 November
2	8	S. E. by E.	N. W.	
4	8	"	"	
6	8	"	"	
8	8	"	"	
10[1]	8			
12	8	"	N. N. W.	
2	8	"	"	
4	8	"	"	
6	8	"	"	
8	8	"	"	
10	8	"	"	Lat. 41 52.
12	8	"	"	Long. 46 53.

1. Course and wind not given.

H.	K.	Course	Wind	26th. November
2	8	S. E. by E.	N. N. W	
4	8	"	"	
6	8	"	"	
8	6	"	"	
10	6	"	"	
12	5	"	"	
2	5	"	"	
4	5	"	"	
6	5	"	"	
8	5	"	"	
10	5	"	"	Lat. 40. 58-
12	5	"	"	Long. 43. 55.
2²	6		W N W	27 November
4	6			
6	6			
8	6			
10	6			
12	6			
2	7			
4	7			
6	7			
8	7			
10	7			Lat. 41—12.
12	7			Long 41—03

2. This day's record is incomplete, as indicated.

H.	K.	Course	Wind	28th November
2	8	E S E	W N W	
4	8	"	"	
6	8	"	"	
8	8	"	"	
10	8	"	"	
12³				
2	9	E S E	"	
4	9	"	"	
6	9	"	"	
8	9	"	"	
10	9	"	"	Lat. 40 37.
12	9	"	"	Long. 36 40.
2	8	E. S. E.	W N W	29th November
4	8	"		
6	8	"		
8	8	"		
10	8	"	N W	
12	8	"	N N W	
2	5	"		
4	5	"		
6	5	"	N W	
8	5	"		Lat. 41—21
10	5	"		Long. 33 16
12	5	"		D R 33.10

3. 12 o'clock not given.

H.	K.	Course	Wind	30th November
2	5	S E by E ¼ E	N. N. W.	
4	5	"		
6	6	"		
8	6	"		
10	6	"		
12	6	"		
2	6	"		
4	6	"		
6	7	"		
8	7	"		
10	7	"		Lat. 41.15
12	9	"		Long. 30 15

H.	K.	Course	Wind	1st December
2	8	S. E. by E. ½ E.	N.	
4	8	"	"	
6	8	"	"	
8	8	"	"	
10	8	"	"	
12	8	"	"	
2	9	"	"	
4	9	"	"	
6	9	"	"	
8	9	"	"	
10	9	"	"	Lat. 40 59
12	9	"	"	Long. 25 50

H.	K.	Course	Wind	2nd December
2	8	S. E.	N.	
4	8	"	"	
6	7	"	"	
8	7	"	"	
10	7	"	"	
12	7	"	"	
2	7	"	"	
4	7	"	"	
6	6	"	"	
8	6	"	"	
10	6	"	"	Lat. 39. 37.
12	6	"	"	Long. 22. 42.

H.	K.	Course	Wind	3rd December
2	6	S. E.	N.	
4	6	"	"	
6	6	"	"	
8	7	"	"	
10	7	"	"	
12	7	"	"	
2	7	"	"	
4	7	"	"	
6	7	"	"	
8	7	"	"	
10	7	"	"	Lat. 38. 55
12	7	"	"	Long. 19° 30′

H.	K.	Course	Wind	4th December
2	7	S. E. by ½ E.	N.	
4	4	"	N. W.	
6	4	"	"	
8	4	"	"	
10	4	"	"	
12	3	"	"	
2	2	"	"	
4	3	"	N.	
6	4	"	"	
8	6	"	"	
10	5	"	"	Lat. 38° 30′.
12	5	"	"	Long. 17 37.

D. R. 17 15

H.	K.	Course	Wind	5th December
2	5	S. E. ½ E.	N. N. E.	
4	5	"	"	
6	3	"	"	
8	2	"	"	
10	2	"	"	
12	2	"	"	
2	2	"	"	
4	1	"	N. E.	
6	2	"	"	
8	3	"	"	
10	3	"	"	
12	3	"	"	

Begins with fresh breeze & clear, sea still running heavy but wind moderating saw a sail to the E 2 P.M. saw she was under very short canvas steering very wild & evidently in distress. Hauled up to speak her & render assistance if necessary, at 3 P.M. hailed her & getting no answer & seeing no one on deck[4] out boat & sent the mate & 2 men on board, sea running high at the time. He boarded her without accident and returned in about an hour and reported her to be the *Mary Celeste* of & from New York for Genoa abandoned with 3½ feet of water in hold &c — &c.

A true Extract

(Signed) FREDERICK SOLLY FLOOD.

4. There seems to be a word (probably "got") missing here.

APPENDIX M

Correspondence between Department of State, Treasury Department, and the British Minister at Washington in March 1873 in regard to documents forwarded from London by Earl Granville, including excerpts from Log of *Dei Gratia* and Log Slate of *Mary Celeste*

DEPARTMENT OF STATE

Washington 14th March 1873

THE HONORABLE GEORGE S. BOUTWELL
Secretary of the Treasury.

SIR: I have the honor to enclose herewith in original, a note of the 11th instant, from the British Minister with its enclosures relating to the circumstances under which an abandoned vessel supposed to be the American Brigantine *Mary Celeste,* has been brought into the harbor of Gibraltar by the British Vessel *Dei Gratia.*

I will thank you to furnish the Department with such information as may be obtainable concerning the *Mary Celeste* as to her ownership and last clearance from the United States &c. &c. The return of the enclosed papers is desired.

I have the honor to be, Sir

Your obedient Servant

HAMILTON FISH.

Enclosure: Sir Edward Thornton to Mr. Fish 11 March 1873
with accompaniments.

Treasury Department, Washington, D. C.

March 24, 1873

SIR:

In compliance with the request contained in your letter of the 14th instant, I have the honor to return herewith the note of the British Minister and the accompanying documents, relative to the Brigantine *Mary Celeste,* found derelict at sea.

A circular letter has been addressed to Collectors of Customs throughout the United States, directing them to furnish any information in regard to the matter which they may be able to obtain, and every effort will be made to ascertain the fate of the persons on board the abandoned vessel.

I am Sir, very respectfully, Your obedient servant,

WM. A. RICHARDSON, *Secretary.*

Hon. Hamilton Fish, Secretary of State

Washington, March 11, 1873

SIR:

In compliance with an instruction which I have received from Earl Granville, I have the honor to transmit herewith copy of a letter together with its inclosures, which has been addressed to the Board of Trade by the Attorney General of Gibraltar relative to the circumstances under which a derelict vessel, supposed to be the American Brigantine *Mary Celeste* has been brought into that Harbour by the British Vessel *Dei Gratia*.

You will perceive that the enquiries which have been instituted into this matter tend to arouse grave suspicions that the Master of the Vessel in question, together with his wife and child, were murdered by the crew who would seem subsequently to have abandoned the Vessel, and are supposed either to have perished at Sea, or to have been picked up by a passing vessel.

It is under these circumstances that I have been instructed to communicate the inclosed documents to you, in order that, if the Government of the United States should think it expedient, investigations may be instituted with a view to obtaining some clue to the cause of the derelict vessel having been abandoned.

I have the honour to be, with the highest consideration, Sir,

Your obedient servant

EDW'D. THORNTON [1]

The Hon'ble. Hamilton Fish

1. British Minister to the United States.

APPENDIX N

Testimony given before Vice-Admiralty Court at Gibraltar, by John Wright, Second Mate, and Seamen Charles Lund, Augustus Anderson and John Johnson, all of the Brigantine *Dei Gratia*

JOHN WRIGHT, sworn, examined by Pisani.

I am Second Mate of the *Dei Gratia*. I remember on the 5th December being on watch on the deck from 12 to 4. I remember sighting a vessel about 1 o'clock on that day p.m. sea time. The vessel was about 6 miles distant on our *port* bow; we were steering S. E. by E. I boarded the vessel with the Mate Deveau and a man named John Johnson to see what was the matter with her. We found no one on board that vessel. I sounded the pump-well and found about 3½ feet of water. I went into the cabin and saw no charts. I had no time or did not take time to look. I did not see anything in the cabin more than in any other cabin. The Hull and spars of the vessel were in good order, the standing rigging was not in very good order — the standing rigging was old — it was not broken but wanted repairing. The sails were furled except lower topsail gib and fore-top stay-sail, those three were set — fore-sail and upper fore top sail were gone. There was water in the cabin, between decks and in the forehouse; the forward hatch and the Lazaret hatches were off, the sky light was in a good state — it was not open. *Johnson remained in the boat along side and did not come on board.* I returned on board my own vessel and did not again return to the *Celeste*. After I returned to my own ship and we wore ship and stood down to the other ship until she the other ship got under way. The Mate Deveau returned to the other ship with two men *Johnny* and *James*. The crew of the *Dei Gratia* numbered all told 8. There was a tolerably heavy sea running when we launched our boat to go to the *Celeste*. We had had heavy weather before that but was then moderating. We were bound for Gibraltar. We sailed keeping sight of the other vessel until 3 o'clock in the night — about the . . . when we lost sight of her. We got to Gibraltar on Tuesday morning. I am sure it was not Thursday afternoon; I had lost sight of the other vessel for three days previously. The derelict arrived at Gibraltar the next day after we did.

Cross-examined by Queen's Proctor. We came to an anchor in Gibraltar between 11 and 12 o'clock one morning and the other vessel arrived the following morning. It was as I have said during my watch that we sighted the derelict; the man at the wheel named Johnson first sighted her and he called to me and showed me the vessel. Our head was then S.E. by East; the head of the other vessel was N.W. by North as far as I could judge. She was on our port bow. When I first saw the vessel it was the state of the vessel's sails that caught my attention. I am sure she had her lower fore top-sail set. She had no after sail on. I should say it was about 2 hours from the time of first seeing to lowering boat to board her. She yawed some but not much—that also attracted my attention. I did not particularly notice the state of her masts and yards—they were all standing—the Royal was bent and furled. I saw that the rigging was out of order—the standing rigging wanted getting up and rattling down—the running rigging I did not notice. I did not notice the state of the peak Halyards. I went down into Cabin. Before I went I assisted sounding the pumps. The pumps were in good state. There was no sounding rod but a piece of iron with a piece of line attached to it—I found no proper sounding rod. I was able to sound with the piece of iron and line attached to it. It was found lying on the deck near the cabin but could only guess from the line being wet the water in the pump—the line as wetted showed about 3 feet and a half. There was no box in one of the pumps and I let the rod down through the box and pipe where the pump should have been. It would take about 15 minutes to remove the box etc. from the pump so as to be able to sound through it. There is a door to the companion stairs—the door was open. The top of the cabin is above the deck—I should say about 10 inch above the deck. The only way of lighting the cabin is by the sky light and the windows three on each side of the cabin and by the companion way when the door is open. The windows were nailed up on the starboard side with plank; they were not nailed up on port side. The windows were shut on port side and would let light in. I could not say whether the windows were fastened up for the voyage—or had been fastened during voyage. On the starboard side the planking was nailed outside the glass; on the port side the windows were shut with glass only and were not broken. When below in the cabin there was plenty of light to see what was on the table. I did not see any of the sky light glass broken. I saw that the Binacle was knocked off its stand; it was lying on deck alongside the wheel; the wheel was not lashed. Nothing was the matter with the wheel. The Binacle had been fastened by two cleets on each side, but I cannot say how it had been fastened to the cleets; the binacle was knocked out of its place but had nothing the matter with it—it was not destroyed. There were only two cleets—neither of them was drawn. I examined the place where the binacle stood; it had slipt in under the cleets and the cleets themselves were not drawn. The compass was in the binnacle; the compass was destroyed. Any force that would remove the binacle would destroy the compass. The glass cover of the compass was knocked off. I left it where it was; I did nothing to it. There were davits to hang a boat astern. They were in good state. I could not tell one way or the other whether a boat had been launched from them. There were no davits on the quarter of the vessel. I saw nothing from which I could judge whether a boat had been upon deck—I saw no lashings cut loose—I saw no ropes on either side showing that a boat had been launched from the ship at all. I observed no remains of any tow line. I saw no spare spars on deck. The ship's anchors and chains were all right and on board, so that there was nothing to show that she had been moored and parted her cable. If she had done so we should have seen it, and did not see it. I went to the galley, the door was open; it was in a bad state. The stove was knocked out of its place. That could have been done by a sea striking the galley and the stove through the door — it would knock the stove out of its place. The sea could come in anywhere, besides from coming from the head could come in from the stern but I never was in a vessel that was pooped. I have been on board a ship where the galley has been carried away on two or three occasions. The Stove was on the starboard side of the door, the cooking utensils were not knocked about — strewn about a good deal of water in the galley. I did not go in and could not see what provisions there were. The door sill is about 9 inches high and would prevent water running out of the galley. There was no place for it to run out and I dont know how long the water had been there; the water could not come down the galley funnel. There was nothing lying on the funnel, the sail was lying alongside it. The forehatch was lying on the port side, three feet from the hatch itself. A sea which would fill the galley would send a lot of water down the hatch way; the Lazarette hatch was open and a good deal of water would have gone down had she been struck by a poop sea, also down the sky light, if struck by a beam sea. The door of the companion faces forward; if a heavy sea were shipped it would come down companion some of it. I did [*sic*] notice any thing on the companion table. I saw nothing particular in the cabin to call my attention. I did not go inside the Captain's Cabin; I stood at the door. I stayed on board about half an hour and about ten minutes near the cabin door. The Main hatch was closed — fastened down. Two spars were lashed there — they were rough spars. I do not know why they were put there.

The evidence of the Witness was read over to him in open Court and he says it is correct to the best of his belief.

EDWARD J. BAUMGARTNER, *Registrar.*

Read in open court at the hearing of the Cause 4th March, 1873.

EDWARD J. BAUMGARTNER, *Registrar.*

CHARLES LUND, sworn, examined by Pisani.

I am one of the crew of the *Dei Gratia* A.B. I remember on the 5th December sighting the *Mary Celeste* — I was not on the watch; I was called up from below and came on deck. I was ordered to board the vessel the second time with the Chief Mate and Anderson. When I went on board it was about four o'clock p.m. or afternoon — and I came with that vessel to Gibraltar. We arrived at Gibraltar on the morning of the 13th and found my own vessel *Dei Gratia* there. During the voyage we kept sight of the *Dei Gratia* until we arrived in the Straits when we lost sight of her. We had a stiff breeze and fair wind all the way until we got into the Straits when it blew hard with rain.

Cross-examined by the Queen's Proctor. We lost sight of our own ship about two days before we reached Gibraltar. I think so, perhaps three. It was not ten or five days, to the best of my recollection it was two or three days that we lost sight of the *Dei Gratia*. I am sure it was two days. It was bad weather. We did not lose any sails nor carry away any of our running rigging or standing rigging nor any sails. The weather was not so bad as to carry away our binacle. When I went on board first the binacle was lying on the deck close to the wheel. We put it into its place again—it may have taken 5 to 10 minutes to put it back again. The binacle was not again carried away by bad weather whilst we were on board. If a sea had come over it might have again struck and carried away the binnacle. I never saw any sea that would do so. We got no water into the galley during the bad weather we were in, but we had to come and close the doors and keep the hatches on. It would not have been prudent to keep the fore-hatch open in such weather as we encountered. If we had kept it open some water would have come in during the rough weather we had in the Straits. The sea never came over our bow and as far as the Lazaret hatch whilst we were on the *Celeste*. The binacle is in a box; it has no glass cover to it. It is a wooden box without any glass cover to it. The compass has a glass over it and also the lights. The sea whilst I was on board never came so far aft as to do any damage to the binacle. The Cabin is flush with the lower deck floor—the top of the cabin is a foot and a half or two feet above the deck. There are, I think, two windows on each side of the cabin. There was wood and canvas nailed over the glass of the [*word missing*] on the starboard side. I cannot say whether the windows on the port side were or were not covered over with wood and canvas or not. I cannot speak to what I am not sure about. I cannot say not being sure I did not see any glass broken in the windows or in the sky light. The sky light was open; one pane of glass in the sky light was split down. The cabin door was open. I went down into the cabin perhaps in a quarter of an hour or ten minutes after I was on board. I did not see anything on the table. I did not go into the pantry. I did not see any bread or food in the cabin. The first time I went into the cabin was for the sounding line. I sounded the well of the *Celeste*—I sounded it with an iron bolt and a piece of line tied to it. The bolt was 6 inches to 1 foot long; I found it and the line in the cabin. I saw no sounding rod. I had no time to look after such things. The chief Mate sounded the pump with my assistance—there was 3 feet and a half. It had been sounded before the first time he went on board. The Chief Mate had sounded it before, and sounded it again the second time—we made it three feet and a half. I did not sound it; it was sounded through the pump pipe where the box should be. There was 3 feet 6. The first thing I did was to pump her dry. It took three hours or more to do so—there was only one pump going. The *Celeste* made a little water afterwards, I cannot say how much—about 20 to 25 strokes. I cannot say how much water she made in the day. I pumped her out morning and evening and 25 strokes each time sucked the pipe. The *Dei Gratia* made more water than the *Celeste*. We found no boats on board—I cannot say how many boats there had been. I am sure there had been a boat at the Main hatch from the fixings there. I cannot say whether there had been any boat at the stern Davits. The standing rigging was old but was taut. She had lower topsail, gib, and foretop staysail I think on the starboard tack. Some of the running rigging was broken; the lee brace of the foretop staysail the peak halyards were broke and gone; the mainsail was furled — perhaps the sail had been furled afterwards. There were no spare spars on deck. The wheel was not damaged in any way. I saw no other damage to the vessel than I have stated — except that two of the sails were gone. I saw davits in the stern of the *Celeste*. I could not see any tackle to them — the boat had lain across the Main hatch. There was a spar lashed across the stern davits from one side to the other. I cannot say whether there could have been a boat lashed there; I think there might have been a boat as well as a spar lashed to the stern davits.

The evidence given by the witness was read over to him and he stated to be correct.

EDWARD J. BAUMGARTNER, Registrar.

The Vice-Admiralty Court is adjourned till tomorrow Saturday, 21 December instant.

The evidence of the last witness is read at the hearing of the Salvage Cause on the 4th March 1873.

EDWARD J. BAUMGARTNER, Registrar, V. A. Court.

Saturday 21st December 1872.   Mary Celeste

The further examination of the witnesses on behalf of the *Dei Gratia* Salvors is proceeded with this day.

AUGUSTUS ANDERSEN — sworn.

I am an A. B. seaman and one of the crew of the *Dei Gratia*. On the 5th December the Captain of my vessel sighted a vessel, and he ordered a boat to be lowered and the Mate Deveau myself and John Johnson got into the boat. I had the watch at the time when we sighted the vessel — she was four to five miles distant when we sighted her. We got into the boat and went on board the other vessel. We found no one board the vessel (the witness it appears did not go to the vessel first trip). I went on board only after the boat had been to the vessel and had returned again to our vessel. I went with the boat the second time only, and sounded the pumps on board the abandoned vessel. I did not go into the Cabin, I was holding on aft. I went to the abandoned vessel in the second boat. I came to Gibraltar in the vessel with Johnson. It was Lund and not Johnson who came with me to Gibraltar in the vessel with the first Mate. We three went in the boat the second trip she made to the vessel. The first thing I did was to sound the pumps. I did not go into the Cabin until I had been on board half an hour. I did not notice anything on the Cabin table, I had not time to do so. I did not take any notice of anything particular in the cabin. The cabin was wet — everything was wet in it, the clothes and all. There was three foot and a half of water in the hold, there was a good deal of water between decks and also in the forward house (up to the combings — Judge). The foresail and upper top sail were gone and lower top-sail hanging by the four corners; the gib and foretop mast staysail were set. I came with this vessel to Gibraltar and arrived on the 13th of this month. We kept company with the *Dei Gratia* until we got to the Straits when we lost sight of her — that was two days before we reached Gibraltar. We had fine weather until we got into the Straits when we had a storm and weather became thick with rain.

Cross-examined by the Queen's Proctor. The Captain first sighted the strange sail. I was on deck at the time—I do not recollect where abouts on deck—I was not at the wheel. Johnson was at the wheel. I was nigh to the wheel at the time the vessel was sighted. I saw the vessel as soon as the Captain drew my attention to it. The vessel was under very short canvas — there was no signal of distress up. I do not recollect how we were steering—we were steering towards Gibraltar. The vessel was on our port bow on the starboard bow (*sic*) heading toward us. She was going pretty steady but she was then too far off for me to tell whether she yawed or not. I do not know whether the wheel was lashed or not when we boarded the vessel. I went up second from the boat immediately after Mate. Her masts and spars were all right; the top gallant and royal yards bent; the standing rigging was all to pieces; the ratlines were all to pieces; the back stays and fore stays were all right. The door of the forward house was open, the fore hatch was off — all open. The cover was all in one and was off. The Lazaret hatch was off; the sky light was open; the Lazaret hatch was in one piece. There was a big hole in one pane of glass on one corner of the sky light, except that the glass was all right. In the cabin there were 3 windows on starboard side, 2 windows on the port side, and 1 window in the fore part facing the bow. All the windows were covered with plank. They are all covered yet — except the one into the Mate's room which was also covered, but he opened it. The cabin window facing the bow was covered also I am sure. The companion door was open — I examined it — there was nothing then the matter with it. I took notice of the Binacle; it was knocked down, lying near the wheel and Lazaret hatch; the compass was broken; the cleets which fastened the binacle were also broken. The Binacle had been fastened on the Cabin house, on the roof of the cabin house. It had been fastened by being lashed to the cleets. The cleets are kind of hooks—there were two one on each side. The cleets had been torn out from the deck and also from the box on one side, and one of the cleets was lying on the deck. The compass was still in the box but broken all to pieces. The glass cover was broken. I did not notice whether the metal of the compass was broken or not—I did not see any needle. The binacle itself had sustained no injury. There were no spars on deck; there were water casks 4 or 5 on deck, all in their proper place; there were no ropes coiled on the deck. I did not see any but there were ropes hanging over the side, there were ropes coiled on deck. The ropes of the running gear were coiled. There was all kind of running gear hanging over her side: sheets and braces, hanging over both sides. The anchors and chains were all in their proper place — the anchor made fast to the cathead.

To Judge. I was present when the pump was sounded. It was sounded with a piece of line and a bolt six or seven inches long. The line and bolt were found in the cabin. The bolt was about 1½ inches thick, the line was fastened to the bolt round the end. There was no hole in it. It had no head to it — it was a piece of iron fastened by having the cord tied round it. We used the same bolt and line to sound with during our voyage to Gibraltar. The Mate found a sounding rod on deck, but I did not see him find it. It was all wet and could not be used. I did not see it — the Mate saw it. I never took notice of the sounding rod myself. I did not see it when I first went on board. I never saw any other sounding rod than the iron bolt and string. The mate told me that there was a sounding rod lying on deck but that it was all wet and could not be used. He did not tell me what he did with it. There was nothing wrong about the vessel. We had hard work to get her into good order to get the gear into order and the sails right. It took us two or three days to set her to rights. On her voyage to Gibraltar the vessel herself was sounded and made little or no water. We got the vessel under sail the same night, but it took us two or three days before we got her all right. We had to pump her out first.

Queen's Proctor reads from the log. She was pumped dry between 8 and 9 o'clock same evening and then sail was set on her.

Memo. The witness is questioned as to what was done on board the *Mary Celeste* from the entries in the Log, and answers yes to every question, and that it is correct as stated in the Log.

The vessel was in a fit state to go round the world with a good crew and good sails. We made Cape Spartel 3 p.m. of 11th, there was then a fresh breeze. I saw our own ship when we were off Cape Spartel. There are a good many lights I dont know the name of and I do not know Ceuta light; I was never in the Straits of Gibraltar before. I shipped on board my vessel at New York but never made this voyage before.

The depositions of the Witness were read over to him and he states that they are correct.

EDWARD J. BAUMGARTNER, *Registrar.*

The evidence of the above witness is read at Court at the hearing of the Cause of Salvage the 4th March 1873.

EDWARD J. BAUMGARTNER, *Registrar.*

JOHN JOHNSON, called, sworn, examined by Pisani, a Russian Lutheran sworn on the New Testament.

My name is John Johnson. I am an able bodied seaman on board the *Dei Gratia.* I do not know what day it was but I do remember meeting or seeing a vessel which vessel is now in Gibraltar. I went in the first boat with John Wright 2nd Mate and the first Mate of the *Dei Gratia* on board this vessel; we went on her deck.

The Witness does not understand English except in a very slight degree. Mr. Pisani proposes that one of the other crew who understands more English should interpret but the Queen's Advocate objects because he can admit nothing.

I did not go on deck, I remained in the boat alongside. I returned back to my own vessel.Yes. And the boat returned a Second time from our vessel *Dei Gratia* to this derelict.

The Queen's Proctor declines to cross-examine the Witness as not understanding the English.

The Judge to the Queen's Proctor. You have the opportunity of seeing the Log of the *Dei Gratia* now if you please and therefore if you do not choose to avail yourself of it it is your own fault.

The Queen's Proctor. I have asked for the Log 20 times a day and not been able to procure it.

Pisani. The Log is here in Court and has been always accessible to the Queen's Proctor.

Pisani. The Mate is here and if the Queen's Advocate or Your Lordship would like to ask him further question about the sounding rod here he is.

The Judge. I dont wish to ask him anything if the Queen's Proctor chooses to do so he may do it. I understood in the first instance that the Captain of the *Dei Gratia* was not to be Examined and I cannot understand what objection there could be made to its production.

Mr. Pisani. Hands in a copy of the Ship's *(Dei Gratia)* Register produced yesterday.

N.B. Certified copy of the Register — also a certified copy of the Log of the *Dei Gratia* to be deposited in the Registry.

OLIVER DEVEAU recalled by the Queen's Proctor.

The book now produced is my ship's Log and is in my handwriting up to the 5th day I left the ship. On the 24th November the Latitude was 41. 49 Long. by Chronometer 50.56.

25th { Latitude   41.52
     { Longitude   46.53

EDWARD J. BAUMGARTNER, *Registrar.*

The evidence as above and Notes are read in court the 4th March 1873.

EDWARD J. BAUMGARTNER, *Registrar.*

Friday 31st January 1873. Vice-Admiralty Court. Adjourned from Wednesday last. Mary Celeste and Cargo, derelict.

The Queen's Advocate.
Cornwell, Proctor for Claimant of the Vessel.
Stokes, Proctor for Owners of Cargo.
Pisani, Proctor for Salvors.

This being the day assigned Cornwell to bring in the proofs of his parties claiming to be the owners of the ship or vessel supposed to be the *Mary Celeste.*

Cornwell then prayed the Judge to admit the claim of his party James H. Winchester as the lawful owner of the said Brig *Mary Celeste* and to decree restitution thereof to him upon payment of salvage and salvage expenses and upon finding sureties to answer all latent claims the Queen's Advocate being present and consenting thereto as also Pisani, Proctor for the Salvors.

The Judge. There are certain matters which have been brought to my notice respecting this vessel my opinion about which I have already very decidedly expressed and which make it desirable and even very necessary that further investigation should take place before the release of the vessel can be sanctioned or before she can quit this port.

The conduct of the Salvors in going away as they have done has in my opinion been most reprehensible and may probably influence the decision as to their claim for remuneration for their services and it appears very strange why the Captain of the *Dei Gratia* who knows little or nothing to help the investigation should have remained here whilst the first Mate and the crew who boarded the *Celeste* and brought her here should have been allowed to go away as they have done.

The Court will take time to consider the Decree for Restitution.[1]

---

[1] The foregoing completes the record of the testimony given by Wright, Lund, Andersen and Johnson. Oliver Deveau was recalled to testify at a session of the Court held on 4 March. A copy of the record of his testimony given at that time will be found in Part I of this narrative.

APPENDIX O

Affidavit of John Austin, Surveyor of Shipping, Gibraltar, Accompanying Frederick Solly Flood's Letter of 22 January 1873 to Board of Trade, Marine Department, London, England[1]

I, John Austin of the City of Gibraltar, Surveyor of Shipping make oath and say.

1. That by desire of Thomas Joseph Vecchio Esqr Marshal of this Honble Court in company with him and Fredk. Solly Flood Esqr H. M's Advocate General for Gibraltar and Proctor for the Queen in her Office of Admiralty on Monday the 23rd day of Dec^{br} last went on board a vessel rigged as a brigantine name unknown supposed to be the *Mary Celeste* then moored in the port of Gibraltar and under an arrest in pursuance of a warrant out of this Honble Court as having been found derelict on the high seas and I then carefully and minutely surveyed and examined the state and condition of the said vessel and was occupied therein for a period of five hours.

2. On approaching the Vessel I found on the bow between two and three feet above the water line on the port side a long narrow strip of the edge of one of her outer planks under the cat-head cut away to the depth of about three eighths of an inch or about one inch and a quarter wide for a length of about 6 or 7 feet. This injury had been sustained very recently and could not have been effected by the weather and was apparently done by a sharp cutting instrument continuously applied thro' the whole length of the injury.

3. I found on the starboard bow but a little further from the stem of the Vessel a precisely similar injury but perhaps an eighth or a tenth of an inch wider wh. in my opinion had been effected at the same time and by the same means and not otherwise.

4. The whole of the Hull — Masts Yards and other Spars were in their proper places and in good condition and exhibited no appearances whatever that the vessel since she had undergone her last repairs or during her last voyage had encountered any seriously heavy weather. Some of her rigging was old but some of her ropes appeared to have been new at the commencement of her last voyage.

5. The peak halyards and throat halyards appeared to be the same with wh. she had been rigged during her last and more than once previous voyage. None of them had been recently spliced and they were all in good working condition. If the peak halyards had been carried away during her last voyage they must have been subsequently spliced wh. was not the case.[2]

---

1. Transcribed from photostatic copy in the author's possession.

2. This seems an effort to contradict the testimony of Mate Deveau and Seaman Lund that the peak halyard was broken. But Deveau would have had to reeve off a new peak

229

6. If the peak halyards had been carried away while the vessel was under sail and the vessel had been abandoned hurriedly and without letting go the throat halyards the gaff would have been carried backwards and forwards by the wind. The jaws of the gaff would thereby have been destroyed and the mainmast would have been cut into but the jaws of the gaff exhibited no signs of an[sic] recent injury and the mainmast was undamaged — in such a case also the Gaff would have ripped the mainsail to pieces.

7. Moreover the main boom would have swayed backward and forward and in the event of there being any strong wind either the sheets would have been carried away or the bolts wld. have been torn out of their deck but they were all uninjured —

8. Upon examining the deck I found the butts and waterways in good condition the pitch in the water ways had nowhere started wh. it must have done extensively if the vessel had encountered seriously bad weather.

9. The Vessel had not bulwarks but was provided with a top gallant rail supported by wooden staunchions [sic] the whole of wh. were uninjured nor was there a single stanchion displaced. The water barrels on deck were in their proper places and secured in the ordinary manner but such that if the vessel had ever been thrown on her beam ends or encountered a very serious gale they wld. have gone adrift and carried away some of the stanchions of the top gallant rail.

10. Returning to the bow of the Vessel I removed the forehatch immediately under wh. was a new hawser wh. had never been used and was perfectly dry — Had any quantity of water found its way thro' this hatch the hawser would have exhibited signs of having been wetted. It exhibited none nor did any other of the articles wh. I observed there.

11. I found a forward deck house thirteen feet square and about six feet in height above the deck.

12. The deck house was made of thin planking painted white the seam between it and the deck being filled in with pitch a very violent sea would have swept the deck house away. A sea of less than very great violence would have cracked the pannelling [sic] and cracked or started the pitch throughout or at least in some parts of the deck.

13. It had not suffered the slightest injury whatever there was not a crack in the planking nor even in the paint nor in the pitch of the deck seams.

14. The port side of the deck house was divided into two cabins the forward one extended between nine feet six and ten feet across the deck and about six feet nine inches fore and aft the after cabin being on the same side was about six feet nine inches by six feet nine inches. The forward cabin entered by a sliding wooden door facing the bow of the ship.

halyard in order to handle the ship, as well as other running gear. Incidentally it seems designed to buttress Mr. Flood's theory of foul-play, which would not have fitted in with the implications associated with the use of the peak halyard as a tow-line, for a tow-line would naturally suggest an intention to return.

15. Close in front of the door of the forward port cabin was a seaman's chest unlocked and at the sides of the door opposite to it was another also unlocked. Both were quite full of seamen's effects of a superior description and mostly quite new. They were perfectly dry and not had the slightest contact with water.

16. Amongst the articles I observed in one of them was a new cigar case with metal clasp not in the slightest degree rusty. It contained nothing but 3 gold studs set with precious stones and a razor also equally unaffected by water. I also particularly noticed a pair of new instep boots and a pair of new high foul weather boots both perfectly clean a quadrant in its case together with a piece of chamois leather all perfectly dry and uninjured and unaffected by water.

17. I also carefully searched for marks of mildew on all the articles particularly on the boots and the rest of the clothing but could not discover any or any other mark of water wh. I believe I must have discovered if the Vessel had encountered any very bad weather.

18. I then examined the after Cabin on the port side wh. I believe to have been the second Mate's and it contained a seaman's chest similiar to those in the forward port Cabin and containing clothes wh. I carefully examined but none of which exhibited the slightest appearance of having been subjected to water.

19. The sills of the doors of these Cabins rise to the height of about a foot above the deck. If water had come into either of them to an extent to have flooded them an inch in depth a great part of the clothing wh. I observed would have shown signs of the water none of wh. were to be seen.

20. The Starboard Side of the Deck house to the extent of about six and a half feet in width aft and about 3¼ feet forward comprised the ships galley and was entered by a sliding door on the after side.

21. The stove and cooking utensils were in good order and exhibited no appearance of having suffered from exposure to water. Had any quantity of water found its way into the galley it would have immediately passed out thro' a scuttle hole on a level with the deck near the stove or thro' a hole wh. I found in the deck near the hearth into the hold.

22. The forward deck house was lighted by two windows on each side those on the port side were covered by a thin sliding shutter. The after window on the Starboard side was uncovered.

23. None of the shutters or of the windows were injured in the slightest degree. Some of them must have been greatly injured or wholly destroyed if the vessel had experienced very bad weather.

24. On the upper deck of the deck house I found the remains of two sails wh. apparently had been split some time or another in a gale and afterwards cut up as large lengths had been cut off with a knife or other sharp instrument and I subsequently found what I believe to be portions of those sails —

25. On going aft I examined a skylight wh. lights both the main cabin

and the Captain's cabin. It consisted of six panes of glass on each side the whole of which had a small piece wanting. Had the ship experienced very bad weather the skylight unless it had been covered which it was not when I surveyed the vessel would have been greatly damaged.

26. The height of the Cabin is increased by means of a false deck raised about 15 inches above the deck of the vessel.

27. The entrance to the Cabin is by means of a companion through a door in the forward side and a sliding hatch.

28. On descending into the main Cabin I found at the foot of the companion an oblong piece of canvas wh. I believe to have formed part of one of the sails which had been split and which I had noticed on the forward house. It had been cut and fitted as a lining for a small recess to which it was carefully fastened with nails or screws and through a small brass hook apparently intended for the purpose of hanging a towel on had been carefully driven into one of the uprights.

29. This piece of canvas had evidently been fixed there before the vessel had sailed on her last voyage. On the port side of the main-cabin was the pantry entered by a door the sill of which was about an inch and a half above the level of the lower deck or floor of the cabin. On the floor of the cabin I found among other things an open box containing moist sugar a bag containing two or three pounds of tea an open barrel containing flour and open box containing dried herrings; also some rice a nutmeg some kidney beans together with several pots of preserved fruits and other provisions in tins covered with paper. The whole of these articles were perfectly dry and had not been in the slightest degree injured or affected by water.

30. On the plate rack was another piece of canvas apparently cut from off the sails which I had observed on the forward house. It was cut into the shape of a towel for which it was apparently used. On the Starboard side of the main cabin was the chief mate's cabin, on a little bracket in which I found a small phial of oil for a sewing machine in its proper perpendicular position a reel of cotton for such a machine and a thimble. If they had been there in bad weather then they wld. have been thrown down or carried away.

31. The chief Mate's bedding was perfectly dry and had not been wetted or affected by water. Underneath his bed place were the vessel's ensign and her private signal W T. The latter had been altered since it had been used. The letter W having been quite recently sown [sic] on.

I also found under the mate's bedplace a pair of heavy Seamen's boots for stormy weather greased cleaned and apparently unused and also two drawers containing various articles.

33. In the lower drawer were a quantity of loose pieces of iron and two unbroken panes of glass which wd. have been broken to pieces had the Vessel encountered any seriously bad weather.

34. In the lower drawer were among other things a pair of log sand glasses and a new log reel without any log line.

35. The whole of the furniture and effects in the cabin were perfectly dry and in good condition. None of the articles had been or were injured or affected by water.

36. In the cabin was a clock without hands and fastened upside down by two screws or nails fixed in the woodwork of the partition, apparently some considerable time previously.

37. On entering the Captain's cabin which is abaft the main cabin I observed and examined a large quantity of personal effects.

38. In the centre of the cabin against the partition was a harmonium in very good condition and near to it a quantity of books mostly of a religious kind and which with the exception of a few which I was informed by the Marshal had been removed by him out of the lowest drawer underneath the Captain's bedplace and which were damaged by water were in Excellently good condition.

39. I found also on the floor of the cabin a little child's high chair in perfectly good condition a medicine chest containing bottles and various medical preparations in good condition.

40. The whole of which articles were uninjured and unaffected by water.

41. The bedding and other effects were perfectly dry they had not been affected by water and were in good condition.

42. I am of opinion that some not large quantity of water had fallen on the floor of the cabin through the sky light and found its way into the bottom drawer under the captain's bedplace.

43. In the cabin I found one of the Vessel's compasses belonging to the binnacle. The card of it had been damaged by water.

44. I also observed in this cabin a Sword in its scabbard which the Marshall informed me he had noticed when he came on board for the purpose of arresting the vessel. It had not[3] affected by water but on drawing out the blade it appeared to me as if it had been smeared with blood and afterwards wiped. Both the cabins were provided with lamps to be lighted by means of petroleum. They and their glasses were uninjured.

45. On the port side of the Captain's cabin was a water-closet near the door of which opposite to a window imperfectly covered on the outside was hanging a bag which was damp and had evidently been much wetted by rain or spray or both coming in at the window.

46. I was informed by the Marshal that upon his going on board the Vessel for the purpose of arresting her he had found the bag full of clothes mostly belonging to a lady and extremely wet.

47. On the Starboard side of the cabins were three windows two of which intended to light the Captain's cabin were covered with canvas similar to that of which the torn sails were made and apparently cut from it the canvas being secured by pieces of plank nailed into the frame work of the cabin the third window intended to light the chief Mate's Cabin no appearance of having ever been covered and the glass was injured on the side

3. Word omitted.

of the Cabin facing the bow of the vessel was another window secured in the same manner and with the same materials as those intended to light the Captain's cabin.

48. On the port side there was a window which lighted the water closet. It was partially covered in the same manner as that last mentioned. There was a port for another window to light the pantry but it had been effectually closed up by a wood made to fit into it.

49. Returning to the deck I found one of the pumps in good order the valve of the other had been removed for the purpose of passing a sounding — apparatus into the well.

50. The sounding apparatus wh. consisted of a metal bolt attached to a line was lying near & was in good order.

51. I then carefully examined the binnacle which I found secured to the deck of the cabin between two battens the original batten on the Starboard Side had been replaced by another roughly made. It was farther secured by cleats on each side.

52 The binnacle was constructed to hold two compasses and a lamp between them with a pane of glass separating the lamp from each compass. Both these panes of glass were cracked perpendicularly and apparently from the heat of the lamp only.

53. One of the compasses was in good working condition and did not appear to have been otherwise during the voyage. The other was missing being the one which I found in the Captain's cabin.

54. The binnacle itself did not appear to have sustained any damage.

55. In my opinion it never could have been carried away by a sea which wd. not have destroyed it & washed it overboard.

56. Such a sea wd. also have swept the decks and carried away the skylight off the cabin the top gallant sail[4] & stanchions and besides doing other damage probably have thrown the Vessel on her beam ends.

57. The whole appearance of the Vessel shows that the Vessel never encountered any such violence.

58. I next examined the after or lazaret hatch which is secured by an iron bar and went into the after hold.

59. I found here barrels of stores and other provisions in good order & condition & in their proper places. The whole of these wd. have been capsized if the Vessel had been thrown on her beam ends or encountered any very violent weather.

60. I also saw there a barrel of Stockholm tar standing in its proper position with the head of the barrel off., none of it appeared to have been used. Had the Vessel encountered any very heavy weather this barrel wd, have been capsized or at all events some of the tar wd. have been spilt, but not a drop of it had escaped.

61. I found no wine or beer or spirits on board. I made the most careful & minute examination through every part of the Vessel to which I had access

4. Probably means "rail."

to discover whether there had been any explosion on board & whether there had been any fire or any accident calculated to create an alarm of an explosion or of fire & did not discover the slightest trace of there having been any explosion or any fire or of anything calculated to create an alarm of an explosion or of fire.

62. The Vessel was thoroughly sound staunch and strong & not making water to any appreciable extent.

63. I gave directions to Ricardo Portunato an experienced Diver minutely & carefully to examine the whole of the hull and bottom of the said Vessel her stem, keel, Sternpost & rudder while I was engaged on board in surveying her, and he remained under water for that purpose for a time amply sufficient for that purpose.

64. I have now perused and considered the paper writing marked A produced & shown to me at the time of the swearing this my affidavit & which purports to be an affidavit by said Ricardo Portunato in this cause on the 7th day of Jany. now instant.

65. Having carefully weighed & considered the contents thereof & all & singular the matters aforesaid I am wholly unable to discover any reason whatever why the said Vessel should have been abandoned.

APPENDIX P

Affidavit of Ricardo Portunato, Diver

In the Vice-Admiralty Court of Gibraltar. The Queen in Her Office of Admiralty Ag't. — The Ship or Vessel name unknown supposed to be called the Mary Celeste *and her Cargo found derelict.*

I, Ricardo Portunato of the City of Gibraltar, Diver make oath and say as follows:

1. I did on Monday the 23rd day of Decbr. last by direction of Thomas Joseph Vecchio Esqr. Marshal of their Honble. Court and of Mr. John Austin Surveyor of Shipping for the port of Gibraltar proceed to a ship or vessel rigged as a Brigantine and supposed to be the *Mary Celeste* then moored in the port of Gibraltar and under arrest in pursuance of a warrant out of their Honble. Court as having been found derelict on the high Seas for the purpose of examining the State and condition of the hull of the said vessel below her water line and of ascertaining if possible whether she had sustained any damage or injury from a collision or from having struck upon any rock or shoal or otherwise howsoever.

2. I accordingly minutely and carefully examined the whole of the hull of the said Vessel and the stern keel, stern post and rudder thereof.

3. They did not nor did any or either of them exhibit any trace of damage or injury or any other appearances whatsoever indicating that the said Vessel had had any collision or had struck upon any rock or shoal or had met with any accident or casualty. The hull Stern, [*sic*] keel Sternpost and rudder of the said Vessel were thoroughly in good order and condition.

4. The said Vessel was coppered the copper was in good condition and order and I am of opinion that if she had met with any such accident or casualty I shld. have been able to discover and shld. have discovered some marks or traces thereof but I was not able to discover and did not discover any.

APPENDIX Q

Analysis by Dr. J. Patron of Supposed Blood-stains

(*Copy*)

Gibraltar, 30th January 1873

At the request of Her Majesty's Attorney General I proceeded on board of the American brig *Mary Celeste* anchored in this Bay for the purpose of ascertaining whether any marks or stains of blood could be discovered on or in her hulk.

After a careful and minute inspection of the deck of the said vessel some red brown spots about a milimetre thick and half an inch in diameter with a dull aspect were found on deck in the forepart of the vessel these spots were separated with a chissel [*sic*] and carefully wrapped in paper No. 1.

Some other similar spots were equally gathered in different parts of the deck and wrapped in papers numbered, 2, 3, and 4.

Paper No. 5 contained a powder grated from a suspicious mark seen on the top-gallant rail part of which was obtained on board and part from a piece of timber belonging to the said vessel in Her Majesty's Attorney General chambers.

I carefully examined the cabin both with natural and artificial light; the floor, the sides of the berths, mattrasses [*sic*] etc. were minutely searched and nothing worth calling attention was seen that could have any relation with the object of my enquiries.

On the 31. January[1] at 2 o'clock I received from the hands of Mr. Vecchio Marshal of the Supreme Court the five papers above mentioned and numbered 1, 2, 3, 4, and 5 and a sword with its sheath found on board the said vessel.

The spots which were in paper No. 1, 2, and 3 were cut in small pieces of about a quarter of an inch long and broad passed through a white thread and suspended half an inch from the bottom of tubes containing a small quantity of distilled water.

The contents of paper No. 4 were put in a small filtering bag as their minuteness would not allow any other process of maceration and the same was done with the contents of paper No. 5.

The maceration went on in the five tubes for two hours and a quarter; the distilled water remaining after this period as clear and bright as in the very beginning of the experiment.

Notwithstanding I left the things as they were till the next day and 23 hours maceration did not produce any alteration in the transparency of the liquid the water being then heated with the spirit lamp as no precipitate or cloudy aspect appeared I consider the experiment over and of a negative character.

The stains on the pieces of timber remained unaltered in their aspect

1. This is the day *following the date of his report.*

and the finger which was passed over them was not tinged or stained in any degree their aspect remaining as it was before maceration.

The contents of paper No. 5 macerated in the bag were then examined with a microscope and nothing particular was seen but a few particles of rust (Carbonate of Iron) and some fragments of vegetable substance (Fibres of Wood).

The sword presented on its blade about the middle and final part some stains of a more suspicious character; although few very small and superficial, their aspect was reddish and in some parts brilliant like albuminous coloured substance, my first impression was that they were really blood stains, examined with an eight or ten diameter magnifying glass these stains presented an irregular and granulated surface; the granules becoming smaller in proportion of their distance from the central and thickest part.

After an hour and three quarters maceration the transparency of the liquid remained unchanged; heat produced no cloudy alteration in it and the result was as negative as in those of the stains found on the deck.

The largest of these reddish spots was carefully grated from the blade and put under a microscope of Doctor Hartnack objective No. 7 and ocular No. 3 corresponding to a magnifying power of 330 diameter. A yellow and imperfectly crystalised substance resembling Citrate of Iron presenting here and there some red granules was seen with some fragments of vegetable ramified fibres; but no blood globules could be detected. Three other stains were tested with Hydrochloric Acid and after a perceptible effervescence a yellow stain was produced of chloride of Iron; the insufficiency of the liquid could not permit of any other experiment.

The blade heated under the flame of the spirit lamp recovered a natural brilliancy after the removal by heat of the superficial crust the sheath of the sword was clean inside and with no mark of any kind.

From the preceding negative experiments I feel myself authorized to conclude that according to our present scientifical knowledge there is no blood either in the stains observed on the deck of the *Mary Celeste* or on those found on the blade of the sword that I have examined.

(Sig'd) J. Patron

M. D.

*Certified to be a true Copy**

Edward J. Baumgartner
Registrar Vice Adm: Court

Gibraltar, 28 *July* 1887

* Quoted from photostatic copy in the author's possession.

APPENDIX R

Inventory Accompanying Letter No. 135, dated 10 March 1873, from Horatio Jones Sprague, American Consul at Gibraltar, to the Department of State, Washington, D. C.

"Inventory of Sailors' effects &c, delivered by the Marshal of the Vice Admiralty Court of Gibraltar, and found on board of the derelict vessel *Mary Celeste.*"

Chest No. 1, containing: a carpet bag; a pair of slippers; a hat; a bag; two vests; three pairs of drawers; a pair of trowsers; three woolen shirts; four cotton shirts; a comforter; six pairs of cotton socks; a pocket book; two pairs of braces; a coat.

Chest No. 2 containing: eight books; a slate; an octant; a cap; two pairs of pants; two undershirts; three white shirts; a colored outside shirt; a coat.

Chest No. 3 containing: two colored shirts; two white shirts; three pairs of pants; an undershirt; two jackets; a package of letters; a vest; a hat; a cap; two comforters; three pocket books.

Chest No. 4 containing: a pair of shoes; a jumper; four vests; two caps; three white shirts; a pair of pants; a Jacket; two pairs of stockings; a pair of mittens; a comforter; two flannel shirts; two outside colored shirts; two pairs of drawers; two white flannel undershirts.

A canvass bag containing pieces of old clothing and bagging.

A canvass bag containing: two pairs of boots; old shoes; a doll.

An harmoniphon.

A child's arm chair.

A bag containing pieces of flannel.

Two lady's hats; one man's hat.

One valise marked D containing: six vests; three linen coats; six pairs of pants.

A canvass bag containing: two sheets; six shirts; one pair of drawers; two towels; three coats; two child's shirts; a pair of child's stockings; a night shirt; two pillow cases.

A trunk marked A containing: a mosquito net; two parcels prints; four parcels of patterns; a small iron stand; a panama hat; a doll; a tool for cutting glass; four pairs of cuffs; two small metal boxes; two handkerchiefs; two neckties; a pair of braces; an envelope containing two free mason's documents; three scarfs; a set of draftsmen; two pairs of drawers; three pairs of pants; two shirts; a child's hood; three waistcoats; three woolen shirts; a pocket book containing $1 in Spanish Gold coin, $1 in American Silver coins, 25 cents in American coppers, together $2.25 cents; a small piece of net; a pair of cloth pants with suspenders; a crinoline; three dresses; two shawls; three coats; three books; a cartoon (*sic*) of ribbons &c.; a piece of cloth; eighteen cloths; two night dresses; a pair of mittens; an old shirt; seven pairs of drawers; two towells (*sic*); five pairs of socks; a piece of cotton cloth; one cap; a piece of flannel; a silver watch; three child's pants; a pair of gloves; two pieces of cotton cloth; two pairs of child's shoes; two music books; a fan; two lady's breast-pins; a small chain.

A sword; a log book; a sewing machine; a silk umbrella; a table cloth.

A trunk marked B containing: two lady's overcoats; a basket of needles, &c.; a cartoon (*sic*) of paper envelopes; three shirt bosoms; two pairs of cuffs; a piece of flannel; two dress bodies; three napkin rings; a box of seidlitz; a cartoon (*sic*) of paper collars; nine books; a parcel of letters; a package of starch; a parasol; two cloths; a bag of shells; two pieces of cotton cloth; a geometry box; a box containing razor, comb and brushes; a box of child's toys; two pairs of cotton stockings; a pair of mittens; a pair of india rubber shoes; a memorandum book; a comforter; a pair socks; an opera glass case; six shirts; two skirts; four waistcoats; two woolen shirts; a pair stockings; three pairs of pants; a pair of drawers; a piece of a dress; a pair gloves; a scale; two parcels of flannels.

A canvass bag marked GWG containing: eight pairs of socks; three under-shirts; three handkerchiefs; a child's undershirt; two pairs of cuffs; three collars; two child's shirts; a napkin; a towell (*sic*); a child's dress; a cotton dress; a child's tie; a child's coat; a shawl; a vest; two pillow-cases; three pairs of drawers; two pairs of woman's pants; four lady's shirts; a small blanket; a piece of a counterpane; a child's petticoat; two morning dresses; three night shirts; three sheets; three shirts; an undershirt.

A chest marked "Arian Martens" containing: four shirts; four pairs of pants; five waistcoats; a morning coat; a woolen shirt; a piece of cloth; two hats; an overcoat; a pair of half-boots; a brush; a cigar case with three studs; six shirt collars; a belt; a cotton cap; a bag containing pieces of cloth; a tin canister containing a German document; a parcel of pieces of cloth; a sextant; a light coat; a razor strop; pieces of flannel; a lamp; a parcel of flax-seed; a straw fan; thirteen books; a paper book; a parcel of papers; a flute.

A trunk marked C containing: fourteen shirts; five pairs of drawers; three vests; six pairs of pants; three towels; ten books; a looking-glass; two pillow-cases; three coats; an undershirt; three pairs of cotton stockings; two albums; a cartoon (*sic*) of paper collars; a hair brush; two boxes containing letters & envelopes; four caps; a pair of slippers; a pair of shoes; a pair of half-boots; nine pairs of socks; a testament; a package of needles and thread; a linen coat; two mittens; a comforter; a gimblet, brush, soap, pins, razor &c.

Gibraltar 6th March 1873

(Signed) G. W. BLATCHFORD, Wrentham, Mass.

(Signed) HORATIO J. SPRAGUE, *U. S. Consul, Gibraltar*

"Inventory of the contents of a desk found on board the American Brig *Mary Celeste* of New York, by the Marshal of the Vice Admiralty Court of Gibraltar, and delivered to me this day, by the said Marshal; the said desk is supposed to belong to Captain B. S. Briggs, the missing Master."[1]

A desk containing: Twenty one letters; an account book; a pocket-book; a ruler; two pieces of sealing wax; four United States postal stamps; a pencil; a paper cover containing sundry papers, envelopes and accounts; wafers; a case of leads; three receipts signed by J. H. Winchester & Co., New York, viz: for $1,500 dated 3rd October 1872; for $500 dated 16th October 1872; for $1,600 dated 22nd October 1872.

Consulate of the United States of America,
   Gibraltar 21*st March* 1873.

(Signed) HORATIO J. SPRAGUE, *U. S. Consul*

[1] This inventory accompanied Consul Sprague's letter No. 138 dated 21 March 1873.

APPENDIX S

Correspondence between German Consul at Gibraltar and Various Persons in Regard to Missing German Seamen

This letter, with its odd phraseology and misspellings, is an exact copy of the photostat in the author's file.

(*Translation.*)

Utersum auf Föhr, 7th February 1885

HIGHLY ESTEEMED MR. CONSUL.

From your valued communication of the 19th ult. I unfolded as Enclosure, copy of a letter of one of your friends from which I note that he as well as myself are convinced that we are on a false track with respect to the crew of the *Mary Celeste* which will become clear to you on perusal of the following.

Before all I must give you some information respecting our local circumstances stating that the Island of Föhr is scarcely 172 square miles large and has not even 5000 inhabitants from which only 130 souls fall to the lot of the village Utersum. The foregoing will prove you that all inhabitants of our village are not only known by me by their names but also are personally acquainted with me. The neighbouring Island of Amrum scarcely shows the number of 600 inhabitants from which the greater part of the male population are likewise personally known to me. In consequence whereof it is not strange nor at all surprising if the personalities of the three missed people can be described by me, the more so on account as I have stated formerly that the two from this place were my former school comrades.[1]

Concerning the letter of the late Chief of this Parish Nickelsen[2] who has brought your friend into erroneous suppositions you will I hope come to the conviction that the object kept by same in view was quite a different one as that supposed by your friend. The first notice of the sad, all now unfortunately still uncleared event of the *Mary Celeste* was communicated to us already in January 1873 and indeed through the Hamburgische Borsenhalle. Later in February the "Secret of the Ocean" as it was called by all newspapers and other small publications besides, appeared insane with all imaginary decorations as you can see from the enclosed print of the *Die Woche*. It is therefore not at all striking if Mr. Nickelsen was partially informed on the 24th March same year respecting the state of the vessel, by one part through the newspapers reports amongst which there were even English & Americans and then also besides through *your own report* dated Gibraltar the 25th February 1873, which you directed to a brother-in-law

1. Presumably the Lorenzen brothers, Volkert and Boz.
2. Presumably the T. A. Nickelsen who, on 24 March 1873 wrote to Consul Sprague.

of the two brethern who had addressed themselves to you and as the original lies before me I copy the following, vis:

Mr. ROLUF TH. WOGENS   *Gibraltar, 25th February 1873*
     Utersum auf Föhr

In answer to your letter of the 14th inst. I inform you that with respect to the American Brigantine I am enabled to report the following.

The said vessel was brought in tow[3] by the English Brigg *Dei Gratia* Captain Morokaise[4] who was bound from New York with a cargo of Petroleum for Gibraltar for orders having been met with in N. L. 38-20 and W. L. 17-30 in an abandoned state. The mate and two of the crew of the *Dei Gratia* were ordered to direct the found vessel to this Port as the same was tight and staunch and Captain Morokaise did not know to which circumstance to attribute that the vessel in question had been abandoned. Silk and other women clothing were found on board the vessel *Mary Celeste* so that it can be supposed that one, or more ladies had been passengers on board of same. It is considered probable that the crew as well as the passengers must have been received by some other vessel as the *Mary Celeste* is tight and staunch so that she will get a fresh crew in order to prosecute, within a few days on her voyage. Should I received any further details respecting the crew in question I will not fail to inform you of same, and in the meantime, I remain with all respect

                 (Signed) FERDINAND SCHOTT
                      Imp. German Consul

Probably it has escaped your memory and you have left unobserved that your foregoing textual letter was written a month before Mr. Nickelsen's communication. That Mr. Nickelsen's writting has failed his object, and even now has given rise to erroneous conclusions, it is very easy if it is considered, that Nickelsen did not know so much of the English language as to use the proper physiology [*sic*], and it can not be expected otherwise although he was a naturalized American Citizen as during his staying in said country he must have rather occupied himself with everything else but with phraseology. The letter of Mr. Nickelsen only touched the subject of the crew and was directed to the American Consul as it was supposed that he was more liable to know more of same than the German one, the more so as the vessel was American property. Your friend appears to consider my former communications inadequate I will therefore do my best this time, as he expresses himself, the truth, nothing but the truth, and the real truth respecting the fate of the three unfortunate seamen missing and does not affect me in the least and indeed simply on account *of the affair being as much in the dark for me now as when the vessel was met with and most difficulty* will be ever cleared up. Neither to this place not to Amrum ever any notice

3. This, in the light of the Court testimony and other authoritative records, is manifestly incorrect, as the vessel was sailed in — not towed — arriving on the day after the arrival of the *Dei Gratia*.

4. Captain Morehouse.

has reached, respecting the fate of the three seamen missing, the relatives know as little about the missing men as myself. The mother of the two brethern[5] is still living and she does not cease to deplore the loss of her two sons. The eldest of whom was married, his wife and daughter are still living here in poor circumstances. The younger brother was betrothed and his bride has married another seaman and also lives in this village. Arian Martens[6]—his wife and children are likewise living in Amrum, in uneasy circumstances. His parents father and mother are both living and I beg to enclose a letter of the old father through which he addresses himself to the aforesaid brother-in-law of the two brethern respecting the narrative which appeared in the Kropper Wochenschan. Of the effects of the two brethern Lorenzen nothing has reached home just because one suppose that it was not worth while claiming them. A short time[7] they got on board the *Mary Celeste* both brethern had lost all their clothing and sundry other effects through shipwreck and same could therefore only be provided with the most necessary articles. Concerning the effects of A. Martens, if they had been claimed by his relatives or not, I am unable to give information what I regret as I will not be able to gather same, But concerning him I know that he had passed his mate's examination and was already navigating several years from Hamburg as such. It is therefore comprehensible that he must have carried with him his effects viz: charts, books, & nautical instruments. It does not lie in my power to describe same. To my best knowledge none of the three seamen has been of a musical nature and it is therefore supposable that it[8] must have belonged to some other member of the crew. The foregoing is more or less all what I know respecting the men, but I must add hereto that same had enjoyed for their class as seamen an extraordinary good education, which is generally the case in all our islands. That same must have lost their lives, I take as a fact, but I cannot admit that they have had a share in any act of violence or in any mutiny which is guaranteed to me the character of the men in question who were of a most pacific disposition.

Your most devoted friend

(Signed)   R. I. LORENZEN

Chief of the Parish

L. S.

5. Volkert and Boz Lorenzen.

6. Meaning that the wife and children of Arian Martens (not Martens himself, member of the missing crew) were still living in Amrum.

7. Word missing.

8. In the inventory sent by Consul Sprague 10 March 1873 (No. 135) to the Department of State, giving details of personal effects found on board *Mary Celeste* there was a chest marked "Arian Martens," which, among other articles contained a flute as well as a sextant and a canister containing a German document.

To Mr. R. O. Wogens, in Utersum,

Amrum May 7th 1884

Esteemed friend.

Yesterday I received a letter from my grandson Anton Mutzen from New York which informs us that he has been speaking with the owners of the *Mary Celeste* that they were, all infamous lies and that the narrative had appeared also two or three years ago in an English journal from which the newspaper *Echo* must have probably extracted it. The vessel has had *no* passengers. The name of the owner is J. Winchester, who resides in New York. In view thereof everything is a lot of lies and inventions.

With a hearty greeting I conclude as your friend

(Signed) Kunot Martens[9]

Anthony's letter was dated 22nd April

9. Father of Arian Martens, one of the missing seamen.

APPENDIX T

Copies of Letters from Frederick Solly Flood to Martin W. Stokes and George F. Cornwell, Proctors, respectively, for Cargo and Vessel interests in proceedings before Vice-Admiralty Court

Mr. Flood's letter to Martin W. Stokes, Proctor for Claimants of Cargo, which the latter failed to acknowledge.

Gibraltar, 18 *April* 1873

The Queen in Her Office of Admiralty

v.

The ship or vessel and her cargo proceeded against as Derelict and as supposed to be the *Mary Celeste* and her cargo.

DEAR SIR:

Herewith I inclose an account of the expenses of Her Majesty in Her Office of Admiralty in the above suit for fees to the Judge, and for fees to the Registrar of the Vice Admiralty Court of Gibraltar together with the Registrar's vouchers for the same.

With a view to save expense I have furnished Mr. Cornwell with a copy of the account only and not of the vouchers.

I should be glad if you and he can examine together the account and the vouchers and arrange for the payment of their expenses.

I have further to acquaint you that it is not my intention to include in the account of expenses in this suit the fees ordinarily payable to H. M's Advocate General and Proctor for the Queen in Her Office of Admiralty.

I am &c &c.

(Signed) FREDERICK SOLLY FLOOD

M. W. STOKES *Esquire.*   *H. M's Advocate General*

Gibraltar, 18 *April* 1873

The Queen in Her Office of Admiralty

v.

The ship or vessel and her cargo proceeded against as Derelict and as supposed to be the *Mary Celeste* and her cargo.

DEAR SIR:

Herewith I enclose an account of the expenses of Her Majesty in Her Office of Admiralty in the above suit for fees to the Judge, and for fees to the Registrar of the Vice Admiralty Court of Gibraltar.

With a view to avoid expense, I have enclosed vouchers to Mr. Stokes only.

I should be glad if you and he can examine together the account and the voucher and arrange for the payment of these expenses.

I have further to acquaint you that it is not my intention to include in the account of expenses in this suit, the fees ordinarily payable to H. M's Advocate General and Proctor for the Queen in Her Office of Admiralty.

I am &c, &c.

(Signed) FRED. SOLLY FLOOD

G. F. CORNWELL *Esqre.*   *H. M's Advocate General*

APPENDIX U

Marriage Certificate — Benjamin Spooner Briggs and Sarah Elizabeth Cobb

THE COMMONWEALTH OF MASSACHUSETTS

COPY OF RECORD OF MARRIAGE

TOWN OF MARION

I, the undersigned, hereby certify that I am Clerk of the Town of Marion, that as such I have custody of the records of marriages required by law to be kept in my office; that among such records is one relating to the marriage of

BENJAMIN SPOONER BRIGGS and SARAH ELIZABETH COBB

and that the following is a true copy of so much of said record as relates to said marriage, namely:

Date of Marriage	SEPTEMBER 9, 1862
Place of Marriage	MARION, MASS.

GROOM	BRIDE
Name, BENJAMIN SPOONER BRIGGS	Name, SARAH ELIZABETH COBB
Age, 27 Color, WHITE	Age, 20 Color, WHITE
Residence, WAREHAM, MASS.	Residence, ROCHESTER, MASS.
Number of Marriage, FIRST	Number of Marriage, FIRST
Single, Widower or Divorced, SINGLE	Single, Widow or Divorced, SINGLE
Occupation, MARINER	Birthplace, ROCHESTER, MASS.
Birthplace, WAREHAM, MASS.	Name of Father, LEANDER COBB
Name of Father, NATHAN BRIGGS	Maiden Name of Mother,
Maiden Name of Mother, SOPHIA M.	JULIA ANN SCRIBNER[1]

Name and official station of person by whom married, LEANDER COBB, PASTOR OF CONG. CHURCH, MARION

Date of Record, JANUARY 12, 1863

And I do hereby certify that the foregoing is a true copy from said records. WITNESS my hand and seal of said Town of Marion on this 14th day of January 1941.

S. W. TAYLOR, *Clerk*

1. The name "Scribner" added, 22 September 1941 by Dr. O. W. Cobb at Easthampton, Massachusetts.

APPENDIX V

Birth Certificate — Arthur Stanley Briggs

THE COMMONWEALTH OF MASSACHUSETTS

UNITED STATES OF AMERICA

CERTIFICATE OF BIRTH

I, the undersigned hereby certify that I hold the office of Clerk of the Town of Marion, County of Plymouth, and Commonwealth of Massachusetts; that the records of Births required by law to be kept are in my custody, and that the following is a true copy from the records of Births, as certified by me.

1. Name of Child   ARTHUR S. BRIGGS
2. Sex   MALE   Color WHITE
3. Date of Birth   SEPTEMBER 20, 1865
4. Place of Birth   MARION, MASS.
5. Name of Father   BENJAMIN S. BRIGGS
6. Occupation of Father   MARINER
7. Birthplace of Father   WAREHAM, MASS.
8. Maiden Name of Mother   SARAH E. COBB
9. Birthplace of Mother   ROCHESTER, MASS. (NOW MARION)
10. Residence of Father   MARION, MASS.
11. Residence of Mother   MARION, MASS.
12. Date of Record   JANUARY 29, 1866

And I do hereby certify that the foregoing is a true copy from said records. WITNESS my hand and seal of said Town of Marion on this 14th day of January 1941.

S. W. TAYLOR, *Clerk*

APPENDIX W

Birth Certificate — Sophia Matilda Briggs

THE COMMONWEALTH OF MASSACHUSETTS

UNITED STATES OF AMERICA

CERTIFICATE OF BIRTH

I, the undersigned hereby certify that I hold the office of Clerk of the Town of Marion, County of Plymouth, and Commonwealth of Massachusetts; that the records of Births required by law to be kept are in my custody, and that the following is a true copy from the records of Births, as certified by me.

1. Name of Child	SOPHIA M. BRIGGS
2. Sex	FEMALE Color WHITE
3. Date of Birth	OCTOBER 31, 1870
4. Place of Birth	MARION, MASS.
5. Name of Father	BENJAMIN S. BRIGGS
6. Occupation of Father	MASTER MARINER
7. Birthplace of Father	WAREHAM, MASS.
8. Maiden Name of Mother	SARAH E. COBB
9. Birthplace of Mother	ROCHESTER, MASS. (NOW MARION)
10. Residence of Father	MARION, MASS.
11. Residence of Mother	MARION, MASS.
12. Date of Record	JANUARY 31, 1871

And I do hereby certify that the foregoing is a true copy from said records. WITNESS my hand and seal of said Town of Marion on this 14th day of January 1941.

S. W. TAYLOR, *Clerk*

APPENDIX X

Letter from Servico Meteorologico dos Açores

Servico Meteorologico dos Açores, Angra do Heroismo, Açores

Angra do Heroismo, Azores Islands, May 27, 1940

MR. CHARLES EDEY FAY, Sunny Crest Farm,
   Grassy Hill Road, Woodbury, Conn., U. S. America

DEAR SIR:

I am very gladly complying with the request in your letter of March 4.

As the records from the stations in the Azores previous to the establishment of the Meteorological Service in the Islands, 1901, are kept in the Lisbon Observatory, I was forced to request the data from the Director of that Observatory, hence the delay in answering your questions.

From the records from Angra do Heroismo and Ponta Delgada, the two only stations existing in 1872, it is concluded that stormy conditions prevailed in the Azores on the 24 and 25 November 1872. A COLD FRONT passed Angra do Heroismo between 3 and 9 P.M. on the 25th. the wind shifting then from SW to NW. The minimum of pressure was 752 mm. and the wind velocity attained to 62 km. at Ponta Delgada at 9 P.M. on the 24th. Calm or light wind prevailed on the forenoon of the 25th., but later, the wind became of a gale force. As usually the wind direction before the cold front was WSW to SW; after the cold front NW. 14 mm. of rain were collected at Angra from noon 24 to noon 25, and 29 mm. at Ponta Delgada.

No record of any earthquake is kept in the registers, neither in the local newspapers which we have searched.

Yours faithfully

(Signed) J. AGOSTINHO
J. AGOSTINHO
Director

INDEX